Beginning Swift Games Development for iOS

■ ■ ■

James Goodwill

Wesley Matlock

Apress®

Beginning Swift Games Development for iOS

ISBN-13 (pbk): 978-1-4842-0401-6

ISBN-13 (electronic): 978-1-4842-0400-9

Managing Director: Welmoed Spahr
Lead Editor: Steve Anglin
Technical Reviewer: Bruce Wade
Editorial Board: Steve Anglin, Louise Corrigan, Jonathan Gennick, Robert Hutchinson,
    Michelle Lowman, James Markham, Susan McDermott, Matthew Moodie, Jeffrey Pepper,
    Douglas Pundick, Ben Renow-Clarke, Gwenan Spearing, Steve Weiss
Coordinating Editor: Mark Powers
Copy Editor: Kim Wimpsett
Compositor: SPi Global
Indexer: SPi Global
Artist: SPi Global
Cover Designer: Anna Ishchenko

Distributed to the book trade worldwide by Springer Science+Business Media New York, 233 Spring Street, 6th Floor, New York, NY 10013. Phone 1-800-SPRINGER, fax (201) 348-4505, e-mail orders-ny@springer-sbm.com, or visit www.springeronline.com. Apress Media, LLC is a California LLC and the sole member (owner) is Springer Science + Business Media Finance Inc (SSBM Finance Inc). SSBM Finance Inc is a Delaware corporation.

For information on translations, please e-mail rights@apress.com, or visit www.apress.com.

Apress and friends of ED books may be purchased in bulk for academic, corporate, or promotional use. eBook versions and licenses are also available for most titles. For more information, reference our Special Bulk Sales–eBook Licensing web page at www.apress.com/bulk-sales.

Any source code or other supplementary material referenced by the author in this text is available to readers at www.apress.com/9781484204016. For detailed information about how to locate your book's source code, go to www.apress.com/source-code/.

To James Gordon Goodwill, Jr.,
my father, who passed away while I was in the middle of writing
this book—he taught me so many things while he was here.

Contents at a Glance

About the Authors... xiii

About the Technical Reviewer xv

Acknowledgments xvii

Introduction xix

■ **Part I: Swift and Sprite Kit** 1

■ **Chapter 1: Setting Up Your Game Scene and Adding Your First Sprites** 3

■ **Chapter 2: Sprite Kit Scenes and SKNode Positioning** 19

■ **Chapter 3: Adding Physics and Collision Detection to Your Game** 33

■ **Chapter 4: Adding Scene Scrolling and Game Control** 47

■ **Chapter 5: Adding Actions and Animations** 59

■ **Chapter 6: Adding Particle Effects to Your Game with Emitter Nodes** 79

■ **Chapter 7: Adding Points and Sound** 97

■ **Chapter 8: Transitioning Between Scenes** 113

■ **Chapter 9: Sprite Kit Best Practices** 127

■Part II: Swift and Scene Kit 141

■Chapter 10: Creating Your First Scene Kit Project................................. 143

■Chapter 11: Building the Scene 155

■Chapter 12: Lighting, Camera, and Material Effects in Scene Kit...................... 169

■Chapter 13: Animating Your Models 181

■Chapter 14: Hit Testing and Collision Detection 189

■Chapter 15: Using Sprite Kit with a Scene Kit Scene 201

■Chapter 16: Advanced Topics and Tips.. 211

■Appendix A: The Swift Programming Language 219

Index.. 245

Contents

About the Authors.. xiii

About the Technical Reviewer xv

Acknowledgments..xvii

Introduction xix

■Part I: Swift and Sprite Kit 1

■Chapter 1: Setting Up Your Game Scene and Adding Your First Sprites 3

What You Need to Know 3

What You Need to Have 3

SuperSpaceMan 4

Creating a Swift Sprite Kit Project.. 4

Starting from Scratch.. 6

    The GameViewController Class... 9

    The GameScene Class.. 11

Adding a Background and Player Sprite 12

Summary... 17

■Chapter 2: Sprite Kit Scenes and SKNode Positioning...19

What Is an SKScene? 19

    The SKScene Rendering Loop 20

    Building the Scene's Node Tree 22

Looking at SKSpriteNode Coordinates and Anchor Points..27

    Coordinates...28

    Anchor Points 30

Summary...32

■Chapter 3: Adding Physics and Collision Detection to Your Game 33

What Is an SKPhysicsBody? 33

Adding Physics to Your Game World...34

 Applying Forces to SKPhysicsBody 35

Adding Collision Detection to Your SKNode..38

    Adding a Node to Collide Into 38

    Adding Collision Detection..39

    Removing the Orb When You Receive a Contact Message 42

Summary...45

■Chapter 4: Adding Scene Scrolling and Game Control..47

Reorganizing the GameScene 47

Adding More Orbs to the Scene...49

Scrolling the Scene 52

Controlling Player Movement with the Accelerometer 54

Summary...58

■Chapter 5: Adding Actions and Animations...59

Refactoring the Orb Node Layout One Last Time...59

Sprite Kit Actions...63

    Using Actions to Move Nodes in the Scene 64

    Using SKActions to Animate Sprites...69

Adding Some Additional Bling to the GameScene...71

Summary...77

■Chapter 6: Adding Particle Effects to Your Game with Emitter Nodes 79

What Are Emitters? 80

Using Particle Emitter Templates 82

Creating a Particle Emitter 82

Adding an Exhaust Trail to the Player 90

Summary 95

■Chapter 7: Adding Points and Sound 97

What Are SKLabelNodes? 97

Changing the Horizontal Alignment of the Label Node 99

Changing the Vertical Alignment of the Label Node 101

Adding Scoring to the Game 105

Adding an Impulse Counter to the Game 108

Adding Simple Sounds to the Game 110

Summary 112

■Chapter 8: Transitioning Between Scenes 113

Transitioning Between Scenes Using SKTransitions 113

Pausing Scenes During a Transition 115

Detecting When a New Scene Is Presented 115

Adding a New Scene to SuperSpaceMan 116

Ending the Game 118

Summary 125

■Chapter 9: Sprite Kit Best Practices 127

Creating Your Own Nodes Through Subclassing 127

Reusing Textures 132

Externalizing Your Game Data 135

Keeping Your Node Tree Pruned 137

Summary 139

■Part II: Swift and Scene Kit 141

■Chapter 10: Creating Your First Scene Kit Project 143

Scene Kit Primer 143

Scene Kit Animation 144

What You Need to Know.. 145

Creating the Scene Kit Project 146

Wiring Up and Building a Scene.. 148

SuperSpaceMan3D... 148

Project Resources... 149

Building the Scene.. 150

Summary 154

■Chapter 11: Building the Scene 155

Scene Graph 155

Scene Kit Editor 157

Render Cycle 160

Scene Kit's Built-in Model Classes.. 161

SCNGeometry Objects 161

Adding Obstacles 163

Using SCNText 167

Starting Screen... 167

Summary... 168

■Chapter 12: Lighting, Camera, and Material Effects in Scene Kit...................... 169

Lighting Up the Scene 169

Materials 171

Appling Materials to Your Obstacles... 174

Adding Textures to Collada Files... 176

Scene Kit Camera Usage 179

Summary... 180

■Chapter 13: Animating Your Models 181

Refactoring the Project.. 181

Starting Animations 182

    PyramidNode 182

    GlobeNode 183

    TubeNode..184

    BoxNode 185

More Animations 186

Summary 188

■Chapter 14: Hit Testing and Collision Detection 189

GameView: Moving the Hero 189

    Writing the Callback Delegate Function 192

    Moving the Camera...193

CoreMotion Framework Introduction... 194

Enemy Node 195

Collision Detection... 196

Summary 200

■Chapter 15: Using Sprite Kit with a Scene Kit Scene 201

Sprite Kit Integration 201

Hooking Up the Controller to the Overlay 203

"Game Over" Screen 206

Bonus Section 208

Summary 209

■Chapter 16: Advanced Topics and Tips... 211

Normal Mapping... 211

Vectors and Various Math Operations 211

Tips.. 213

Summary 218

■**Appendix A: The Swift Programming Language** **219**

Variables and Constants **220**

Flow of Control **221**

if 222

switch 222

for Loops 224

while Loops 225

Functions **226**

Variadic Parameters 227

Tuples 227

Nested Functions 228

Functions Returning Functions 229

Passing Functions As Parameters 231

inout Parameters 232

Closures **233**

Classes **234**

Extending Classes 236

Computed Properties 237

Structures **238**

Enumerations **239**

Protocols **240**

Extensions **242**

Generics **243**

Index **245**

About the Authors

James Goodwill is a nine-time published author of books about leading technologies such as Grails, Groovy, iOS, Objective C, Java Servlets, JavaServer Pages (JSP), Tomcat, and Struts. He is a senior enterprise iOS and Java consultant in the Denver metro area and frequent speaker and article writer. You can find additional resources about Sprite Kit, Swift, and James himself at his blog at www.jgoodwill.org. You can also follow James on Twitter at https://twitter.com/jamesgoodwill.

Wesley Matlock is a professional independent iOS consultant in the Kansas City metro area. He has more than 19 years of development experience in several different platforms. He first started doing mobile development on the Compaq iPaq in the early 2000s. Today he enjoys developing on the iOS platform and bringing new ideas to life. You can find additional resources about Scene Kit, Swift and Wesley himself at his blog at wesleymatlock.com. You can also follow Wesley on Twitter at https://twitter.com/wes_matlock.

About the Technical Reviewer

Bruce Wade is the founder of Warply Designed Inc. (www.warplydesigned.com), a company specializing in using game technology for real-world applications. He has more than 16 years of software development experience with a strong focus on 2D/3D animation and interactive applications primarily using Apple technology.

Acknowledgments

This book could not have been written without the incredible folks at Apress. The idea of a Swift iOS gaming book began with a conversation with Steve Anglin and came to life with a great discussion about gaming and Apple with Michelle Lowman. Mark Powers and James Markham kept the book on the rails and brought it safely into the station. Bruce Wade made sure all of the technical statements made sense and the code compiled and ran successfully. I thank you all.

I want to send out a special thanks to Wes Matlock for taking over the Scene Kit section of the book when my father passed. I just did not have the time or energy to complete the second section of the book, and Wes stepped in without hesitation.

I also want to thank Deborah Saez for the wonderful artwork in the book. I highly recommend her. She is both very talented and a very hard worker. You can find her at www.deborahsaez.com/. Look her up.

Finally and most importantly, I want to thank the three girls in my life: Christy (my wonderful wife) and our daughters, Abby (who did a great review of the book) and Emma (who supplied a ton of inspiration). You three are the most important people in my life.

—James Goodwill

Introduction

Which Version of Swift Is Covered in This book?

This book covers version 1.1 of Swift. Swift 1.2 is currently in beta and under a nondisclosure agreement (NDA). When 1.2 is released, we will update the source in this book at both the Apress.com web site and James Goodwill's blog at www.jgoodwill.org. Please be aware that you will need to update your source when 1.2 is released.

What This Book Is

Game apps are one of the most popular categories in the Apple iTunes App Store. Well, the introduction of the new Swift programming language will make game development even more appealing and easier to existing and future iOS app developers. In response, James Goodwill, Wesley Matlock, and Apress introduce you to this book, *Beginning Swift Games Development for iOS*.

In this book, you'll learn the fundamental elements of the new Swift language as applied to game development for iOS in 2D and 3D worlds using both Sprite Kit and Scene Kit, respectively.

What You Need to Know

This book assumes you have a basic understanding of how to create applications for the iPhone using Xcode. You will also need a basic understanding of Apple's new programming language, Swift 1.1. We assume that you can download, install, and use the latest version of Xcode to create an application and run it on the iPhone simulator.

What You Need to Have

In terms of hardware, you need an Intel-based Macintosh running Mountain Lion (OS X 10.8) or later. Regarding software, you need Xcode 6.2 since that is the current version to include Swift 1.1. You can download Xcode from the App Store or Apple's developer web site at http://developer.apple.com.

What's in This Book?

In Chapter 1, you'll learn about what Sprite Kit is and how you create a new Sprite Kit game using Xcode. You will then dive in and create the beginnings of a Sprite Kit game starting from scratch. You will learn about SKNodes and their subclasses, and you'll use an SKSpriteNode to add both a background node and a player node.

In Chapter 2, we will step back a bit and give you a deeper look at Sprite Kit scenes, including how scenes are built and why the order they are built in can change your game. The chapter will close with a discussion of Sprite Kit coordinate systems and anchor points as they relate to SKNodes.

In Chapter 3, you'll work with Sprite Kit's physics engine and collision detection. The chapter will begin with a discussion of SKPhysicsBody—the class used to simulate collision detection. You will then turn on gravity in the game world and see how that affects the nodes. After that, you will add a touch responder to propel the playerNode up into space, and finally you will learn how to handle node collisions.

In Chapter 4, you'll start adding some real functionality to your game. You'll begin by making some small changes to the current GameScene. After that, you will add additional orb nodes to collide into. You will then add scrolling to your scene, allowing you to make it look like the player is flying through space collecting orbs. Finally, you will start using the phone's accelerometer to move the player along the x-axis.

In Chapter 5, you'll refactor the orb node's layout one last time with the goal of enhancing playability. After that, you will learn how you can use SKActions to move an SKSpriteNode back and forth across the scene and then make that same node rotate forever. The chapter will close with a look at how you can add colorizing effects to an SKSpriteNode using a colorize action.

In Chapter 6, you'll see how to define particle emitters and how to leverage them in Sprite Kit games. After that, you will learn how you can use them to add engine exhaust to the playerNode whenever an impulse is applied to the physicsBody.

In Chapter 7, you'll see how you can use SKLabelNodes to add text to your Sprite Kit games. Specifically, you'll see how you how to add a label that keeps up with the number of impulses remaining for the spaceman to use, and then you'll see how you can add scoring to the game to keep up with the number of orbs the spaceman has collected.

In Chapter 8, you'll learn how to implement scene transitions using Sprite Kit's SKTransition class. You will look at some of the different types of built-in transitions Sprite Kit makes available to you. You will also see how you can control each scene during a transition. At the end of the chapter, you will take your newfound knowledge and add a menu scene to your SuperSpaceMan game.

In Chapter 9, you'll learn some Sprite Kit best practices; specifically, you will see how you can create your own subclasses of SKSpriteNode so that you can better reuse your nodes. You will then move on to changing your game to load all the sprites into a single texture atlas that you can reference when creating all future sprites. After that, you will move on to externalizing some of your game data so that designers and testers can change the game play. Finally, you will close out the chapter when you prune your node tree of all nodes that have fallen off the bottom of the screen.

In Chapter 10, you'll learn about what Scene Kit is and how to create a new Scene Kit game using Xcode. You will then dive in and create the beginnings of a Scene Kit game starting from scratch. You will learn to about SCNScene and SCNodes with a Scene Kit primer.

In Chapter 11, you'll learn more about the scene graph and some of the basics of Scene Kit. You will start to create your game by loading the spaceman from his Collada file. You will also learn about the Scene Kit primitive geometries by adding these as objects for the spaceman to avoid.

In Chapter 12, you'll learn how Scene Kit uses lighting and the type of lighting that is available to you in Scene Kit. You will also examine how materials are added onto the SCNNode, as well as how the camera is used within the scene.

In Chapter 13, you'll learn about the basics of animating the objects in your game. You will see a couple of different ways to animate the nodes to give you more than one way to do your animations. Once you have completed this chapter, all of your objects will move within the scene.

In Chapter 14, you'll learn about collision detection within the scene. You will learn how to move the spaceman around the scene. Once you have the spaceman moving, you will learn how to detect when the spaceman runs into an obstacle.

In Chapter 15, you'll learn how to use a Sprite Kit scene within the Scene Kit scene. The chapter will show you how to create a screen to show you a timer that you will start when the user starts the game. The chapter will also show you how to display a "game over" screen and then restart the game.

In Chapter 16, you'll get some tips and tricks on using the Xcode editor. We will also explain some of the vectors and matrix methods in some detail to give you a better understanding of what those methods are doing behind the scenes.

In Appendix A, you'll take a quick (you might say a "swift") look at each of the features in the Swift programming language. We'll start by describing each feature and then cement your knowledge through consecutive examples.

Part **I**

Swift and Sprite Kit

In this part of this book, we will cover the basics of Sprite Kit including how you render and animate sprites, add physics and collision detection, and control your game play with the accelerometer. You will also look at how you add particle emitters to enhance the appearance of your game. We will cover everything you need to know to create your own Sprite Kit game.

Chapter 1

Setting Up Your Game Scene and Adding Your First Sprites

Sprite Kit is Apple's exciting 2D game framework released in September 2013 with iOS 7. It is a graphics rendering and animation framework that gives you the power to easily animate textured images, play video, render text, and add particle effects. It also includes an integrated physics library. Sprite Kit is the first-ever game engine formally built into the iOS SDK.

In this chapter you will learn what Sprite Kit is and how you create a new Sprite Kit game using Xcode. You will then move on and create the beginnings of a Sprite Kit game starting from scratch. You'll learn about SKNodes and their subclasses, and you'll also use an SKSpriteNode to add both a background node and a player node to your game.

What You Need to Know

This section of this book assumes you have a basic understanding of how to build iPhone applications using Xcode and the Xcode Simulator. It also assumes you have a basic knowledge of the iOS/Mac programming language Swift. If you are not familiar with Swift, there is a brief introduction in the appendix at the back of this book.

This book will not cover how to program. It will focus only on Sprite Kit game programming.

What You Need to Have

To complete all of the examples in the book, you will need to have an Intel-based Macintosh running OS X 10.8 (Mountain Lion) or newer. You will also need Xcode 6+ installed. You can find both of these in the Apple App Store.

SuperSpaceMan

I feel the best way to learn anything is to do it. Therefore, in this book you are going to dive right in and create your own game. You will start off with the basic code for a 2D game, and you will add new features to the game as I introduce new topics with each chapter. At the end of the book, you will have a complete game.

The game you are going to create is inspired by Sega's popular Sonic Jump Fever (https://itunes.apple.com/us/app/sonic-jump-fever/id794528112?mt=8). It is a vertical scroller that accelerates the main character through obstacles and collectables, increasing your score as you collect rings.

This game will be similar, in that it is a vertical scroller, but your main character is going to be a space man who hurtles through space collecting power orbs while trying to avoid black holes that will destroy him.

Creating a Swift Sprite Kit Project

Before you can get started, you will need to create a Swift Sprite Kit project. So, go ahead and open Xcode and complete the following steps:

1. Select the menu File ➤ New ➤ Project.

2. Select Application from the iOS group.

3. Then select the Game icon. The choose template dialog should now look like Figure 1-1.

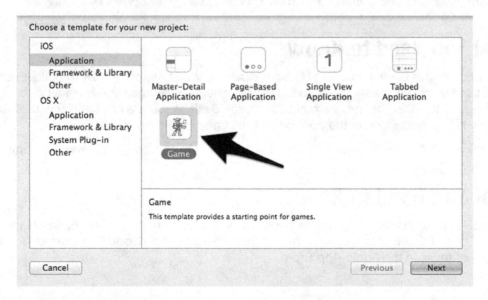

Figure 1-1. The choose template dialog

4. To move on, click the Next button.

5. Enter **SuperSpaceMan** for Product Name, **Apress** for Organization Name, and **com.apress** for Organization Identifier.

6. Make sure Swift is the selected language, Sprite Kit is the selected game technology, and iPhone is the selected device.

7. Before you click the Next button, take a look at Figure 1-2. If everything looks like this image, click the Next button and select a good place to store your project files and click the Create button.

Figure 1-2. The choose project options dialog

> **Note**   You will notice you are creating an iPhone-only game. This is only because the game you are creating lends itself better to the iPhone. Everything I will cover in this book translates to the iPad just as well.

You now have a working Sprite Kit project. Go ahead and click the Play button to see what you have created. If everything went OK, you will see your new app running in the simulator.

> **Note**   The Xcode simulator may take awhile to start on some slower machines. Simulating Sprite Kit can be very taxing on your processors.

It does not do a whole lot yet, but there is more to it than the displaying of the universal "Hello, World!" Tap the simulator screen a few times. You will see rotating space ships displayed wherever you tap. Depending on where you tapped, you should see something similar to Figure 1-3.

Figure 1-3. The Sprite Kit sample application

Starting from Scratch

While the standard Sprite Kit template works great, you are going to be starting from scratch. Starting from nothing will allow you to see all the working parts in a Sprite Kit game and give you a much better understanding of what you are creating.

The first thing you need to do is make sure your game runs only in portrait mode. To do this, follow these steps:

1.   Select the SuperSpaceMan project in the Project Explorer.

2.   Then select SuperSpaceMan from Targets.

3.   Deselect Landscape Left and Landscape Right.

At this point, your target settings should look like Figure 1-4.

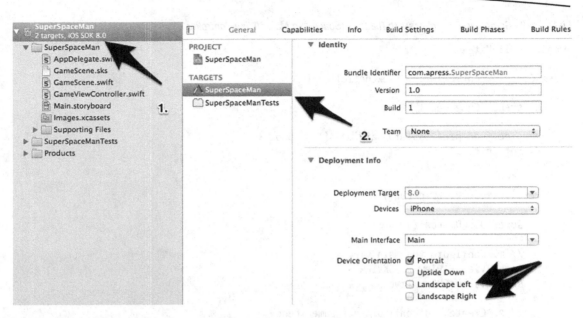

Figure 1-4. *The SuperSpaceMan target settings*

The next thing you need to do is delete the file GameScene.sks. You will not be using the level editor in this book. You can find this file in the SuperSpaceMan group. Delete this file and then open GameScene.swift and replace its contents with the class in Listing 1-1.

Listing 1-1. GameScene.swift: The SuperSpaceMan Main GameScene

```
import SpriteKit

class GameScene: SKScene {

    required init?(coder aDecoder: NSCoder) {

        super.init(coder: aDecoder)
    }

    override init(size: CGSize) {

        super.init(size: size)

        backgroundColor = SKColor(red: 0.0, green: 0.0, blue: 0.0, alpha: 1.0)
    }
}
```

There is one more change you need to make before examining your baseline project. Open GameViewController.swift and replace its contents with the Listing 1-2 version of the same class.

Listing 1-2. GameViewController.swift: The SuperSpaceMan Main UIViewController

```
import SpriteKit

class GameViewController: UIViewController {

    var scene: GameScene!

    override func prefersStatusBarHidden() -> Bool {
        return true
    }

    override func viewDidLoad() {

        super.viewDidLoad()

        // 1. Configure the main view
        let skView = view as SKView
        skView.showsFPS = true

        // 2. Create and configure our game scene
        scene = GameScene(size: skView.bounds.size)
        scene.scaleMode = .AspectFill

        // 3. Show the scene.
        skView.presentScene(scene)
    }
}
```

Save all your changes and click the Play button once more. Wow, um. That was not very exciting. If you made all the changes, you should now be staring at a totally black screen with only the current frame rate displayed. This was the intent. You truly are starting from nothing.

Let's take a moment and examine each component of your new game. First, open Main.storyboard. Everything here should look pretty normal. You should see a single storyboard with a single UIViewController. Expand Game View Controller Scene in the Story Board Explorer and select Game View Controller, as shown in Figure 1-5.

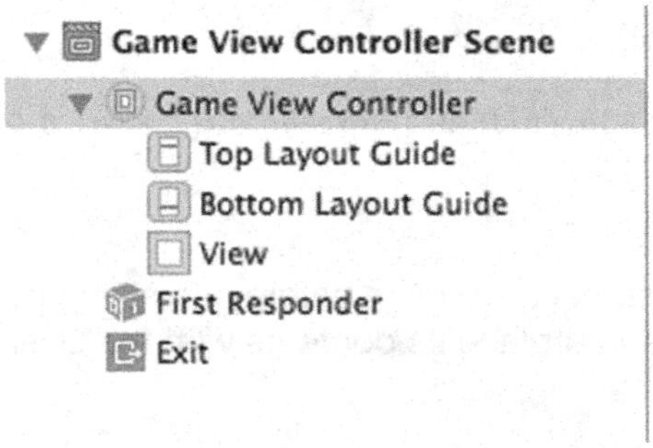

Figure 1-5. Game View Controller Scene

Now expand the Utilities view on the right side of Xcode and click Show the Identity inspector button. You will see the custom class of this UIViewController is your GameViewController.swift. Figure 1-6 shows you this connection.

Figure 1-6. The custom class GameViewController

There is one last thing to look at before you get back to the code portion of this tour. Go back to the Utilities view and select the Connections inspector. Notice the View outlet is connected to your GameViewController.view. Figure 1-7 shows this connection.

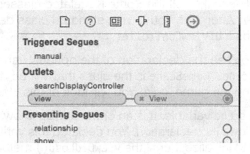

Figure 1-7. The View outlet

The point of going through this examination of the storyboard is to show that while Sprite Kit is used to create games, the technology used to create games is just like what you would use to create any modern iOS app.

The GameViewController Class

Let's get back to the code. You can ignore AppDelegate.swift—it is the same boilerplate code you use to start all iOS Swift applications. GameViewController.swift is the best starting point. I included it earlier, but for the sake of convenience it is listed here again:

```
import SpriteKit

class GameViewController: UIViewController {

    var scene: GameScene!

    override func prefersStatusBarHidden() -> Bool {

        return true
    }
```

```
    override func viewDidLoad() {

        super.viewDidLoad()

        // 1. Configure the main view
        let skView = view as SKView
        skView.showsFPS = true

        // 2. Create and configure our game scene
        scene = GameScene(size: skView.bounds.size)
        scene.scaleMode = .AspectFill

        // 3. Show the scene.
        skView.presentScene(scene)
    }
}
```

Starting with the first line of this controller, you see a simple import including the Sprite Kit framework. This line makes all the Sprite Kit related classes available to your `GameViewController`. After that, you have a standard class definition—the `GameViewController` extends a `UIViewController`.

After the class definition, you see the declaration of the optional variable scene, which is declared as the type `GameScene`. `GameScene` is the class that will be doing most of your work. It is where you will be adding the game logic. You will look at this class in the next section.

Notice one thing about the `scene` variable. It is an optional. You know it is an optional because an exclamation point (!) follows its declaration. You declared this variable as an optional because you are not going to initialize it until the `viewDidLoad()` method fires and Swift requires you to initialize all properties in a class either at their declaration or in the `init()`. If you don't initialize a property in either of these locations, then you must declare the property as optional. You will see the use of optionals throughout all of the examples in this book.

After the scene declaration, you see an override of the `UIViewController`'s `viewDidLoad()` method. Here you return `true` because you don't want a status bar displayed in the game.

The next thing to check out is the `viewDidLoad()` method. This is where you really start to see your first active Sprite Kit code. The first thing you do, after calling `super.viewDidLoad()`, is to configure your main view. In the first step, you downcast your standard `UIView` to an `SKView`. The `SKView` is the view that will host your game scene mentioned earlier. For the most part, the `SKView` acts much like any `UIView`, with the exception that it has a collection of game-related properties and utility methods like the line following the downcast.

```
skView.showsFPS = true
```

This property of the `SKView` is used to show or hide the frames per second the application is rendering—the higher, the better.

After configuring the main view, you create and configure the `GameScene`.

```
scene = GameScene(size: skView.bounds.size)
scene.scaleMode = .AspectFill
```

The first line creates a new instance of the GameScene initializing the size to match the size of the view that will host the scene. After that, you set scaleMode to AspectFill. The scaleMode (implemented by the enum SKSceneScaleMode) is used to determine how the scene will be scaled to match the view that will contain it. Table 1-1 describes each of the available scaleMode properties.

Table 1-1. *The SKSceneScaleModes*

SKSceneScaleMode	Definition
SKSceneScaleMode.Fill	The Fill scaleMode will fill the entire SKView without consideration to the ratio of width to height.
SKSceneScaleMode.AspectFill	The AspectFill mode will scale the scene to fill the hosting SKView while maintaining the aspect ratio of the scene, but there may be some cropping if the hosting SKView's aspect ratio is different. This is the mode you are using in this game.
SKSceneScaleMode.AspectFit	The AspectFit mode will scale the scene to fill the hosting SKView while maintaining the aspect ratio of the scene, but there may be some letterboxing if the hosting SKView's aspect ratio is different.
SKSceneScaleMode.ResizeFill	The ResizeFill mode will modify the size of the scene to fit the hosting view exactly.

> **Note** When setting the scaleMode property of the scene, you are using a shortened syntax to represent the mode you are setting, specifically, the .AspectFill mode. You can use this dot syntax because you know the type of the scaleMode property is an SKSceneScaleMode, which is an enum containing all of the scale modes.

Once you have the view and the scene configured, there is only one last thing to do—present the scene. This is done with the last line in viewDidLoad().

```
skView.presentScene(scene)
```

The GameScene Class

Now that I have walked you through each line of the GameViewController class, it is time to talk about the GameScene class. Again, for convenience's sake, I am including the source for the GameScene.swift file a second time:

```
import SpriteKit

class GameScene: SKScene {

    required init?(coder aDecoder: NSCoder) {

        super.init(coder: aDecoder)
    }
```

```
override init(size: CGSize) {

    super.init(size: size)

    backgroundColor = SKColor(red: 0.0, green: 0.0, blue: 0.0, alpha: 1.0)
    }
}
```

As you look over GameScene, you will notice there is really not much to it. It extends SKScene and implements two init() methods; the first init() that takes an NSCoder can be ignored. You had to add this only because a Swift class does not inherit its parent's constructors. The init() you are interested in is the second method, which takes a CGSize parameter that represents the size you want the scene to be (in this case, the size you passed in from the GameViewController). After that, you pass the size to your superclass and then set the background color to black.

While there is not a whole lot to your current GameScene, this is where you will be doing almost all of your Sprite Kit work. SKScenes and the classes that extend them are the root nodes of all Sprite Kit content, and your GameScene will grow considerably as you move along in this book.

Adding a Background and Player Sprite

I have talked enough for one chapter. Let's get back to the game itself. In this, the last section of this chapter, you are going to just jump in and add a game background and a player sprite to your scene and see how they look.

Before you can do this, you need some image files. You can find all of the necessary assets for this book in the file assets.zip found at Apress.com. Go ahead and download and unzip this file.

Inside the unzipped folder you will find two folders one named Images and another named sprites.atlas. Now copy the entire spites.atlas folder directly into the SuperSpaceMan folder of the same project.

Next, open the Image.xcassets folder in Xcode. You will see a figure similar to Figure 1-8.

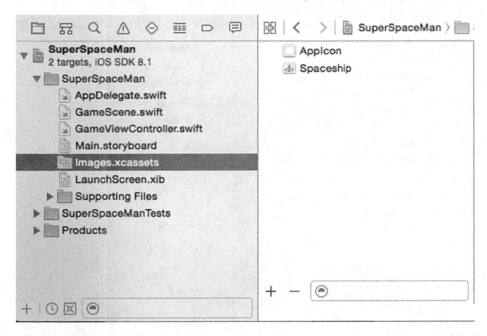

Figure 1-8. Adding Image Assets

Next, using Finder, browse to the Images folder in the previously downloaded zip file and finally select the three folders inside the Images directory and drag them onto the xcassets palette directly below the SpaceShip asset. When the files have been added, your xcassets palette will look like Figure 1-9.

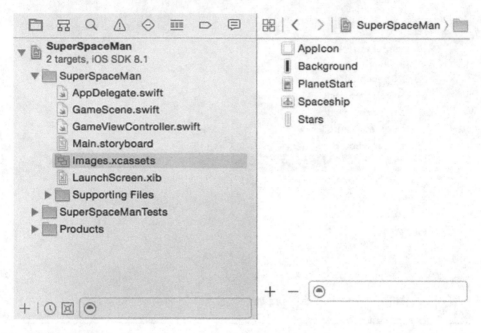

Figure 1-9. The Added Image Assets

Now that you have all of the images added to your project, let's put some of them to good use. Go back to GameScene.swift and add the following two lines to the beginning of the GameScene class:

```
let backgroundNode : SKSpriteNode?
var playerNode : SKSpriteNode?
```

Here you are adding two optionals, backgroundNode and playerNode, both of which are SKSpriteNodes. An SKSpriteNode is a descendent of an SKNode, which is the primary building block of almost all Sprite Kit content. SKNode itself does not draw any visual elements, but all visual elements in Sprite Kit based applications are drawn using SKNode subclasses. Table 1-2 defines the main descendants of SKNode that render visual elements.

Table 1-2. The Descendants of SKNode That Render Visual Elements

Class	Description
SKSpriteNode	A node that is used to draw textured sprites
SKVideoNode	A node that presents video content
SKLabelNode	A node that is used to draw text strings
SKShapeNode	A node that is used to draw a shape based upon a Core Graphics path
SKEmitterNode	A node that is used to create and render particles
SKCropNode	A node that is used to crop child nodes using a mask
SKEffectNode	A node that is used to apply Core Image filters to its child nodes

In this book you will be using three subclasses of SKNode: SKSpriteNode, SKLabelNode, and SKEmitterNode.

After adding the two SKSpriteNodes, add the following lines to the bottom of the GameScene.init(size: CGSize) method:

```
// adding the background
backgroundNode = SKSpriteNode(imageNamed: "Background")
backgroundNode!.anchorPoint = CGPoint(x: 0.5, y: 0.0)
backgroundNode!.position = CGPoint(x: size.width / 2.0, y: 0.0)
addChild(backgroundNode!)
```

The first line of this snippet creates an SKSpriteNode with an image named Background, which you just added to your Images.xcassets folder.

In this case you are drawing the background image. The next line of code determines where the new node will be anchored in your scene. Don't worry too much about this at the moment. I will be discussing anchor points in great detail in the next chapter. Just know that the anchor point of (0.5, 0.0) sets the anchor point of the background node to the bottom center of the node.

Next, you set the position of the backgroundNode. Here you are setting the node's position to an x-coordinate half the width of the scene, which is in the middle of the scene, and setting the y-coordinate to 0.0, which is the bottom of the scene.

The final line in the snippet adds the backgroundNode to your scene. To see what you have just accomplished, save your work and run the application again. You should now see your background displayed, as shown in Figure 1-10.

Figure 1-10. The backgroundNode added to the GameScene

That was easy enough. Now, let's add your player to your scene. Adding the player node is just as easy as adding the background. Take a look at the following snippet:

```
// add the player
playerNode = SKSpriteNode(imageNamed: "Player")
playerNode!.position = CGPoint(x: size.width / 2.0, y: 80.0)
addChild(playerNode!)
```

As you can see, you are creating a new SKSpriteNode using the image named Player. You then set the position of the playerNode and add it to the scene. Notice one difference here. You did not set the anchor point of the playerNode. This is because the default anchor point of all SKNodes is (0.5, 0.5), which is the center of the node. Again, don't worry about the positions or anchorPoints for now. I will be discussing them in the next chapter.

Go ahead and add this snippet to the bottom of the GameScene.init() method and save your changes. Now run the application one more time. You will now see the SuperSpaceMan positioned in front of the previously added backgroundNode, as shown in Figure 1-11.

Figure 1-11. The playerNode added to the GameScene

After making these changes, your new GameScene.swift file should look like Listing 1-3.

Listing 1-3. GameScene.swift: The modified GameScene.swift

```
import SpriteKit

class GameScene: SKScene {

    let backgroundNode : SKSpriteNode?
    var playerNode : SKSpriteNode?

    required init?(coder aDecoder: NSCoder) {

        super.init(coder: aDecoder)
    }

    override init(size: CGSize) {

        super.init(size: size)

        backgroundColor = SKColor(red: 0.0, green: 0.0, blue: 0.0, alpha: 1.0)

        // adding the background
        backgroundNode = SKSpriteNode(imageNamed: "Background")
        backgroundNode!.anchorPoint = CGPoint(x: 0.5, y: 0.0)
        backgroundNode!.position = CGPoint(x: size.width / 2.0, y: 0.0)
        addChild(backgroundNode!)

        // add the player
        playerNode = SKSpriteNode(imageNamed: "Player")
        playerNode!.position = CGPoint(x: size.width / 2.0, y: 80.0)
        addChild(playerNode!)

    }
}
```

Summary

In this chapter you learned what Sprite Kit is and how you create a new Sprite Kit game using Xcode. You then dove in and created the beginnings of a Sprite Kit game starting from scratch. You learned about SKNodes and their subclasses, and you used an SKSpriteNode to add both a background node and a player node.

In the next chapter, you will dig a little deeper into Sprite Kit and discuss the details of the SKScene, including the coordinate system and anchor points. You will also look at how a scene's node tree is constructed.

Chapter 2

Sprite Kit Scenes and SKNode Positioning

In the previous chapter I talked about what Sprite Kit was and how you can use it to create 2D games. I then jumped right in and showed how to start working with the SKSpriteNode to create a background and player sprite and then showed how to add them to a game scene.

In this chapter, I am going to step back a bit and give you a deeper look at Sprite Kit scenes, including how scenes are built and why the order they are built in can change your game. I will close the chapter with a discussion of Sprite Kit coordinate systems and anchor points as they relate to SKNodes.

What Is an SKScene?

I used the SKScene object in the previous chapter to host the background and player nodes, but I really did not explain the scene I was using. I just used it to add the sprites and called it a day. It is now time to dig in and see how SKScene really works. I'll start by defining an SKScene object.

An SKScene object represents a scene of content in a Sprite Kit game. An SKScene object inherits from SKEffectNode, SKNode, UIResponder, and, of course, NSObject. It is constructed first by creating the scene and then by adding *n* number of other SKNodes to it. The scene plus all of its child nodes are called the *node tree*, and the scene is the *root* of the node tree. The nodes contained in a scene provide the content the scene will animate and render for display.

The following are the steps you performed in the previous chapter to create the node tree. They are the basic steps you will complete whenever setting up a game scene.

1. Create the `GameViewController`.

2. Have the `GameViewController` create its `UIView`.

3. Inside the `GameViewController.viewDidLoad()`, downcast the `UIView` to an `SKView` and set the `showFPS` property to true.

    ```
    let skView = view as SKView
    skView.showsFPS = true
    ```

4. Create an instance of the `SKScene` named `GameScene`, passing it its size in the constructor and setting the `scaleMode` property.

    ```
    scene = GameScene(size: skView.bounds.size)
    scene.scaleMode = .AspectFill
    ```

5. Inside the `init()` of the `GameScene`, add the `SKSpriteNode` objects to the scene.

    ```
    backgroundNode = SKSpriteNode(imageNamed: "Background")
    backgroundNode!.anchorPoint = CGPoint(x: 0.5, y: 0.0)
    backgroundNode!.position = CGPoint(x: size.width / 2.0, y: 0.0)
    addChild(backgroundNode!)

    playerNode = SKSpriteNode(imageNamed: "Player")
    playerNode!.position = CGPoint(x: size.width / 2.0, y: 80.0)
    addChild(playerNode!)
    ```

6. Present the complete scene in the `GameViewController`. `viewDidLoad()` method.

    ```
    skView.presentScene(scene)
    ```

At this point, you have a complete scene with a complete node tree. You can always add more nodes as the game progresses, but these are the basic steps that you will complete whenever you create a new `SKScene`.

The SKScene Rendering Loop

In this section, I will describe what happens after the `SKScene` is presented by the `SKView`. In a more traditional iOS application, you would render the view's content only once, and it would stay static until the model that the view is presenting changes. This is fine for a business app, but a game has the potential to constantly change.

Because of this dynamic characteristic, Sprite Kit is constantly updating the scene and its contents. This constant updating is called the *rendering loop* (see Figure 2-1).

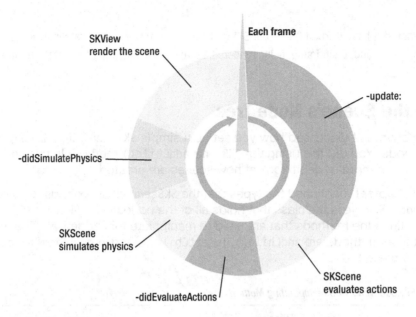

Figure 2-1. *The Sprite Kit rendering loop*

Each iteration of this loop generates the next frame in the scene. The steps involved in generating the next frame of a scene are as follows:

1. The scene calls its update() method. This is where you will have most of your game logic. More often than not, you will be moving nodes around, adding new actions to existing nodes, and handling user input. (I will talk about the update() method in Chapter 4.)

2. The scene next performs all programmed actions on its children. In this step, the scene will execute any actions you may have set up in step 1. (I will talk about actions in Chapter 5.)

3. The scene then calls the didEvaluateActions() method. This is where you would put any post-action game logic. An example would be testing the position of a node, after the actions were performed, and responding accordingly.

4. Next the scene executes any physics simulations on physics bodies in the scene. (I will discuss physics in Chapter 3.)

5. The scene calls the didSimulatePhysics() method. This is much like the didEvaluateActions() method in that this is where you would add any game logic to be performed after all the physics simulations are completed. This is your last chance to perform any game logic before the scene is rendered.

6. The scene is rendered.

You will see examples of each step in the rendering loop as you progress through each chapter of this book.

> **Note** When you have `showsFPS` in your `SKView`, you will see how many frames your game is rendering per second. Each frame, being rendered, represents a single iteration of the render loop.

Building the Scene's Node Tree

Earlier in this chapter, I discussed how you set up a simple `SKScene` with a background node and a player node. You did this using the `SKScene.addChild()` method. In this section, you are going to take a more in-depth look at how scenes are created.

Earlier in this chapter I mentioned the types that the `SKScene` class extends. One of those types is `SKNode`. `SKNode` is the class that holds all of the nodes in an `SKScene` object's node tree. It also defines the methods that are used to manipulate this node tree. The most common of these methods are `addChild()`, `insertChild()`, and `removeFromParent()`, as described in Table 2-1.

Table 2-1. The SKNode Node Tree Manipulating Methods

Method	Purpose
(1) `addChild()`	The `addChild(_:)` method adds a node to the end of the receiver's collection of child nodes.
(2) `insertChild(_:atIndex:)`	The `insertChild(_:atIndex:)` method inserts a child node at a specific position in the receiver's collection of child nodes.
(3) `removeFromParent()`	`removeFromParent()` removes the receiving node from its parent.

These are the three methods you will use to build the scene's node tree. The easiest way to see how these methods work is through a simple example. Take a look at the following sequence:

```
var gameScene = SKScene(size: CGSizeMake(320.0, 568.0))

var node1 = SKSpriteNode()
var node2 = SKSpriteNode()
var node3 = SKSpriteNode()

gameScene.addChild(node1)
gameScene.addChild(node2)
gameScene.addChild(node3)
```

Here you are creating an `SKScene` named gameScene. You then create three nodes and add them to the gameScene. At this point, the gameScene's node tree looks like Figure 2-2.

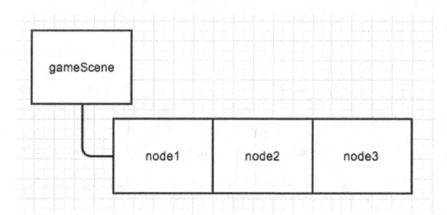

Figure 2-2. The gameScene's children property after adding three nodes

At this point, the node tree contains three nodes—node1, node2, and node3 (in that order). Now, if you executed the following snippet, you would have a node tree that looked like Figure 2-3:

```
var node4 = SKSpriteNode()
gameScene.insertChild(node4, atIndex: 2)
```

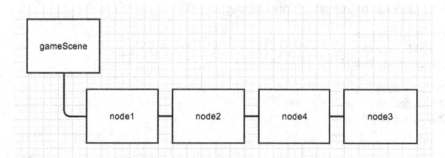

Figure 2-3. The gameScene's node tree after inserting a fourth node

The children property now contains four nodes, with node4 being inserted between node2 and node3. Let's do one last thing and remove a node.

```
node2.removeFromParent()
```

By invoking node2's removeFromParent method, you have removed node2 from its parent, which is gameScene in this case. Now the node tree looks like Figure 2-4.

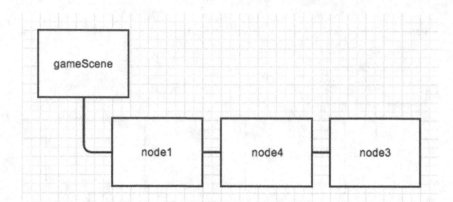

Figure 2-4. The gameScene's node tree after removing node4

There is one last thing you need to look at, and that is nested nodes. Because the node tree is part of SKNode and because SKSpriteNode is extended from SKNode, it can have nested nodes. The nice thing about nesting related nodes is that when you change the parent node, the same changes will be applied to all the child nodes.

To see how nested nodes are represented in the node tree, let's go back to the node tree represented by Figure 2-4. If you want to nest additional nodes inside node4, you can do so by executing the following snippet right after the previously executed node2.removeFromParent(). Figure 2-5 represents the results of this snippet.

```
var node4a = SKSpriteNode()
var node4b = SKSpriteNode()
var node4c = SKSpriteNode()

node4.addChild(node4a)
node4.addChild(node4b)
node4.addChild(node4c)
```

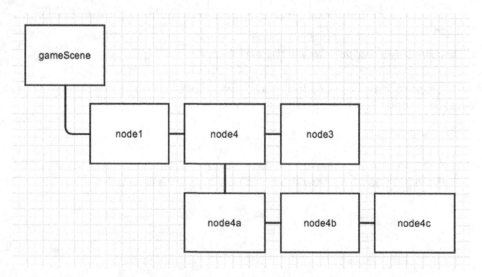

Figure 2-5. The gameScene's node tree with nodes nested inside node4

Rendering the Node Tree

Now that you know how to build the node tree, it is time to look at how the node tree is rendered. The order in which you add nodes to your scene is important. When the scene is rendered at the end of the rendering loop, it is rendered in reverse order of the way it was built. Let's use the node tree represented by Figure 2-3 as an example. When this node tree is rendered, the scene will render each node in the following order:

1. node3
2. node4
3. node2
4. node1

Notice the last node rendered was the first node added to the scene. Nested nodes are also rendered in the reverse order they were added. If you were to render the node tree represented by Figure 2-5, it would be rendered in the following order:

1. node3
2. node4
   a. node4c
   b. node4b
   c. node4a
3. node1

This is important because, based upon the position of each node, there could be some overlapping of nodes in the scene, which could lead to partial or completely hidden nodes.

It is also important because of the way Sprite Kit performs hit testing. When Sprite Kit processes a touch event or mouse event, it walks the scene to find the closest node that wants to receive the event. If the first node doesn't want the event, Sprite Kit checks the next closest node and repeats this process until the event is handled or ignored. Just like the scene rendering order, the order in which hit testing is performed is the reverse of the drawing order.

To see how this looks using the sample app, replace the current contents of the GameScene.init() method with the following code:

```
super.init(size: size)

backgroundColor = SKColor(red: 0.0, green: 0.0, blue: 0.0, alpha: 1.0)

// adding the background
backgroundNode = SKSpriteNode(imageNamed: "background")
backgroundNode!.anchorPoint = CGPoint(x: 0.5, y: 0.0)
backgroundNode!.position = CGPoint(x: size.width / 2.0, y: 0.0)
addChild(backgroundNode!)
```

```
// add the player
var playerNode1 = SKSpriteNode(imageNamed: "Player")
playerNode1.position = CGPoint(x: size.width / 2.0, y: 80.0)
addChild(playerNode1)

var playerNode2 = SKSpriteNode(imageNamed: "Player")
playerNode2.position = CGPoint(x: size.width / 2.0, y: 100.0)
addChild(playerNode2)

var playerNode3 = SKSpriteNode(imageNamed: "Player")
playerNode3.position = CGPoint(x: size.width / 2.0, y: 120.0)
addChild(playerNode3)
```

In this snippet, three player nodes are being added to the scene, each of them 20 points below the most recently added node. To see the results, run the project again. You will see the overlapping players, with the first player added on top, as shown in Figure 2-6.

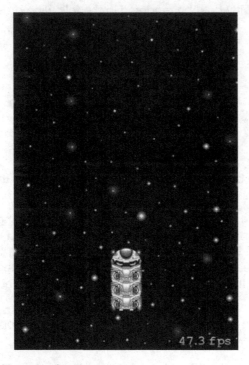

Figure 2-6. The gameScene's with overlapping player nodes

Searching the Node Tree

There is one last topic I want to cover before moving on to the coordinate system and anchor points: how you search the node tree. Something I have not discussed yet is the name property of the SKNode. The SKNode.name property is a String property that can be used to identify a unique sprite or a group of sprites.

An example of this would be to give the unique playerNode a name of Player. Assuming you were inside the GameScene and you did give the playerNode a name of Player, you could then search the GameScene for a unique node named Player using the following line of code:

```
childNodeWithName("Player")
```

This method returns an optional SKNode. If more than one child shares the same name, then the first node in the children array would be returned. If no child with this name was found, then return would have no value.

Another example might be to name a collection of sprites with the same name. For example, you could name a collection of sprites with the same circular texture, such as orb. You could then search for all sprites with that name and apply the set of actions in one call. This can be done using SKNode's enumerateChildNodesWithName() method.

This method searches for all nodes with the passed-in name and then executes the code in the block on each node found. Again, assuming you were inside the GameScene and you have added several sprites all named orb, you could search for all the orb nodes and execute a block on each one using the following snippet:

```
enumerateChildNodesWithName("orb", usingBlock: {
    node, stop in
    // do something with node or stop
})
```

Everything looks pretty straightforward here except for the parameters being passed to the block every time a node with the name orb is found. The first parameter is a reference to the node that was found—no problem. The second parameter, stop, is a pointer to a Boolean that can be used to stop the iteration. If you want to stop iterating over each node found, set the stop parameter's memory property to true like the following example.

```
stop.memory = true
```

Looking at SKSpriteNode Coordinates and Anchor Points

So far, I have talked about how you create an SKScene object and how it is rendered. I am now going to talk about how you position nodes in a scene. Let's begin by looking at the scene's coordinate system. Before you begin, be sure to change the GameScene.init() method back to the following:

```
init(size: CGSize) {

    super.init(size: size)

    backgroundColor = SKColor(red: 0.0, green: 0.0, blue: 0.0, alpha: 1.0)

    // adding the background
    backgroundNode = SKSpriteNode(imageNamed: "Background")
    backgroundNode!.anchorPoint = CGPoint(x: 0.5, y: 0.0)
```

```
    backgroundNode!.position = CGPoint(x: size.width / 2.0, y: 0.0)
    addChild(backgroundNode!)

    // add the player
    playerNode = SKSpriteNode(imageNamed: "Player")
    playerNode!.position = CGPoint(x: size.width / 2.0, y: 80.0)
    addChild(playerNode!)
}
```

Coordinates

When a scene is first initialized, its `size` property is set in its initializer, as you saw earlier. The size of the scene denotes the size of the visible portion of the scene. It does not define the entire size of the game world. You can think of the size of the scene as the viewport into the game world.

By default, an `SKScene`'s origin is placed in the bottom-left corner of the view presenting it. The coordinate representing this origin is (0, 0). Going back to the game from the previous chapter, add this line of code to the `GameScene.init()` method immediately following the call to the `super.init()`:

```
println("The size is (\(size.width), \(size.height)).")
```

Now run the application again using the iPhone 4s simulator. After you do, look in the console window. You will see the following output:

```
The size is (320.0, 480.0).
```

This is the size of the scene running on an iPhone 4s. You can try this again running on either of the iPhone 5 or 6 simulator. These values tell you the size of your scene (the viewport into your game world).

If you want to position `SKNode` objects into the visible world of your game, you have to set their positions inside the range of (0, 0) to (320, 480) on the iPhone 4s or from (0, 0) to (320, 568) on the iPhone 5s. Take a moment and play around with the coordinate system. Go back to the `GameScene.init()` method and change the position of the `playerNode` using the following line:

```
playerNode!.position = CGPoint(x: size.width / 2, y: size.height / 2)
```

With this change, you are positioning the `playerNode` in the center of the scene. To see the position change, run the app in the simulator again. You will now see your player in the middle of your scene, as shown in Figure 2-7.

Figure 2-7. *The playerNode in the middle of the scene*

Make one more position change before you move on. Change playerNode's position using the following line of code:

```
playerNode!.position = CGPoint(x: size.width, y: size.height)
```

As you can see, the new position is set to the maximum (x, y) of the viewable area in the scene. Run the app in the simulator again. You will see your player in the upper-right corner of your scene, as shown in Figure 2-8.

Figure 2-8. The playerNode at the top right of the scene

While you successfully positioned your player in the upper-right corner of the scene, you will notice something a little odd—only the bottom-left quarter of the playerNode is visible. You will see why this is in the next section when I focus on anchor points.

Anchor Points

As you saw in the previous section, when you positioned the playerNode in the top-right corner of the scene, only the bottom-left quarter of the node was visible in the scene. This is because the default anchor point for SKSpriteNodes is positioned at the center of the node.

A sprite's anchorPoint property is used to set the point in the SKSpriteNode's frame in which the sprite's position property will be applied. This sounds a little complicated, but it is really pretty straightforward. Take a look at Figure 2-9.

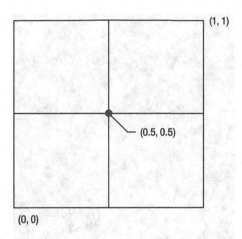

Figure 2-9. *SKSpriteNode's anchor point unit coordinate system*

This figure shows an SKSpriteNode's anchor point coordinate system. Notice the dot at position (0.5, 0.5). This is the default anchor point. Take a look at Figure 2-10 to see some common anchor points.

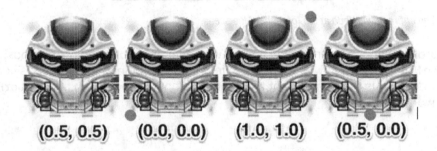

Figure 2-10. *An SKSpriteNode's some example anchor points*

In this figure there are four common anchor points as they relate to the sprites they are applied to. Looking at these examples, you can see that if you want to position the playerNode at the top-rightmost position of the scene and still have the entire spriteNode visible in the scene, then you would need to set the sprite's anchorPoint property to (1.0, 1.0). Do that now by adding the following line of code directly after playerNode's construction.

```
playerNode!.anchorPoint = CGPoint(x: 1.0, y: 1.0)
```

Now run the application once more. You will now see the entire playerNode positioned at the top right of the scene, as shown in Figure 2-11.

Figure 2-11. The entire playerNode at the top right of the scene

To get a handle on anchor points, play around with different anchor points and positions of the `playerNode` and see how each of the different anchor points affect the positioning of the `playerNode`. It is really important to understand how the `position` and `anchorPoint` properties work together.

> **Note**   When you are finished playing around with the `playerNode`'s position and anchor point, revert all of your code changes until the project is back to where you left it in Chapter 1.

Summary

In this chapter I covered quite a bit of information including what `SKScenes` are and how they are built. I also talked about the `SKScene` rendering loop and how the order the scene's node tree is constructed can affect the look and interactivity of the nodes. I closed the chapter with a look at a scene's coordinate system and node anchor points.

In the next chapter, I will cover Sprite Kit's physics engine and collision detection. That chapter will be a lot of fun, and you will start seeing your game coming to life.

Chapter 3

Adding Physics and Collision Detection to Your Game

In the previous chapter I covered quite a bit of information including what SKScene objects are and how they are built. I also talked about the SKScene rendering loop and how the order that the scene's node tree is constructed in can affect the look and interactivity of the nodes. I closed the chapter with a look at a scene's coordinate system and node anchor points.

In this chapter, I will cover Sprite Kit's physics engine and collision detection. I will begin the chapter with a discussion of SKPhysicsBody—the class used to simulate collision detection. You will then turn on gravity in the game world and see how that affects the nodes. After that, you will add a touch responder to propel the playerNode up into space, and I will close this chapter with a discussion of how to handle node collisions.

What Is an SKPhysicsBody?

To simulate physics in a Sprite Kit game, you add a physics body to a scene or node. A physics body, implemented by the Sprite Kit class SKPhysicsBody, is a simulated object attached to a node in the scene's node tree. The SKPhysicsBody class uses the properties of the node such as the position and velocity, combined with its own properties, to simulate how physical forces are applied to the simulated game world. It does the calculations to perform these simulations with each iteration of the render loop.

There are three types of physics bodies. There is a dynamic volume, a static volume, and an edge. A dynamic volume is a physical body with a volume and a mass that is affected by collisions and forces in the physics simulation. Nodes with a dynamic volume attached to them are the active nodes in games.

A physics body with a static volume is just like a dynamic volume, except forces and collisions do not affect them. Static volume bodies are often used as barriers in a game. When a dynamic body collides with a static body, the dynamic body is affected by the collision, and the static body remains constant.

An edge is a static body without volume. The simulation never moves an edge, and an edge's mass will not affect the simulation of other nodes. Edges represent negative space within a scene.

Adding Physics to Your Game World

The easiest way to see how all this works is to just do it. Let's begin by creating and associating an SKPhysicsBody with the playerNode. Add the following lines of code to the GameScene's .init(size: CGSize) method immediately following the construction of the playerNode:

```
playerNode!.physicsBody =
    SKPhysicsBody(circleOfRadius: playerNode!.size.width / 2)
playerNode!.physicsBody!.dynamic = true
```

Take a look at these two lines of code. The first line creates an SKPhysicsBody passing the initializer a parameter named circleOfRadius with a CGFloat for the value. Sprite Kit provides a handful of standard shapes for physics bodies, including circles (circleOfRadius), rectangles (rectangleOfSize), and a path-based polygon (polygonFromPath). The most efficient of these shapes is the circle, and the most inefficient is the path-based polygon.

Because the circle is the most efficient node shape, it will be the shape used for all of physics bodies in this game. The value passed to the constructor, in this instance, is the width of the playerNode divided by 2. I am using this value because I want to create a circle around the playerNode starting from its center with a radius of half the width of the node. This will result in a circle that surrounds the playerNode completely. If there were an SKPhysicsBody(circleOfDiameter:) constructor, then I would not need to divide the width by 2, but there is no such constructor.

Let's get back to the second line of this snippet. The second line turns the playerNode into a physics body with a dynamic volume. It will now respond to gravity and other physical bodies in the scene. Once you have made these changes, your new player setup code should look like the following.

```
// add the player
playerNode = SKSpriteNode(imageNamed: "Player")

playerNode!.physicsBody =
    SKPhysicsBody(circleOfRadius: playerNode!.size.width / 2)
playerNode!.physicsBody!.dynamic = true

playerNode!.position = CGPoint(x: size.width / 2.0, y: 80.0)
addChild(playerNode!)
```

Now, go back to Xcode and run the application once again. If you were not paying close attention, you would see only the background node of the game. This is because the default gravity setting in Sprite Kit matches the earth's gravitational forces, and the player node is now falling rapidly to the center of the earth.

To slow things down, you need to play around with the game world's gravity settings until you have a gravitational force you are happy with. Go back to the GameScene.init (size: CGSize) method and add the following line immediately following the super.init(size: size) invocation; then run the application again:

```
physicsWorld.gravity = CGVectorMake(0.0, -0.1);
```

Now you will see the player slowly drift off the bottom of the screen. What you have done here is modify the world's gravity using the SKScene's physicsWorld.gravity property and setting it to a value that slows the playerNode's descent considerably.

Notice the value you set the gravity property to is a vector with a value of 0.0 for the x-coordinate and a value of -0.1 for the y-coordinate. You set the x-coordinate to a value of 0.0 because gravity exerts force only along the y-axis. The result of this vector is a force that results in a gravitational force pulling toward the bottom of the scene.

While setting the y-coordinate to -0.1 helps us to see the playerNode fall off the scene, it is not practical for game play. A more reasonable value would be -2.0. Set the gravity property to CGVectorMake(0.0, -2.0) and try running it again. You will see the player fall off the screen, but it will be at a rate more conducive to game play.

> **Note**   In this section you modified the world's gravity property to a value that was not consistent with the earth's real gravity. I had you do this because you are not trying to match the earth's gravity but are instead trying to create a simulated game world that is fun for your players. You will find yourself doing this often as you start creating your own games. After all, it is about your players having fun, not matching the real world.

Applying Forces to SKPhysicsBody

At this point you have your player responding to the physical properties of your game world, and you have also adjusted the gravitational forces that pull the player off the bottom of the visible scene. This is great, but watching your character fall of the screen is not going to be a whole lot of fun. It is now time to apply some forces to the player to allow him to fight gravity and stay in the visible scene. The two most common methods of changing the velocity of an SKPhysicsBody are applying a force and applying an impulse.

When applying a force to an SKPhysicsBody, you apply the force for a length of time based on the amount of time that passes between invocations of the rendering loop. Forces are generally used for continuous velocity changes. You apply forces using the SKPhysicsBody's applyForce() method.

When you apply an impulse to an SKPhysicsBody, you are applying an instantaneous change to the body's velocity that is independent of the amount of simulation time that has passed. Impulses are used when you need to apply an immediate change to a node's velocity. You apply impulses using the SKPhysicsBody's applyImpulse() method. The game is going to use impulses to modify the player's velocity and will therefore use the applyImpulse() method.

Before you can apply an impulse to the player's physics body, you need to give the user the ability to tell the game when to apply the impulse. Because SKNode extends UIResponder and SKScene is an SKNode, you can test for touches in the scene by overriding the GameScene's UIResponder.touchesBegan() method. To do this, you need to complete two steps.

Add the following line of code that turns on user interaction in the scene immediately before the line of code that creates your backgroundNode:

```
userInteractionEnabled = true
```

And then override the UIResponder.touchesBegan() by adding the following method to the GameScene class:

```
override func touchesBegan(touches: NSSet, withEvent event: UIEvent) {

    playerNode!.physicsBody!.applyImpulse(CGVectorMake(0.0, 40.0))
}
```

Add this method to the bottom of the GameScene class definition and rerun the SuperSpaceMan application. While the application is running, tap the screen as many times as you need to get the player to fly back into the scene. The number of taps it takes will depend on how far the playerNode fell out of the scene.

After playing around with the touch responder, take a look at the single line of code in the touchesBegan() method. This line applies an impulse to the playerNode's physics body every time you tap the screen. The direction and strength of the impulse depend upon the vector you pass to the applyImpulse() method. In this case, you are creating a vector with an x-value of 0.0 (because you want to apply the impulse only linearly along the y-axis) and a y-value of 40.0, which results in a pulse that springs the player in the opposite direction of gravity.

Before moving on, play around with the y-value used to create this vector. It will help you understand how this value affects the size of the pulse. When you are finished, put the y-value back to 40.0 and let's move on.

Once you have the player visible in the scene, tap the screen until the player is at the top of the visible scene and watch him fall. One thing to note about the way the playerNode descends is that the player falls as if it has no surface area to dampen its velocity. This does not look quite right.

To fix this problem, Sprite Kit's SKPhysicsBody provides a linearDamping property. This property, which has a default of 0.1, is used to reduce a physics body's linear velocity to simulate fluid or air friction. In this case, you are simulating air friction. To see how you can use this property, add the following line of code immediately after the positioning of the playerNode and run the application again:

```
playerNode!.physicsBody!.linearDamping = 1.0
```

Now tap the screen until the player reaches the top of the screen and let it fall once more. This time, the playerNode will fall more slowly, simulating the resistance of falling through air.

Before moving on to the collision detection section of this chapter, make sure your modified GameScene.swift file looks like Listing 3-1.

Listing 3-1. GameScene.swift: The SuperSpaceMan Main Modified GameScene

```swift
import SpriteKit

class GameScene: SKScene {

    let backgroundNode : SKSpriteNode?
    var playerNode : SKSpriteNode?

    required init?(coder aDecoder: NSCoder) {

        super.init(coder: aDecoder)
    }

    override init(size: CGSize) {

        super.init(size: size)

        physicsWorld.gravity = CGVectorMake(0.0, -2.0);

        backgroundColor = SKColor(red: 0.0, green: 0.0, blue: 0.0, alpha: 1.0)

        userInteractionEnabled = true

        // adding the background
        backgroundNode = SKSpriteNode(imageNamed: "Background")
        backgroundNode!.anchorPoint = CGPoint(x: 0.5, y: 0.0)
        backgroundNode!.position = CGPoint(x: size.width / 2.0, y: 0.0)
        addChild(backgroundNode!)

        // add the player
        playerNode = SKSpriteNode(imageNamed: "Player")

        playerNode!.physicsBody =
            SKPhysicsBody(circleOfRadius: playerNode!.size.width / 2)
        playerNode!.physicsBody!.dynamic = true

        playerNode!.position = CGPoint(x: size.width / 2.0, y: 80.0)
        playerNode!.physicsBody!.linearDamping = 1.0
        addChild(playerNode!)
    }

    override func touchesBegan(touches: NSSet, withEvent event: UIEvent) {

        playerNode!.physicsBody!.applyImpulse(CGVectorMake(0.0, 40.0))
    }
}
```

Adding Collision Detection to Your SKNode

At this point, the game has a `playerNode` that responds to gravity and impulses; it's now time to add another node that your player can interact with. In this section, you are going to add another sprite that represents an orb in your game. You will begin by adding the orb and positioning it above the player. After that, you will modify the orb's properties so the player and orb interact naturally in the game. And finally, you will add code that will detect collisions between the player and the orb and remove the orb from the scene when they collide.

Adding a Node to Collide Into

Let's get started. The first thing you are going to do is add the orb sprite to the `GameScene` at a position a little to the left and above the player. The image you are going to use for the orb is in the `sprites.atlas` collection and is named `PowerUp`. There is nothing special about adding this sprite—you do so just like you added the player. First add the declaration of the new node to the `GameScene` immediately following the declaration of the `playerNode`.

```
let orbNode : SKSpriteNode?
```

After adding the declaration of the `orbNode`, add this code to the end of the `GameScene.init(size: CGSize)` method:

```
orbNode = SKSpriteNode(imageNamed: "PowerUp")
orbNode!.position = CGPoint(x: 150.0, y: size.height - 25)
orbNode!.physicsBody =
    SKPhysicsBody(circleOfRadius: orbNode!.size.width / 2)
orbNode!.physicsBody!.dynamic = false
addChild(orbNode!)
```

As you look over this snippet, you will see that it looks similar to the code you used to add the `playerNode` with a couple exceptions. First, the `orbNode` is being positioned 25 points from the top of the scene and a little to the left of the player. The second thing to notice is that the `orbNode.physicsBody.dynamic` property is being set to `false`. This is because you don't want this node to react to other nodes. You want the `playerNode` to pass through the scene collecting power-up orbs to fuel its ascent. This is why you have given the `orbNode`'s `physicsBody` a static volume.

Go ahead and run the app again. This time, tap the screen until the `playNode` collides with the `orbNode`. Because the `playerNode` is a dynamic body, it bounces off and goes spinning into the distance, and because the `orbNode` is a static body, it remains constant.

This is pretty cool for so little coding. But before moving on to detecting the collision and removing the orb, you need to do one more thing. As you will have noticed when the `playerNode` collided with the `orbNode`, the `playerNode` started to spin. This is a correct response in a lot of cases, but for this game you want the `playerNode` to just keep blasting through the orbs without spinning off. Sprite Kit provides a simple method of preventing these rotations. It does so with the physicsBody.allowsRotation property. Add the following line of code immedietly before the playerNode is added to the scene:

```
playerNode!.physicsBody!.allowsRotation = false
```

Now run the app again. This time when the player collides with the orb, it will bounce off but will not spin.

Adding Collision Detection

You now have your playerNode and orbNode colliding and reacting to the collisions properly. It is time to add explicit code that will detect collisions between the player and the orb and remove the orb from the scene when they collide.

When you run your game, you do see the collision between the orb and player, but what you want to do now is detect when that collision occurs and remove the orb that was part of the collision. Later in the game you will be adding a fuel element so that the orbs will provide fuel for the player to ascend higher and higher.

To be able to detect when SKNodes come into contact with each other, you first implement the Sprite Kit protocol SKPhysicsContactDelegate in the GameScene class and then implement the methods needed in your game. The SKPhysicsContactDelegate protocol defines two methods used to detect when SKNodes touch each other: the didBeginContact and the didEndContact() methods. The following snippet shows the protocol:

```
protocol SKPhysicsContactDelegate : NSObjectProtocol {

    optional func didBeginContact(contact: SKPhysicsContact!)
    optional func didEndContact(contact: SKPhysicsContact!)
}
```

The method names make their function pretty straightforward. The didBeginContact() method is invoked when the contact first begins, and the didEndContact() method is invoked when contact ends. For this game, you are interested only in the first method, didBeginContact(), because you don't want the playerNode to pass through the orb. You want the orb to be removed from the scene as soon as the playerNode contacts the orb.

Go back to the GameScene.swift file and change the class definition to the following:

```
class GameScene: SKScene, SKPhysicsContactDelegate
```

After you change your class definition, add this implementation of the didBeginContact() method to the end of the GameScene class:

```
func didBeginContact(contact: SKPhysicsContact!) {

    println("There has been contact.")
}
```

Finally, you need to make the GameScene the delegate of the scene's physicsWorld.contactDelegate. This is done by adding the following line in the GameScene.init(size: CGSize) method directly after the call to the super.init(size: size):

```
physicsWorld.contactDelegate = self
```

Adding Bit Masks to Your SKPhysicsBody

Everything is wired up to receive contact notifications, so the next thing you need to do is tell Sprite Kit which objects you are interested in receiving contact notifications. You do this using a concept called *bit masks*.

The SKPhysicsBody has three bit mask properties you can use to define the way your physics body interacts with other physics bodies in a game world: collisionBitMask, categoryBitMask, and contactTestBitMask. Each of these properties is described in Table 3-1.

Table 3-1. *The SKPhysicsBody's Three Bit Mask Properties*

Method	Purpose
1. collisionBitMask	Defines the collision categories that your SKPhysicsBody will bump into. All other physics bodies will be passed through.
2. categoryBitMask	Defines the collision categories a physics body belongs.
3. contactTestBitMask	Determines which categories this physics body makes contact with. An example, used in your game, would be coming in contact with the orb. You want Sprite Kit to tell you when the playerNode comes into contact with the orbNode.

At the moment, the app has only two nodes: a player and an orb. This makes it easy to categorize them. You can put the player into the category CollisionCategoryPlayer and all the orb nodes (there is only one at the moment) into a category named CollisionCategoryPowerUpOrbs. These two category bit masks are defined here:

```
let CollisionCategoryPlayer      : UInt32 = 0x1 << 1
let CollisionCategoryPowerUpOrbs : UInt32 = 0x1 << 2
```

Here are two bit masks, CollisionCategoryPlayer and CollisionCategoryPowerUpOrbs, each of which is an unsigned 32-bit integer. This is an important thing to note because collision bit masks are 32 bits, and you can have only 32 unique categories. Go ahead and add these two lines to the GameScene immediately following the declaration of the orbNode and before the first init() method:

```
let CollisionCategoryPlayer      : UInt32 = 0x1 << 1
let CollisionCategoryPowerUpOrbs : UInt32 = 0x1 << 2
```

Let's see how to set up the collision detection properties using the two nodes. First let's start with the playerNode. The following three lines set up the player's collision properties:

```
playerNode!.physicsBody!.categoryBitMask = CollisionCategoryPlayer
playerNode!.physicsBody!.contactTestBitMask = CollisionCategoryPowerUpOrbs
playerNode!.physicsBody!.collisionBitMask = 0
```

The first line of code associates the playerNode.physicsBody's category bit mask to the CollisionCategoryPlayer. The second line tells Sprite Kit that whenever your physics body comes into contact with another physics body belonging to the category CollisionCategoryPowerUpOrbs, you want to be notified. The final line, setting the playerNode.physicsBody's collisionBitMask to 0, tells Sprite Kit not to handle collisions for you. The game is going to be doing this itself in the didBeginContact() method. Go ahead and add these three lines to the GameScene.init(size: CGSize) method immediately after this line:

```
playerNode!.physicsBody.allowsRotation = false
```

Next, let's move on to configuring the orbNode's phsyicsBody. Setting up the orbNode's physics body is even easier than setting up the playerNode and can be done with only two lines of code.

```
orbNode!.physicsBody!.categoryBitMask = CollisionCategoryPowerUpOrbs
orbNode!.physicsBody!.collisionBitMask = 0
```

The first line associates the orbNode's physics body to the category CollisionCategoryPowerUpOrbs, and the second line, just like when configuring the player, is set to 0 because you are going to handle collisions yourself. There is one thing to note here. When configuring the orb node, you are not setting a contactTestBitMask. You are not doing this because it is not necessary. You will be notified of the contact because you already set this up in the playerNode. Add these two lines to the GameScene.init(size: CGSize) method immediately before adding the orbNode to the scene:

At this point, you have both nodes configured for collision detection, and whenever the playerNode comes into contact with the orbNode, the didBeginContact() method will be invoked. Let's give it a try. Save all your changes and run the application—paying attention to the console as you are tapping the screen. Now when the player comes into contact with the orb, you will see the following text printed in the console:

```
There has been contact.
```

Also, notice that this time the player passes through the orb. This is because you set the physics bodies' contactTestBitMask property to 0 in both nodes.

Removing the Orb When You Receive a Contact Message

The last thing you are going to do is add the functionality needed to remove the orbNode when the playerNode comes into contact with it. To do this, you need to make a couple of changes. First, as mentioned in Chapter 2, SKNodes have a name property that is used to identify a single node or group of nodes, so you need to use this property to tell you that the player runs into an orb. To name the orbNode, add the following line of code to the GameScene.init(size: CGSize) method right before you add orbNode to the scene:

```
orbNode!.name = "POWER_UP_ORB"
```

The last thing you need to do is modify the didBeginContact() method to see whether the node being contacted by the player SKNode has a name property equal to POWER_UP_ORB and, if it does, remove the node from the scene. The modified didBeginContact() method is shown here:

```
func didBeginContact(contact: SKPhysicsContact) {

    var nodeB = contact.bodyB!.node!

    if nodeB.name == "POWER_UP_ORB" {

        nodeB.removeFromParent()
    }
}
```

The first thing to look at in this method is the parameter being passed to the method. Here you have a contact parameter with a type of SKPhysicsContact. The SKPhysicsContact contains all of the information you need to handle a node contact. The SKPhysicsContact class contains five properties to help you determine the characteristics of the contact. Each of these is defined in Table 3-2.

Table 3-2. *The SKPhysicsContact Properties*

Method	Purpose
bodyA	The bodyA property, an SKPhysicsBody, represents first body in the contact. (This will be the playerNode.)
bodyB	The bodyB property, an SKPhysicsBody, represents second body in the contact. (This will be the orbNode.)
contactPoint	The contactPoint, a CGPoint, represents the contact point between the two physics bodies in the scene coordinates.
collisionImpulse	The contactImpulse, a CGFloat, specifies how hard these two bodies struck each other using newton-seconds as the unit of measure.
collisionNormal	The collisionNormal, a CGVector, specifies the direction of the collision.

You are interested only in the second of these properties, bodyB. Getting back to the didBeginContact() method, notice the second line of the method. Here you are referencing the contact's bodyB property, which as I mentioned earlier is an SKPhysicsContact. Once you have this reference, you can then get the SKNode instance from the bodyB.node property, which represents the second node in the collision.

Once you have the second SKNode in the collision, you can check to see whether it has a name of POWER_UP_ORB. If it does, then you invoke the node's removeFromParent() method, which, as it sounds, removes the orbNode from the scene.

Go ahead and replace the contents of the current didBeginContact() with this version and run the app one last time. This time, when the playerNode collides with the orbNode, the orbNode disappears from the scene.

At the end of this chapter, the new GameScene.swift should look like Listing 3-2.

Listing 3-2. GameScene.swift: The SuperSpaceMan GameScene with Collison Detection

```
import SpriteKit

class GameScene: SKScene, SKPhysicsContactDelegate {

    let backgroundNode : SKSpriteNode?
    var playerNode : SKSpriteNode?
    let orbNode : SKSpriteNode?

    let CollisionCategoryPlayer      : UInt32 = 0x1 << 1
    let CollisionCategoryPowerUpOrbs : UInt32 = 0x1 << 2

    required init?(coder aDecoder: NSCoder) {

        super.init(coder: aDecoder)
    }

    override init(size: CGSize) {

        super.init(size: size)

        physicsWorld.contactDelegate = self

        physicsWorld.gravity = CGVectorMake(0.0, -2.0);

        backgroundColor = SKColor(red: 0.0, green: 0.0, blue: 0.0, alpha: 1.0)

        userInteractionEnabled = true

        // adding the background
        backgroundNode = SKSpriteNode(imageNamed: "Background")
        backgroundNode!.anchorPoint = CGPoint(x: 0.5, y: 0.0)
        backgroundNode!.position = CGPoint(x: size.width / 2.0, y: 0.0)
        addChild(backgroundNode!)
```

```
        // add the player
        playerNode = SKSpriteNode(imageNamed: "Player")

        playerNode!.physicsBody =
            SKPhysicsBody(circleOfRadius: playerNode!.size.width / 2)
        playerNode!.physicsBody!.dynamic = true

        playerNode!.position = CGPoint(x: size.width / 2.0, y: 80.0)
        playerNode!.physicsBody!.linearDamping = 1.0
        playerNode!.physicsBody!.allowsRotation = false
        playerNode!.physicsBody!.categoryBitMask = CollisionCategoryPlayer
        playerNode!.physicsBody!.contactTestBitMask =
            CollisionCategoryPowerUpOrbs
        playerNode!.physicsBody!.collisionBitMask = 0
        addChild(playerNode!)

        orbNode = SKSpriteNode(imageNamed: "PowerUp")
        orbNode!.position = CGPoint(x: 150.0, y: size.height - 25)
        orbNode!.physicsBody =
            SKPhysicsBody(circleOfRadius: orbNode!.size.width / 2)
        orbNode!.physicsBody!.dynamic = false
        orbNode!.physicsBody!.categoryBitMask = CollisionCategoryPowerUpOrbs
        orbNode!.physicsBody!.collisionBitMask = 0
        orbNode!.name = "POWER_UP_ORB"
        addChild(orbNode!)
    }

    override func touchesBegan(touches: NSSet, withEvent event: UIEvent) {

        playerNode!.physicsBody!.applyImpulse(CGVectorMake(0.0, 40.0))
    }

    func didBeginContact(contact: SKPhysicsContact!) {

        var nodeB = contact.bodyB!.node!

        if nodeB.name == "POWER_UP_ORB" {

            nodeB.removeFromParent()
        }
    }
}
```

Summary

In this chapter I discussed Sprite Kit's physics engine and collision detection. I began the chapter with a discussion of the `SKPhysicsBody`. You then turned on the game world's gravity, which pulled the player down the length of the scene. After that, you added a touch responder to propel the `playerNode` back up into space. Finally, I closed the chapter with a discussion on how to handle collsions.

In the next chapter, you will add scrolling to the scene so that the player can fly higher in the scene without flying off the top of the scene. You will end the chapter by adding accelerometer integration to give additional controls to the player.

Chapter 4

Adding Scene Scrolling and Game Control

In the previous chapter I discussed Sprite Kit's physics engine and collision detection. I started with a discussion of `SKPhysicsBody`. You then turned on the game world's gravity and added a touch responder to propel the `playerNode` up into space. Finally, I closed out the chapter with a discussion of how to handle collisions.

In this chapter, you will start adding some real functionality to your game. You are going to begin by making some small changes to the current `GameScene`. After that, you will add additional orb nodes to collide into. You will then add scrolling to your scene, allowing you to make it look like the player is flying through space collecting orbs. And finally, you will start using the phone's accelerometer to move the player along the x-axis.

Reorganizing the GameScene

Before you move on to adding scrolling and the accelerometer, you need to do some small code changes in the existing `GameScene`. In previous chapters, there was a lot of code that showed how to do certain things in Sprite Kit. The changes you will be making here are reorganizational changes focused on setting up the game for continued game development.

The first thing you need to change is the strength of gravity in the game's physics world. You are going to do this by changing the vector that represents gravity's force from (0.0, -0.2) to (0.0, -0.5). Go ahead and find where you set the `physicsWorld.gravity` property and change it to the following:

```
physicsWorld.gravity = CGVectorMake(0.0, -5.0)
```

To prepare the scene for the next section where you will start scrolling the different layers in the game scene, you need to add another layer to your scene to hold all of the sprites. You will do this by adding another `SKSpriteNode` named `foregroundNode`. This node will hold

all of the sprites that will affect game play. So, let's add this node and add the player to it.
First, add the following declaration of the foregroundNode immediately after the declaration
of the backgroundNode:

```
let foregroundNode  : SKSpriteNode?
```

Next, create and add the following foregroundNode instance directly after where you added
the backgroundNode to the scene:

```
foregroundNode = SKSpriteNode()
addChild(foregroundNode!)
```

Now find the location in the init() method where you added the playerNode and orbNode to
the scene and change the addChild() invocations to the following:

```
foregroundNode!.addChild(playerNode!)
foregroundNode!.addChild(orbNode!)
```

Once you have the playerNode and orbNode added to the new foregroundNode, find where
you are setting the position of the playerNode and change its position property using the
following CGPoint:

```
playerNode!.position = CGPoint(x: self.size.width / 2.0, y: 180.0)
```

Now find where you are setting the playerNode.physicsBody.dynamic property and turn off
the player's dynamic volume.

```
playerNode!.physicsBody!.dynamic = false
```

You are doing this so the player does not fall off the screen if you don't tap the screen in
time. Next, add the following new property to the GameScene immediately after the definition
of the orbNode:

```
var impulseCount = 4
```

Now change the touchesBegan() method to match the following:

```
override func touchesBegan(touches: NSSet, withEvent event: UIEvent) {

    if !playerNode!.physicsBody!.dynamic {

        playerNode!.physicsBody!.dynamic = true
    }

    if impulseCount > 0 {

        playerNode!.physicsBody!.applyImpulse(CGVectorMake(0.0, 40.0))
        impulseCount--
    }
}
```

This snippet is turning the player's dynamic volume back on, if it was off, so the player will start reacting to gravity again. After that, it checks the impulseCount property. If it is greater than 0, then it applies an impulse to the player and decrements the impulseCount property by 1.

The purpose of this code is to put the game in an initial start state with the player stationary until you tap the screen to start. When the screen is tapped the first time, the game begins.

The impulseCount property was added to introduce a new game element. The game is going to use the impulseCount property to give the user a limited number of impulses that can be used for thrusts. The impulseCount property will increment each time the playerNode comes into contact with an orb and decrement every time the player taps the screen. This means the user must be good at collecting orbs, or they will eventually fall into oblivion and lose the game.

The next thing that needs to be changed is how the orb nodes are added to the scene. You want to add many more. Before adding additional nodes, the code that currently adds the nodes needs to be removed.

To remove this code, start by removing the orbNode property from the top of the GameScene class. Find the following line in the declarations section of the GameScene and remove it:

```
let orbNode : SKSpriteNode?
```

And then remove all of the following lines, which were used earlier to add the single node:

```
orbNode = SKSpriteNode(imageNamed: "PowerUp")
orbNode!.position = CGPoint(x: 150.0, y: size.height - 25)
orbNode!.physicsBody = SKPhysicsBody(circleOfRadius: orbNode!.size.width / 2)
orbNode!.physicsBody!.dynamic = false
orbNode!.physicsBody!.categoryBitMask = CollisionCategoryPowerUpOrbs
orbNode!.physicsBody!.collisionBitMask = 0
orbNode!.name = "POWER_UP_ORB"

foregroundNode!.addChild(orbNode)
```

Adding More Orbs to the Scene

The game scene is ready to start adding some real game components. The first is going to be a collection of additional orb nodes. The orbs will be laid out in two lines above the player. The first line of orbs, a collection of 20, will be centered and will start 100 points above the playNode with 140 points in between each node's anchorPoint. The second set of orb nodes will also be a string of 20 nodes, but they will be 50 points to the right of the player. The code to add the first set of orb nodes is shown in the following snippet:

```
var orbNodePosition = CGPointMake(playerNode!.position.x,
                         playerNode!.position.y + 100)

for i in 0...19 {

    var orbNode = SKSpriteNode(imageNamed: "PowerUp)

    orbNodePosition.y += 140
    orbNode.position = orbNodePosition
```

```
orbNode.physicsBody = SKPhysicsBody(circleOfRadius: orbNode.size.width / 2)
orbNode.physicsBody!.dynamic = false

orbNode.physicsBody!.categoryBitMask = CollisionCategoryPowerUpOrbs
orbNode.physicsBody!.collisionBitMask = 0
orbNode.name = "POWER_UP_ORB"

foregroundNode!.addChild(orbNode)
}
```

As you look over this code, you will see a variable named orbNodePosition that has an x-coordinate matching the playerNode's x-coordinate and a y-coordinate that is 100 points above the playerNode.

After that, there is a for loop that adds 20 orbNode objects centered above the player, with each node 140 points above the previous node's anchorPoint. Go ahead and add this code to the bottom of the GameScene's init() method, and then let's move on to the second set of orbNode objects.

To add the second set of nodes, you will use the following, similar code:

```
orbNodePosition = CGPointMake(playerNode!.position.x + 50, orbNodePosition.y)

for i in 0...19 {

    var orbNode = SKSpriteNode(imageNamed: "PowerUp")

    orbNodePosition.y += 140
    orbNode.position = orbNodePosition
    orbNode.physicsBody = SKPhysicsBody(circleOfRadius: orbNode.size.width / 2)
    orbNode.physicsBody!.dynamic = false

    orbNode.physicsBody!.categoryBitMask = CollisionCategoryPowerUpOrbs
    orbNode.physicsBody!.collisionBitMask = 0
    orbNode.name = "POWER_UP_ORB"

    foregroundNode!.addChild(orbNode)
}
```

As you look over this code, you will see that the only change is the modification of the variable orbNodePosition. The value of the orbNodePosition's x-coordinate is increasing by 50, and everything else is the same. You could easily refactor this code into a method and pass it the new x-coordinate, but the goal here is to see how everything works. It will be refactored in the next chapter. Before moving on, go ahead and add this code after the previous loop in the GameScene's init() method.

After you have all of this code added to the game scene, run the application. Your screen will now look like Figure 4-1.

Figure 4-1. The modified scene with additional orbs

The last thing that needs to be done before adding the scrolling to the game is to change how orb contacts are handled. If you remember from the previous chapter, whenever the playerNode came into contact with an orbNode, the orbNode was removed from the scene. This is still going to happen, but now the contact is going to also increment the impuleCount variable, giving the player additional impulses. To do this, change the current didBeginContact() method to the following:

```
func didBeginContact(contact: SKPhysicsContact!) {

    var nodeB = contact!.bodyB!.node!

    if nodeB.name == "POWER_UP_ORB"  {

        impulseCount++
        nodeB.removeFromParent()
    }
}
```

The new didBeginContact() increases the impulseCount property each time the player comes into contact with an orb and then removes the orb. Now the player has additional fuel to keep from crashing into the planet's surface below.

To see this change in action, save your changes and run the game again. This time when you tap the screen, the player will be thrust upward and hit the first orb, then hit the second, and so on, until it flies off the top of the screen. If you tap long enough, the player will eventually run out of impulses and fall back through the bottom of the game.

Scrolling the Scene

In this section you are going to start adding movement to your game world. Before making any additional code changes, go back to Xcode and select the first background image in the Images.xcassets folder (Arrow 1), as shown in Figure 4-2. With the first background selected (Arrows 2 & 3), expand the Utilities section of Xcode (Arrow 4) and then click the Show Attributes Inspector button (Arrow 5). Notice the Image properties (Arrow 6). The height of the image is much greater than any of the currently available devices (Arrow 6).

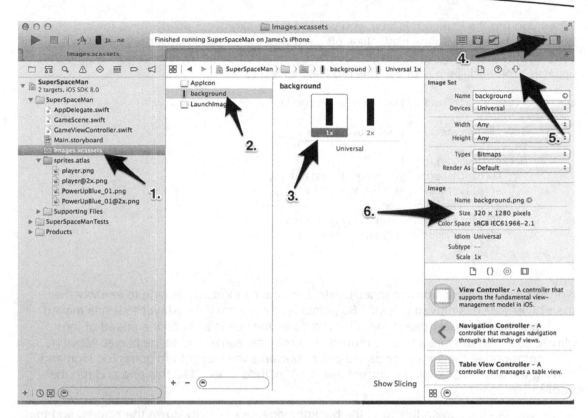

Figure 4-2. The background image size

The reason the background is so much bigger is because it is going to scroll downward to simulate the playerNode flying up through space. This is going to be accomplished by making use of the update() method in the game's rendering loop.

The first step to scroll the background is to change the position of the background based upon the location of the player in the game. Every time the player goes higher in the scene, the background will be moved down in the scene. The following code, which you will need to add to the GameScene in a moment, does just this:

```
override func update(currentTime: NSTimeInterval) {

    self.backgroundNode!.position =
        CGPointMake(self.backgroundNode!.position.x,
        -((self.playerNode!.position.y - 180.0)/8))
}
```

This implementation of the update() method changes the position of the background node based upon the current position of the player. Specifically, it sets the position of the backgroundNode to its same x-value but uses a y-value that is 180 points below the position of the player, which is then divided by 8. Don't worry about these numbers at the moment. I will talk about them a lot more in just a moment. Go ahead and add this update method to the end of the GameScene and then run the game again.

When you tap the screen this time, you will see the background slowly move toward the bottom of the scene as the player flies off the top of the screen. That's pretty cool, but the player is still flying out of the scene. There needs to be one more change made to the update() method. Take a look at this modified update():

```
override func update(currentTime: NSTimeInterval) {

    if playerNode!.position.y >= 180.0 {

        backgroundNode!.position =
            CGPointMake(backgroundNode!.position.x,
            -((playerNode!.position.y - 180.0)/8))
        foregroundNode!.position =
            CGPointMake(foregroundNode!.position.x,
            -(playerNode!.position.y - 180.0))
    }
}
```

Notice there have been two changes made. First the method is checking to see whether the playerNode has moved at least 180 points up the scene. If the playerNode has moved this high, then the backgroundNode is moved down the scene at 1/8th the speed of the player, and then the foreground is moved at exactly the same rate as the player. Moving the foreground at the same rate as the player prevents the player from going too high and leaving the scene. Change the current update() method to look like this one and run the application again.

When you tap the screen this time, the background moves slowly down the screen, and the SuperSpaceMan does not fly off the top of the screen. This is great except for one thing. When the playerNode gets to the top of the first line of orbs, the player can go no higher because the next set of orbs are to the right, and the player has no way of getting to them. This problem will be solved in the next section of this chapter when I show you how to add horizontal movement to the player using the accelerometer.

Controlling Player Movement with the Accelerometer

In the previous section of this chapter, the player ran into a problem when the next set of orbs needed to continue up the scene were 50 points to the right but the player had no horizontal movement to reach them. You will now fix this problem by using the phone's accelerometer to control the player's movement along the x-axis.

To use the accelerometer in your game, you first need to add the CoreMotion framework to your GameScene. You do this by adding the following import statement to the top of your GameScene.swift file:

```
import CoreMotion
```

After this, you need to add two properties. The first will hold an instance to the CMMotionManager object that will be used to monitor horizontal movement, and the second will hold a CGFloat value representing the acceleration along the x-axis. Add these two variables to the GameScene directly after the impulseCount variable added earlier:

```
let coreMotionManager = CMMotionManager()
var xAxisAcceleration : CGFloat = 0.0
```

This code creates an instance of the CMMotionManager and stores it in the constant coreMotionManager. The next line creates a CGFloat variable, xAxisAcceleration, and initializes it with the value 0.0.

Let's talk a little about what a CMMotionManager does. A CMMotionManager object is the object used to get access to the motion services provided by iOS. These services include access to the accelerometer, magnetometer, rotation rate, and other device motion sensors.

You are specifically interested in the acceleration along the x-axis of the device. This information is accessed using the accelerometer. You will be using the CMMotionManager to get the accelerometer to update the app on a specific interval with the current device acceleration. The code to do this is shown here:

```
self.coreMotionManager.accelerometerUpdateInterval = 0.3
self.coreMotionManager.startAccelerometerUpdatesToQueue(NSOperationQueue(), withHandler: {

    (data: CMAccelerometerData!, error: NSError!) in

        if let constVar = error {

            println("There was an error")
        }
        else {

            self.xAxisAcceleration = CGFloat(data!.acceleration.x)
        }
})
```

Take a moment to look at this code. The first line tells the coreMotionManager the interval, in seconds, that the accelerometer will use to update the app with the current acceleration. This value is set to 3/10 of a second; this provides a pretty smooth update rate. You can play around with this value and see how it affects the app.

The second line of this code actually starts the accelerometer updates. It does this using the startAccelerometerUpdatesToQueue() method, which takes two parameters. The first is the queue that the operation should be run on, and the second is the closure that will be handling each of the updates.

The closure is the interesting part of these two parameters. It has two optional parameters passed to it. The first contains the accelerometer data, and the second contains an error if there was one. As you look over this closure, you will see that it first tests and make sure it did not encounter an error. If it did, it prints a message to the console and ignores this update.

If it did not encounter an error, the method grabs the x-acceleration out of the CMAccelerometer's acceleration property and stores it in the class's xAxisAcceleration property. Go ahead and add this code to the touchesBegan() method of the GameScene just after the playerNode.physicsBody.dynamic property is set to true. This modified touchesBegan() method is shown here:

```
override func touchesBegan(touches: NSSet, withEvent event: UIEvent) {

    if !playerNode!.physicsBody!.dynamic {

        playerNode!.physicsBody!.dynamic = true

        self.coreMotionManager.accelerometerUpdateInterval = 0.3
        self.coreMotionManager.startAccelerometerUpdatesToQueue(NSOperationQueue(),
        withHandler: {

            (data: CMAccelerometerData!, error: NSError!) in

            if let constVar = error {

                println("There was an error")
            }
            else {

                self.xAxisAcceleration = CGFloat(data!.acceleration.x)
            }
        })
    }

    if impulseCount > 0 {

        playerNode!.physicsBody!.applyImpulse(CGVectorMake(0.0, 40.0))
        impulseCount--
    }
}
```

Now it is time to do something with this information. At first using the update() method would seem like the logical location to put this data to use, but the update() method is invoked before the render loop has evaluated all of the physics bodies in the scene. It is possible that colliding with another node in the scene could have altered the player's velocity along the x-axis, and this change should take place prior to altering the player's velocity with the accelerometer. While this cannot happen in this game, because the playerNode is the only dynamic volume in the game, it is good to be aware of.

Given that all the physics changes should be evaluated before the player's velocity on the x-axis is modified, there is really only one place in the render that can process accelerometer changes, and that is in the render loop's `didSimulatePhysics()` method. To override the current `didSimulatePhysics()`, add the following code to the bottom of the `GameScene`:

```
override func didSimulatePhysics() {

    self.playerNode!.physicsBody!.velocity =
                        CGVectorMake(self.xAxisAcceleration * 380.0,
                        self.playerNode!.physicsBody!.velocity.dy)

    if playerNode!.position.x < -(playerNode!.size.width / 2) {

        playerNode!.position =
            CGPointMake(size.width - playerNode!.size.width / 2,
            playerNode!.position.y);
    }
    else if self.playerNode!.position.x > self.size.width {

        playerNode!.position = CGPointMake(playerNode!.size.width / 2,
                                    playerNode!.position.y);
    }
}
```

Once you have added this code to the `GameScene`, save it, and this time run the app on your physical iPhone. The simulator will not simulate accelerometer activity. When the app is running on your device, tap the screen and try to collect all of the `orbNodes`. Remember, the more orbs you collect, the more impulses the player will have to keep going.

Once you have played around with the accelerometer a bit, let's look at the code you just added. The first line is where the `playerNode`'s velocity is changed. This is done by creating a new vector with the most recent accelerometer x-acceleration value multiplied by 380.0 as the x-value, then using the player's current velocity along the y-axis, and finally making this the player's new overall velocity.

After the player's velocity is modified, there are two `if` statements to determine whether the player is flying off the scene either to the left or to the right. If either of these two conditions occurs, the player is moved to the opposite side of the scene. Notice when the location of the `playerNode` is tested, the test is checking to see whether half of the `playerNode` is off the scene. This is done because the `playerNode`'s anchor point is (0.5, 0.5).

There is one last change that needs to be made, and that is to turn off accelerometer updates when the `GameScene` is no longer used. To do this, add the following `deinit()` method to the bottom of the `GameScene` and save your changes:

```
deinit {

    self.coreMotionManager.stopAccelerometerUpdates()
}
```

Summary

In this chapter you started to add some real functionality to your game. You began by making some small restructuring changes to the beginning of the game. After that you added additional orbNodes to collide with. After adding the new orbNodes, you added scrolling to your game scene, making it look like the player was flying through space collecting orbs. And finally, you closed out the chapter using the phone's accelerometer to move the player along the x-axis.

In the next chapter, you will continue adding new game elements as well as start animating your SKSpriteKitNodes. That is the chapter where you will start turning your game into a real, playable game.

Chapter 5

Adding Actions and Animations

In the previous chapter, you started to add some real functionality to your game. You began by making some small restructuring changes to the beginning of the game. After that, you added additional orbNode objects to collide with. After adding the new orbNode objects, you added scrolling to your game scene to make it look like the player was flying through space collecting orbs. Finally, you closed out the chapter using the phone's accelerometer to move the player along the x-axis.

In this chapter, you will refactor the orb node's layout one last time with the goal of enhancing playability. After that, I will show you how you can use SKActions to move an SKSpriteNode back and forth across the scene and then make that same node rotate forever. I am going to close out the chapter with a look at how you can add colorizing effects to an SKSpriteNode using a colorize action.

Refactoring the Orb Node Layout One Last Time

Before I start talking about SKActions, a few changes need to be made to the way the orb nodes are laid out. In the previous chapter, I mentioned refactoring the layout of the orb nodes. In this section, I want to not only refactor the layout of the nodes into a method but also modify the layout of the orb nodes one last time. The goal of this modification is to lay out the orbs in a little more gamelike manner. This new method is shown here:

```
func addOrbsToForeground() {

    var orbNodePosition = CGPoint(x: playerNode!.position.x, y: playerNode!.position.y + 100)
    var orbXShift : CGFloat = -1.0

    for _ in 1...50 {
```

```
        var orbNode = SKSpriteNode(imageNamed: "PowerUp")

        if orbNodePosition.x - (orbNode.size.width * 2) <= 0 {

            orbXShift = 1.0
        }

        if orbNodePosition.x + orbNode.size.width >= self.size.width {

            orbXShift = -1.0
        }

        orbNodePosition.x += 40.0 * orbXShift
        orbNodePosition.y += 120
        orbNode.position = orbNodePosition
        orbNode.physicsBody = SKPhysicsBody(circleOfRadius: orbNode.size.width / 2)
        orbNode.physicsBody!.dynamic = false

        orbNode.physicsBody!.categoryBitMask = CollisionCategoryPowerUpOrbs
        orbNode.physicsBody!.collisionBitMask = 0
        orbNode.name = "POWER_UP_ORB"

        foregroundNode!.addChild(orbNode)
    }
}
```

As you look at this method, you will see there is really nothing too special about it. It begins by setting the initial position of the first orb to be 100 points directly above the player node. It then adds 50 orbs, 40 points apart on the x-axis and 120 points apart on the y-axis, moving from right to left on the scene until all of the nodes have been added. Go ahead and add this method to the GameScene directly after the init() method.

Once you have the addOrbsToForeground() method added to the game scene, then you need to add a call to invoke this method. Add the following method invocation to the end of the GameScene's init() method.

```
addOrbsToForeground()
```

Before invoking this new method, you need to remove the old orb-adding code from the init() method. To do so, find the following code and remove it from the init():

```
var orbNodePosition = CGPointMake(playerNode!.position.x, playerNode!.position.y + 100)

for i in 0...19 {

    var orbNode = SKSpriteNode(imageNamed: "PowerUp")

    orbNodePosition.y += 140
    orbNode.position = orbNodePosition
    orbNode.physicsBody = SKPhysicsBody(circleOfRadius: orbNode.size.width / 2)
    orbNode.physicsBody!.dynamic = false
```

```
    orbNode.physicsBody!.categoryBitMask = CollisionCategoryPowerUpOrbs
    orbNode.physicsBody!.collisionBitMask = 0
    orbNode.name = "POWER_UP_ORB"

    foregroundNode!.addChild(orbNode)
}

orbNodePosition = CGPointMake(playerNode!.position.x  + 50, orbNodePosition.y)

for i in 0...19 {

    var orbNode = SKSpriteNode(imageNamed: "PowerUp")

    orbNodePosition.y += 140
    orbNode.position = orbNodePosition
    orbNode.physicsBody = SKPhysicsBody(circleOfRadius: orbNode.size.width / 2)
    orbNode.physicsBody!.dynamic = false

    orbNode.physicsBody!.categoryBitMask = CollisionCategoryPowerUpOrbs
    orbNode.physicsBody!.collisionBitMask = 0
        orbNode.name = "POWER_UP_ORB"

    foregroundNode!.addChild(orbNode)
}
```

Once you have made and saved all of these changes, run the app again and take a look at the new layout. It should look like Figure 5-1.

Figure 5-1. *The new orb layout*

After restarting the app, play around with the new layout. It's a lot more fun than just going straight up.

Sprite Kit Actions

In Sprite Kit whenever you want to move, modify, or perform some action on an SKNode, you are going to be, more often than not, applying that change using an SKAction. Apple defines an SKAction as follows: "An action is an object that defines a change you want to make to the scene." There are many different uses for SKActions, but some of the more common uses of SKActions are as follows:

> Animating a node through a series of textures
>
> Modifying the position of a node using its position property
>
> Changing the visibility of a node using its hidden property
>
> Adjusting the translucency of a node using its alpha property
>
> Modifying the size of a node using its size property
>
> Playing simple sounds
>
> Colorizing a node

To use an SKAction, you have to perform only two steps: you create the action you want to perform, and you tell the node you want to perform it on to run the action. An example of this that would move a node to the right side of the scene over a period of two seconds is shown here:

```
var moveRightAction = SKAction.moveToX(size.width, duration: 2.0)
sampleNode.runAction(moveRightAction)
```

Another really cool feature of SKActions is the ability to chain actions together. Take a look at this example:

```
var moveRightAction = SKAction.moveToX(size.width, duration: 2.0)
var moveLeftAction = SKAction.moveToX(0.0, duration: 2.0)
var actionSequence = SKAction.sequence([moveRightAction, moveLeftAction])
sampleNode.runAction(actionSequence)
```

This bit of code will begin by moving the node to the right of the scene, and then when that action is finished, it will move the same node to the left side of the scene. Another nice feature of SKAction is the ability to repeat an action. Take a look at this snippet:

```
var moveRightAction = SKAction.moveToX(size.width, duration: 2.0)
var moveLeftAction = SKAction.moveToX(0.0, duration: 2.0)
var actionSequence = SKAction.sequence([moveRightAction, moveLeftAction])
var moveAction = SKAction.repeatActionForever(actionSequence)
sampleNode.runAction(moveActionSequence)
```

Here you see the previous example, but now there is another action, repeatActionForever, that will run the moveAction forever. That's all it took—one line to make all the previous actions run forever.

While this is a simple set of SKAction examples, there is almost no limit to how you can leverage actions in your games. In the following sections of this chapter, I will show you how to use some of this same code to move a collection of nodes back and forth across the scene while also rotating the node through a collection of textures, giving the illusion of node rotation.

Before moving on, there is one thing you should note. Take a look at all the methods used to create the SKActions. Note that all of these methods are class methods. This is the pattern used to create all SKActions. Currently there are no extensions of the SKAction class.

Using Actions to Move Nodes in the Scene

In the previous section, I told you I was going to show you how to move a collection of nodes back and forth across the game scene. You have already seen how to do this using the moveToX, sequence, and repeatForever actions.

The node that will be moving across the scene is a new node. If you open the sprites.atlas folder, you will see several BlackHoleX.png images. Select the first image in the list, BlackHole0.png. It should look like Figure 5-2.

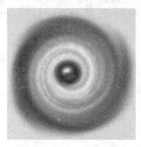

Figure 5-2. The BlackHole node

The purpose of this node will be to represent a black hole moving back and forth across the scene. If the player node comes into contact with this node, the player will stop responding to the physics world and slowly fall to their death.

To add this new node to the scene, you need to create a new SKSpriteNode instance and pass it the BlackHole0 image. You can find the code to do this in the following method, named addBlackHolesToForeground():

```
func addBlackHolesToForeground() {

    var blackHoleNode = SKSpriteNode(imageNamed: "BlackHole0")
    blackHoleNode.position = CGPointMake(size.width - 80.0, 600.0)
    blackHoleNode.physicsBody =
        SKPhysicsBody(circleOfRadius: blackHoleNode.size.width / 2)
    blackHoleNode.physicsBody!.dynamic = false
    blackHoleNode.name = "BLACK_HOLE"

    foregroundNode!.addChild(blackHoleNode)
}
```

You have seen all this code before. It starts by creating a new instance of the blackHoleNode using the image named BlackHole0. It then adds the node to the scene, sets the properties of the node's physicsBody, and names the node BLACK_HOLE. Go ahead and add this code immediately following the addOrbsToForeground() method. And then add a call to invoke the addBlackHolesToForeground() method right before the invocation of the addOrbsToForeground() method.

After you have made these changes, run the app again. This time you will see the blackHoleNode suspended up and to the right of the player node, as shown in Figure 5-3.

Figure 5-3. *The BlackHole node added to the scene*

Before moving on to performing actions on this node, the code to handle contacts between the playerNode and the blackHoleNode needs to be added to the GameScene class. You have seen all of this code before. So, I will be going over it quickly without too much explanation.

First the categoryBitMask of the blackHoleNode needs to be configured, and the playNode's contactBitMask needs to be modified to include the blackHoleNode's categoryBitMask. To do this, add this definition of the CollisionCategoryBlackHoles constant directly below the other two category definitions, as shown here:

```
let CollisionCategoryPlayer : UInt32 = 0x1 << 1
let CollisionCategoryPowerUpOrbs : UInt32 = 0x1 << 2
let CollisionCategoryBlackHoles : UInt32 = 0x1 << 3
```

Next, set the blackHoleNode.physicsBody's categoryBitMask and collisionBitMask, as shown in the following snippet. Add these lines directly before the blackHoleNode is added to the foreground in the addBlackHolesToForeground() method.

```
blackHoleNode.physicsBody!.categoryBitMask = CollisionCategoryBlackHoles
blackHoleNode.physicsBody!.collisionBitMask = 0
```

After you have configured the blackHoleNode.physicsNody's bit masks, you need to add the CollisionCategoryBlackHoles to the playerNode.physicsBody's contactTestBitMask, as shown next. Find where the playerNode.physicsBody's contactTestBitMask is being set and modify it to look like this line:

```
playerNode!.physicsBody!.contactTestBitMask =
    CollisionCategoryPowerUpOrbs | CollisionCategoryBlackHoles
```

There is one more change you need to make, and that is to modify the didBeginContact() method so that it tests for the BLACK_HOLE node whenever nodes come into contact with the playerNode. The simplest way to do this is to add an if else condition to the current if statement in the method. This change is shown in the following snippet:

```
if nodeB.name == "POWER_UP_ORB" {

    impulseCount++
    nodeB.removeFromParent()
}
else if nodeB.name == "BLACK_HOLE" {

    playerNode!.physicsBody!.contactTestBitMask = 0
    impulseCount = 0
}
```

Make this change to the didBeginContact() method and run the app again. When you play this time, try to make the player come into contact with the new black hole. When you do, you will notice the player quits responding to taps and contact with other nodes and then slowly falls until it falls through the bottom of the scene. At this point, the game is essentially over.

All right, it is finally time to use some SKActions. If you remember from the previous section, there are two steps involved when using an SKAction. First you create the action you would like to use, and second you tell the node that you want to apply the action to run the action. Let's begin with the action sequence used earlier in this chapter.

```
let moveLeftAction = SKAction.moveToX(0.0, duration: 2.0)
let moveRightAction = SKAction.moveToX(size.width, duration: 2.0)
let actionSequence = SKAction.sequence([moveLeftAction, moveRightAction])
let moveAction = SKAction.repeatActionForever(actionSequence)
```

As you look at this code, you will recognize it from earlier in the chapter when I first introduced SKActions. The first line creates an action that will move the node that runs it to point 0.0 on the x-axis, and the second line moves the node back to the far-right side of the scene. After this, both of these actions are used to create a sequence of actions, and this new action is stored in the variable actionSequence. Finally, the actionSequence is used to create a repeating action using the SKAction.repeatActionForever() class method. After you have looked this code over a bit, copy it to the top of the addBlackHolesToForeGround() method.

The final step to make the black hole move back and forth across the scene is to tell the blackHoleNode to actually run the action. This is done using the following single line:

```
blackHoleNode.runAction(moveAction)
```

Add this line to the end of the addBlackHolesToForeground() method and run the app again. This time you will see the black hole moving back and forth across the scene for as long as the game is being run.

There is one more thing I want to do with the addBlackHolesToForeground() method before moving on. You may have noticed the name of the addBlackHolesToForeground() method mentions more than one black hole. This was intentional. I think the game needs several black holes to make it more difficult to play. Take a look at the new addBlackHolesToForeground() method shown here:

```
func addBlackHolesToForeground() {

    let moveLeftAction = SKAction.moveToX(0.0, duration: 2.0)
    let moveRightAction = SKAction.moveToX(size.width, duration: 2.0)
    let actionSequence = SKAction.sequence([moveLeftAction, moveRightAction])
    let moveAction = SKAction.repeatActionForever(actionSequence)

    for i in 1...10 {

        var blackHoleNode = SKSpriteNode(imageNamed: "BlackHole0")

        blackHoleNode.position = CGPointMake(self.size.width - 80.0, 600.0 * CGFloat(i))
        blackHoleNode.physicsBody = SKPhysicsBody(circleOfRadius: blackHoleNode.size.width / 2)
        blackHoleNode.physicsBody!.dynamic = false
        blackHoleNode.physicsBody!.categoryBitMask = CollisionCategoryBlackHoles
        blackHoleNode.physicsBody!.collisionBitMask = 0
        blackHoleNode.name = "BLACK_HOLE"
```

```
        blackHoleNode.runAction(moveAction)

        self.foregroundNode!.addChild(blackHoleNode)
    }
}
```

As you look at this code, you will notice it iterates over a for loop 10 times, adding another black hole every 600 points above the previous black hole. As it does so, it tells each new node to run the moveAction created earlier. To see this change in action, use this code to replace the current addBlackHolesToForeground() method and run the app. When you run the app this time, you will see additional black holes going up the length of the scene.

Using SKActions to Animate Sprites

In this section I will show you how to leverage SKActions to animate the black hole nodes that you just added to the scene. In doing so, I will be introducing you to a couple of new classes: SKTexture and SKTextureAtlas.

An SKTexture is an object that holds an image that is used by SKSpriteNodes, SKShapeNodes, or as the particles created by an SKEmitterNode. You have been using SKTexture throughout this book when you have created an SKSpriteNode. Each image used to create an SKSpriteNode was internally represented as an SKTexture.

An SKTextureAtlas is a collection of SKTexture objects created from a texture atlas stored in an application's resource bundle. Go back to your project in Xcode and open the folder named sprites.atlas. You will see all of the images, except background images, used in this game. If you wanted to load all of the images in this atlas folder into an SKTextureAtlas, you would execute the following code:

```
let textureAtlas = SKTextureAtlas(named: "sprites.atlas")
```

This single line reads all of the individual files in the sprites.atlas folder and adds them to the SKTextureAtlas each as an SKTexture that can be looked up by the original file name. Add this line to the top of the addBlackHolesToForeground() method, and let's move on.

To retrieve an SKTexture, you would use the SKTextureAtlas.textureNamed() method, passing it the name of the texture you want to retrieve. An example of this that retrieves the first black hole texture in the textureAtlas is shown here:

```
let frame0 = textureAtlas.textureNamed("BlackHole0")
```

This line of code retrieves the SKTexture represented by the name BlackHole0 and stores it in the constant frame0.

To create an animation using all of the black hole images, you would retrieve each of them from the textureAtlas and add them to an array that represents the order each texture will be displayed in the animation. This code is shown in the following snippet:

```
let frame0 = textureAtlas.textureNamed("BlackHole0")
let frame1 = textureAtlas.textureNamed("BlackHole1")
let frame2 = textureAtlas.textureNamed("BlackHole2")
let frame3 = textureAtlas.textureNamed("BlackHole3")
let frame4 = textureAtlas.textureNamed("BlackHole4")

let blackHoleTextures = [frame0, frame1, frame2, frame3, frame4]
```

Once you have examined this code, add it to the top of the addBlackHolesToForeground() method immediately after the creation of the textureAtlas.

Now, all you have to do to animate the black holes is to create a new action using the SKAction.animateWithTextures() method, passing it the array of textures and the time, in seconds, each frame is to be displayed. Take a look at the following lines:

```
let animateAction =
    SKAction.animateWithTextures(blackHoleTextures, timePerFrame: 0.2)
let rotateAction = SKAction.repeatActionForever(animateAction)
```

The first line creates an action that will display each texture in the textureAtlas array for 2/10ths of a second. To make the black hole nodes animate forever, the second line creates another action that will perform the animation action forever. To see your new animation in action, copy all of this code to the top of the addBlackHolesToForeground() method immediately after the blackHoleTextures array and then add the following line, which will run the action, right before you add each blackHoleNode to the scene:

```
blackHoleNode.runAction(rotateAction)
```

When you have made all of these changes to the addBlackHolesToForeground() method, the new method will look like the following:

```
func addBlackHolesToForeground() {

    let textureAtlas = SKTextureAtlas(named: "sprites.atlas")

    let frame0 = textureAtlas.textureNamed("BlackHole0")
    let frame1 = textureAtlas.textureNamed("BlackHole1")
    let frame2 = textureAtlas.textureNamed("BlackHole2")
    let frame3 = textureAtlas.textureNamed("BlackHole3")
    let frame4 = textureAtlas.textureNamed("BlackHole4")

    let blackHoleTextures = [frame0, frame1, frame2, frame3, frame4]

    let animateAction =
        SKAction.animateWithTextures(blackHoleTextures, timePerFrame: 0.2)
    let rotateAction = SKAction.repeatActionForever(animateAction)
```

```
        let moveLeftAction = SKAction.moveToX(0.0, duration: 2.0)
        let moveRightAction = SKAction.moveToX(size.width, duration: 2.0)
        let actionSequence = SKAction.sequence([moveLeftAction, moveRightAction])
        let moveAction = SKAction.repeatActionForever(actionSequence)

        for i in 1...10 {

            var blackHoleNode = SKSpriteNode(imageNamed: "BlackHole0")

            blackHoleNode.position = CGPoint(x: size.width - 80.0, y: 600.0 * CGFloat(i))
            blackHoleNode.physicsBody =
                SKPhysicsBody(circleOfRadius: blackHoleNode.size.width / 2)
            blackHoleNode.physicsBody!.dynamic = false
            blackHoleNode.physicsBody!.categoryBitMask = CollisionCategoryBlackHoles
            blackHoleNode.physicsBody!.collisionBitMask = 0
            blackHoleNode.name = "BLACK_HOLE"

            blackHoleNode.runAction(moveAction)
            blackHoleNode.runAction(rotateAction)

            foregroundNode!.addChild(blackHoleNode)
        }
    }
```

Once you have made all of these changes, save your work and run the application again. This time you will see that as the black holes are moving back and forth across the scene, they are also rotating as they are animated through each of the textures in the blackHoleTextures array.

Adding Some Additional Bling to the GameScene

Now that you have all the orbs laid out nicely and the black holes are animating back and forth across the game scene, it is time to add a little more bling to make the game scene look just a little better. Specifically, I will show how to add some additional stars to the scene, a planet surface, and finally I will show how to colorize the playerNode when it comes into contact with a black hole.

Let's get started with adding some stars to the background. First, open the Images. xcassets folder in Xcode and select the image Stars. To add this image to the scene, first add a declaration statement that will hold the reference to the SKSpriteNode referencing the Stars image. This declaration should be added to the GameScene directly after the backgroundNode declaration.

```
let backgroundNode  : SKSpriteNode?
let backgroundStarsNode  : SKSpriteNode?
```

After adding the declaration, add the following lines to the `GameScene.init(size: CGSize)` method immediately after the line that adds the `backgroundNode` to the scene:

```
addChild(backgroundNode!)

backgroundStarsNode = SKSpriteNode(imageNamed: "Stars")
backgroundStarsNode!.anchorPoint = CGPoint(x: 0.5, y: 0.0)
backgroundStarsNode!.position = CGPoint(x: 160.0, y: 0.0)
addChild(backgroundStarsNode!)
```

There is one last thing you need to do before running the app and checking out the new stars, and that is to move the stars in relation to the `playerNode`. Moving the stars in relation to the player is pretty straightforward, but I do want to add a little coolness. I want to do this by moving the stars at a slightly different rate than the background. I have modified the `update()` method to do just this. Take a look:

```
override func update(currentTime: NSTimeInterval) {

    if playerNode!.position.y >= 180.0 {

        backgroundNode!.position = CGPointMake(backgroundNode!.position.x,
            -((playerNode!.position.y - 180.0)/8));

        backgroundStarsNode!.position = CGPointMake(backgroundStarsNode!.position.x,
            -((playerNode!.position.y - 180.0)/6))

        self.foregroundNode!.position = CGPointMake(self.foregroundNode!.position.x,
            -(self.playerNode!.position.y - 180.0));
    }
}
```

Notice the bolded section of the modified `update()` method. With these two lines I am moving the stars relative to the `playerNode`, but I am moving them at a slightly slower rate than the `backgroundNode`. This gives the illusion that the `backgroundStarsNode` is closer to the viewport of the scene. Make this change to the `update()` method and run the application again. When the game is first launched, you will see a scene that looks like Figure 5-4.

Figure 5-4. *A layer of stars added to the scene*

Go ahead and start playing the game. When you go higher and higher in the scene, you will notice that the stars are moving just a bit faster than the background. This effect is called *parallelaxation*.

The next thing I want to do is add the perception that the `playerNode` is starting on a planet's surface. Go back to Xcode and, once again, open the `Images.xcassets` folder and find the `PlanetStart` image. This is the image that will act as the planet's surface.

Adding this new image to your scene is not complicated, and you have seen it before. The only difference from adding the stars to the scene is that you are going to move the planet at the same rate as the background node. This will make the planet's surface fall away as the player gets higher and higher in the scene.

Let's go ahead and do this. First, add a new `SKSpriteNode` declaration directly following the declaration of the `backgroundStarsNode`.

```
let backgroundStarsNode : SKSpriteNode?
let backgroundPlanetNode : SKSpriteNode?
```

Next, insert the code to add the `backgroundPlanetNode` to the scene. This code should immediately follow the addition of the `backgroundStarsNode`, as shown here:

```
addChild(backgroundStarsNode!)

backgroundPlanetNode = SKSpriteNode(imageNamed: "PlanetStart")
backgroundPlanetNode!.anchorPoint = CGPoint(x: 0.5, y: 0.0)
backgroundPlanetNode!.position = CGPoint(x: 160.0, y: 0.0)
addChild(backgroundPlanetNode!)
```

Now, find the line of code that sets the position of the `playerNode` (in the `init(size: CGSize)` method) and change the `position` to match the following:

```
playerNode!.position = CGPoint(x: size.width / 2.0, y: 220.0)
```

Finally, modify the `update` method to move the `backgroundPlanetNode` at the same rate as the `backgroundNode`.

```
override func update(currentTime: NSTimeInterval) {

    if playerNode!.position.y >= 180.0 {

        backgroundNode!.position =
            CGPointMake(backgroundNode!.position.x,
            -((playerNode!.position.y - 180.0)/8));

        backgroundStarsNode!.position =
            CGPointMake(backgroundStarsNode!.position.x,
            -((playerNode!.position.y - 180.0)/6));
```

```
    backgroundPlanetNode!.position =
        CGPointMake(backgroundPlanetNode!.position.x,
        -((playerNode!.position.y - 180.0)/8));

    foregroundNode!.position = CGPointMake(foregroundNode!.position.x,
        -(playerNode!.position.y - 180.0));
    }
}
```

Once you have made all of these changes, run the app again and admire your handwork.
You should now see a planet resting at the bottom of the scene and the playerNode standing
on top of it. Tap the screen a few times. The planet and the background will move together,
giving the impression that the playerNode is flying off the planet's surface and into space.
Figure 5-5 shows the new scene.

Figure 5-5. *A planet's surface added to the scene*

There is one last change I would like to make. If you have had the player run into a black hole recently, you will know that it is a bit anticlimactic. I want to add a visual indicator that shows the player is dead. A simple way to do this is to use a colorize action. A colorize action will blend a second color into an SKNode over a specified interval. An example creation of colorizeAction is shown here:

```
SKAction.colorizeWithColor(UIColor.redColor(), colorBlendFactor: 0.5, duration: 1)
```

This action, when run on an SKNode, will blend a red color with a blend factor of 0.5 over a period of 1 second. This is similar to what I would like to apply to the playerNode when it comes into contact with a black hole. Take a look at the last two lines of this modified didBeginContact's method:

```
func didBeginContact(contact: SKPhysicsContact!) {

    var nodeB = contact!.bodyB!.node!

    if nodeB.name == "POWER_UP_ORB"  {

        impulseCount++
        nodeB.removeFromParent()
    }
    else if nodeB.name == "BLACK_HOLE"  {

        playerNode!.physicsBody!.contactTestBitMask = 0
        impulseCount = 0

        var colorizeAction = SKAction.colorizeWithColor(UIColor.redColor(),
            colorBlendFactor: 1.0, duration: 1)
        playerNode!.runAction(colorizeAction)
    }
}
```

These two lines create a colorize action that will fully blend a red color to the playerNode over a period of one second whenever the player runs into a black hole. Make these changes and run the application one more time. When you run it this time, be sure to run the player into a black hole. Notice how, when he does, he will slowly turn red and fall to the planet's surface—much better.

Summary

In this chapter, you refactored the orb node's layout one last time with the goal of enhancing playability. After that, you saw how to use SKActions to move an SKSpriteNode back and forth across the scene and then make that same node rotate forever. At the end of the chapter, you took a look at how you can add colorizing effects to an SKSpriteNode using a colorize action.

In the next chapter, I will focus on using particle emitters and how they can be leveraged in Sprite Kit games. After that, I will show you how they can be used to add engine exhaust to the playerNode whenever an impulse is applied to the physicsBody.

Chapter 6

Adding Particle Effects to Your Game with Emitter Nodes

In the previous chapter, you refactored the orb node's layout and saw how you could use SKActions to move an SKSpriteNode back and forth across the scene while making that same node rotate forever. At the end of the chapter, you looked at how you can add colorizing effects to an SKSpriteNode using a colorize action.

In this chapter, I will show you how to define particle emitters and how to leverage them in Sprite Kit games. After that, I will show you how you can use them to add engine exhaust to the playerNode whenever an impulse is applied to the physicsBody.

> **Note** I will cover only the properties that I will be using in the SuperSpaceMan game.
> If you want to see the complete list of properties, check out the Apple Developer docs at
> https://developer.apple.com/library/ios/documentation/SpriteKit/Reference/
> SKEmitterNode_Ref/index.html and https://developer.apple.com/library/ios/
> documentation/IDEs/Conceptual/xcode_guide-particle_emitter/Introduction/
> Introduction.html.

What Are Emitters?

Particle emitters are a really cool and easy-to-use feature provided by Sprite Kit. You can use them to create special effects that simulate anything from fire to rain. Sprite Kit implements these effects using the class `SKEmitterNode`.

An `SKEmitterNode` object is a node that creates and renders small particle sprites. These sprites are owned by Sprite Kit and are not directly accessible by your game. You will not be able to modify the individual sprites yourself, but you can modify the properties of the `SKEmitterNode` instance.

You can create particle emitters by hand, but it is much easier to create a particle emitter using Xcode's built-in Particle Emitter Editor. The Particle Emitter Editor is a graphical editor built into Xcode that provides a visual environment in which you can design custom particle effects. Figure 6-1 shows Xcode's Particle Emitter Editor.

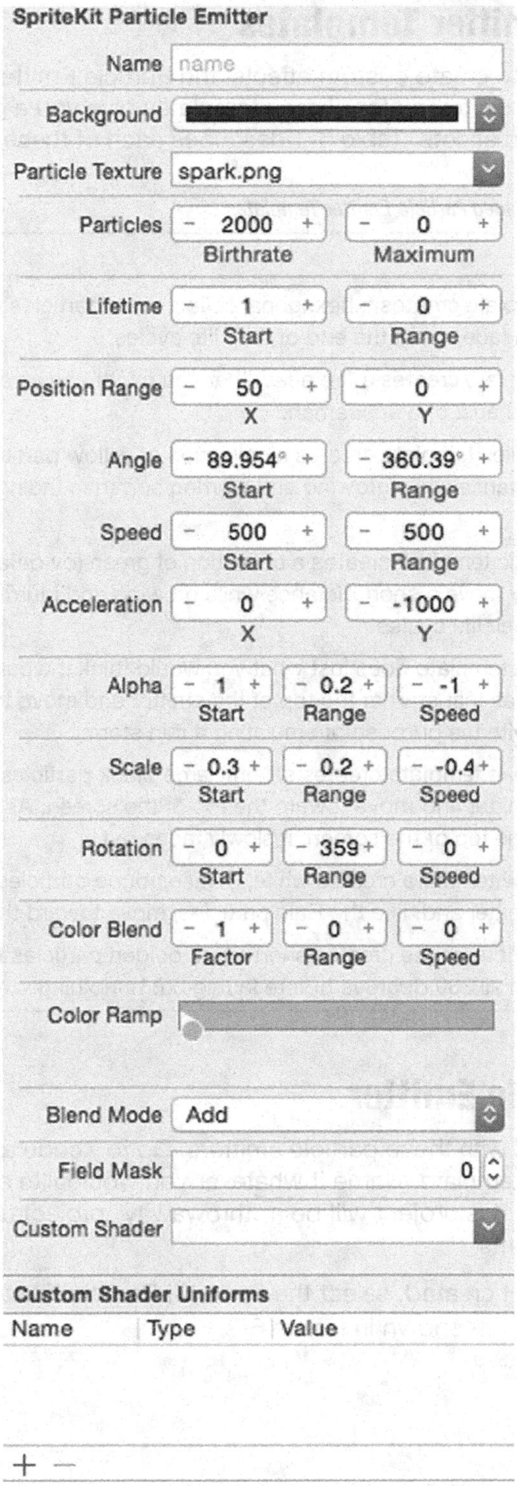

SpriteKit Particle Emitter

Name	name
Background	▮▮▮▮▮▮▮▮▮▮▮▮▮▮ ◇
Particle Texture	spark.png ⌄

Particles	− 2000 +	− 0 +
	Birthrate	Maximum

Lifetime	− 1 +	− 0 +
	Start	Range

Position Range	− 50 +	− 0 +
	X	Y

Angle	− 89.954° +	− 360.39° +
	Start	Range

Speed	− 500 +	− 500 +
	Start	Range

Acceleration	− 0 +	− -1000 +
	X	Y

Alpha	− 1 +	− 0.2 +	− -1 +
	Start	Range	Speed

Scale	− 0.3 +	− 0.2 +	− -0.4 +
	Start	Range	Speed

Rotation	− 0 +	− 359 +	− 0 +
	Start	Range	Speed

Color Blend	− 1 +	− 0 +	− 0 +
	Factor	Range	Speed

Color Ramp	▬▬▬▬▬▬▬▬▬●▬

Blend Mode	Add ◇
Field Mask	0 ◇
Custom Shader	⌄

Custom Shader Uniforms

Name	Type	Value

＋ −

Figure 6-1. Xcode's Particle Emitter Editor

Using Particle Emitter Templates

In addition to being able to create custom effects, the Particle Emitter editor offers a collection of prebuilt particle templates. These templates give you a great starting point for creating your own custom effects. Table 6-1 describes each of these templates.

Table 6-1. *The Xcode's Prepackaged Particle Emitter Templates*

Template Name	Use
Bokeh	This template creates a hexagonal collection of particles that grow and blur and then fade out at the end of their life cycles.
Fire	This template creates a fire effect that you might use as a torch or, just maybe, as the exhaust of a spaceman.
Fireflies	The Fireflies template creates a collection of yellow particles that randomly move a short distance while growing and blurring and then fading out at the end of their life cycles.
Magic	The Magic template creates a collection of green (by default) particles that also randomly move a short distance while growing and blurring before fading out at the end of their life cycles.
Rain	The Rain template does just what you would think it would; it creates a collection of particles that start at the top of the emitter and move toward the bottom of the screen with the purpose of emulating a rain storm.
Smoke	The Smoke template creates several large black particles that start at the bottom of the emitter and move toward the top of the screen. As each particle moves toward the top of the screen, it slowly fades out.
Snow	The Snow template creates white, diffuse, round particles that start at the top of the emitter and, like the Rain particles, move toward the bottom of the screen.
Spark	The Spark template creates short-lived, golden particles that burst out of the emitter in all 360 degrees before fading out to nothing.

Creating a Particle Emitter

Let's start playing around with these particle emitters. Go to Xcode and create a new iOS project, using the Game template. Name it whatever you would like and save the project wherever you would like. This project will be a "throwaway" project used only as a play area for your emitter experiments.

Once you have the project created, select the SpriteKit Particle File template from the iOS ➤ Resource category, as shown in Figure 6-2.

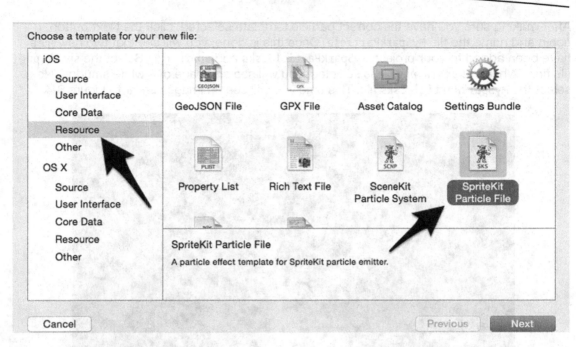

Figure 6-2. The Choose Template dialog

Now click the Next button and select the Spark particle template, as shown in Figure 6-3.

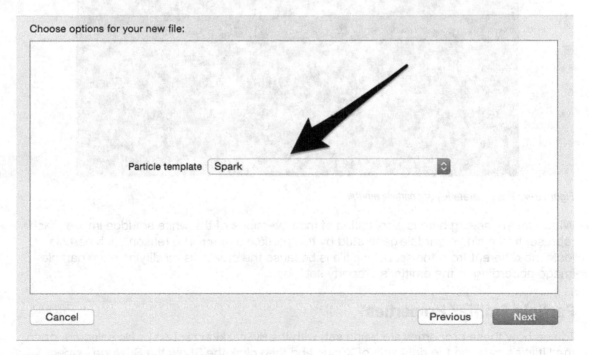

Figure 6-3. The Choose File Options dialog

After making sure you have the correct particle template selected, click the Next button again and name the file MySparkParticle. Once this is done, you will see that two new files have been added to your project, MySparkParticle.sks and spark.png. Select the spark.png file first. When the spark.png file is selected, you will see an image of a white smudge. Next, select the MySparkParticle.sks file. This time you will see an image similar to Figure 6-4.

Figure 6-4. The generated spark particle emitter

What you are seeing here is a collection of many versions of the white smudge image, each representing a single particle generated by this particle emitter. The reason each particle looks so different from the spark.png file is because the emitter is modifying each particle image according to the emitter's property settings.

Particle Emitter Properties

To see how these properties are being set, with the MySparkParticle.sks file selected, open the Utilities pane on the right side of Xcode and then click the Show the SKNode inspector button. This will show each of the properties of the current particle emitter. You can see these attributes in Figure 6-5.

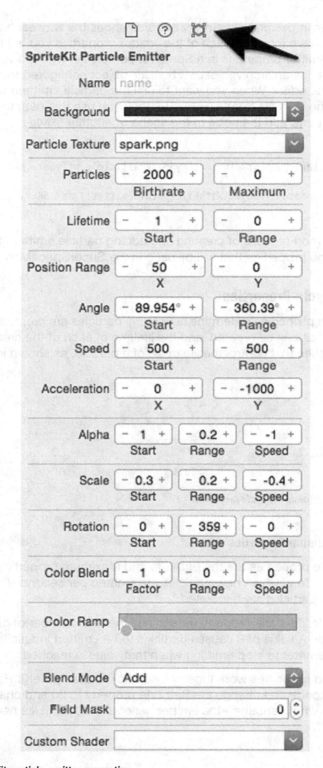

Figure 6-5. The SpriteKit particle emitter properties

Each of the properties in this particle emitter editor changes the way each of the particles is emitted. Once you have modified each of the emitter properties you are interested in, Xcode will save the emitter properties in a Sprite Kit particle file with the .sks extension. The resulting file contains an archived SKEmitterNode object configured to run the particle effects designed in the editor. When you want to use the particle emitter in your game, you first get the path to the .sks file from mainBundle; then you use this path to unarchive the SKEmitterNode object and add the node to the scene or another SKNode.

```
let pathToEmitter =
    NSBundle.mainBundle().pathForResource("MySparkParticle", ofType: "sks")
let emitter =
    NSKeyedUnarchiver.unarchiveObjectWithFile(pathToEmitter!) as? SKEmitterNode
addChild(emitter!)
```

This is the most common process of creating and adding particle emitters to your game. Let's take a look at the properties that will be used in the SuperSpaceMan game.

The Particle Life-Cycle Properties

The particle life-cycle properties determine how many particles are created, the maximum number of particles that can be created, and the lifetime of each of the created particles. There are four properties that control the life cycle of a particle, as shown in Figure 6-6.

Figure 6-6. The Sprite Kit particle life-cycle properties

The Birthrate and Maximum Properties

The first two life-cycle properties are the Birthrate and Maximum properties. The Birthrate property defines the rate at which new particles are emitted per second. The higher the value, the faster new particles are generated.

The Maximum particle life-cycle property determines the total number of particles to be emitted by the emitter. A value of 0 causes particles to be emitted indefinitely. Any other value will cause the emitter to stop emitting when that value is reached.

To see how these two properties work together, go back to the SpriteKit Particle Emitter properties editor in Xcode and change the Birthrate property to 20 and change the Maximum property to 0. Watch what happens—the emitter generates 20 particles per second.

Now leave the Birthrate property at 20, change the Maximum property to 20, and check out how the emitter changes. This time, the emitter will emit 20 particles over 1 second and then stop for 1 second and then emit another 20 particles. It will repeat this process forever. When you have finished playing around with these two properties, change the Birthrate property back to 2000 and the Maximum property back to 0.

The Start and Range Properties

The next two particle life-cycle properties are the Start and Range properties. These properties control the lifetime of the emitted particles. The Start property controls the average length of time in seconds that a particle is visible. When the time elapses, the particle fades away.

The Range property provides a method of varying the time a particle is on the screen. When you set this property to any number other than 0, then a random number between 0 and the entered number is generated. Half of that number is then randomly added or subtracted to the Start value to produce the final lifetime of the particle. If you enter 0, then all particles will stay visible for the same amount of time.

The Particle Movement Properties

There are four sets of properties that affect the movement of particles being emitted, as shown in Figure 6-7 and described in the following sections.

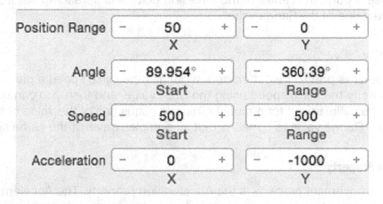

Figure 6-7. The Sprite Kit particle movement properties

The Position Range Property

The Position Range property defines the area in which the emitted particles are created. The particles are created within a rectangle defined by the Position Range property's X and Y values.

To see how this works, go back to the `MySparkParticle.sks` file and change the Position Range property's X value to 300 and the Y value to 300 and watch how this affects the emission of the particles. You will now see the particles are being emitted in a 300-by-300 box. Play around with these properties until you are comfortable with how they work.

The Angle Property

The next particle movement property is the Angle property. The Angle property defines the angle at which particles travel away from the creation point in counterclockwise degrees. There are two Angle values: Start and Range.

The Start value defines the direction, in degrees, that a particle is emitted, and the Range value defines the number of degrees, plus or minus half of the number value, that the particle's initial angle varies. This all sounds complicated, so let's play around with these values and see what happens.

If you look at the initial value of the spark emitter's Angle property, you will see that it is roughly 90 degrees, and the Range property is set to roughly 360 degrees. The easiest way to see how these values affect particle emission is to set both the Start and Range values. Currently, Range is set to 360 degrees, which says the particle emission range is a complete circle. Reduce the Range value to 90 degrees, set the Start value to 0 degrees, and see what happens. You will now see that the particles start out being emitted to the right of the screen and spread out to roughly 45 degrees above and below their initial emission point.

Now increase the Start value to 90 degrees. Notice how the particles are now beginning their life being emitted straight up. Increase the Start value by another 90 degrees, making it 180 degrees. This time the particles are being emitted to the left side of the screen. After playing around with these values, you will see that the Start value goes from 0 to 360 degrees counterclockwise around the center of the emission point and spreading out from the Start value by half the value of the Range value.

The Speed Property

The Speed property is pretty straightforward. It defines the initial speed a particle moves at creation. You specify the initial speed using the Start value, and then you can use the Range value to adjust the initial speed for a particle, plus or minus half of the value of the Range value. Setting the Range value to 0 means that all particles travel at the same speed.

The Acceleration Property

The final particle movement property is the Acceleration property. The Acceleration property controls the degree to which a particle accelerates or decelerates after emission in terms of both X and Y directions. You use the X value to apply acceleration along the x-axis, and you use the Y value to apply acceleration along the y-axis.

It is common to use the Acceleration property to simulate a gravity effect. The easiest way to see how this works is to change all the emitter properties so that they match the values in Figure 6-8.

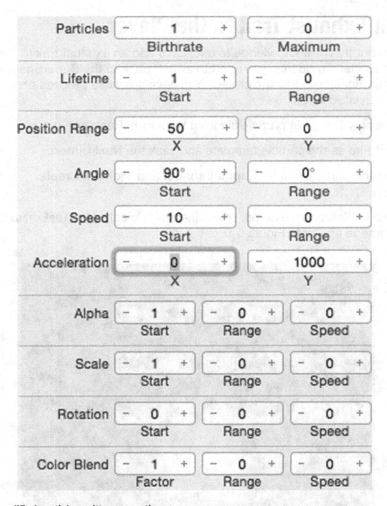

Particles	−	1	+	−	0	+
		Birthrate			Maximum	
Lifetime	−	1	+	−	0	+
		Start			Range	
Position Range	−	50	+	−	0	+
		X			Y	
Angle	−	90°	+	−	0°	+
		Start			Range	
Speed	−	10	+	−	0	+
		Start			Range	
Acceleration	−	0	+	−	1000	+
		X			Y	

Alpha	−	1	+	−	0	+	−	0	+
		Start			Range			Speed	
Scale	−	1	+	−	0	+	−	0	+
		Start			Range			Speed	
Rotation	−	0	+	−	0	+	−	0	+
		Start			Range			Speed	
Color Blend	−	1	+	−	0	+	−	0	+
		Factor			Range			Speed	

Figure 6-8. The modified particle emitter properties

If you don't see a property in this figure, then you don't have to worry about changing it. After you have made these changes, you will see a single particle moving straight up along the y-axis. The reason the particle is going straight up is because all of the acceleration is along the y-axis.

Change the X value for the Acceleration property to 500 and see what happens. The particle now moves up the y-axis and to the right along the x-axis. Next, change the X value for the Acceleration property to -500. You will now see that the particle is again moving up along the y-axis, but this time it is moving left along the x-axis. This is because you applied a negative X acceleration.

Adding an Exhaust Trail to the Player

It is now time to put this new knowledge to use. Let's add an exhaust trail to the playerNode using a particle emitter. To do this, you need to switch back to the SuperSpaceMan project and add a new particle emitter to the project. You have seen this process previously, but here are the abbreviated steps:

1. Add a new Sprite Kit particle file from the iOS ➤ Resource group.

2. Select Fire as the particle template and click the Next button.

3. Name the particle emitter **EngineExhaust** and click the Create button.

Once you have completed these steps, select the newly created EngineExhaust.sks file. You will see an image similar to Figure 6-9.

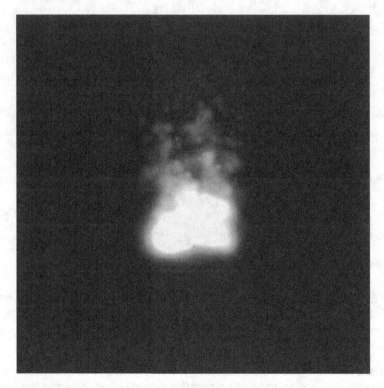

Figure 6-9. The default fire particle emitter

This looks really good, but to emulate exhaust emitting from the spaceman as he flies up the scene, the angle of the emitting fire needs to be rotated by 180 degrees. To make this happen, change the Start value for the Angle property to 270 degrees, and to resize the emitted flame's width, reduce the Position Range's X value to 23. Figure 6-10 shows these changes.

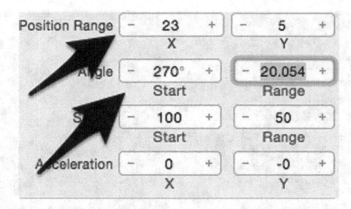

Figure 6-10. *The inverted fire particle emitter property changes*

Once you have made these changes, you will see that the fire is now being emitted toward the bottom of the screen, and the width of the flame has been reduced. This looks much better, but I think it would look even better if the flames were a little subtler. The easiest way to make this happen is to reduce the Birthrate value of the particles being emitted. Do this by reducing the particle Birthrate value to 100, as shown in Figure 6-11.

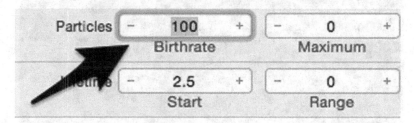

Figure 6-11. *The reduced particle Birthrate value changes*

Awesome. Save your changes, and let's take a look at the new particle emitter shown in Figure 6-12.

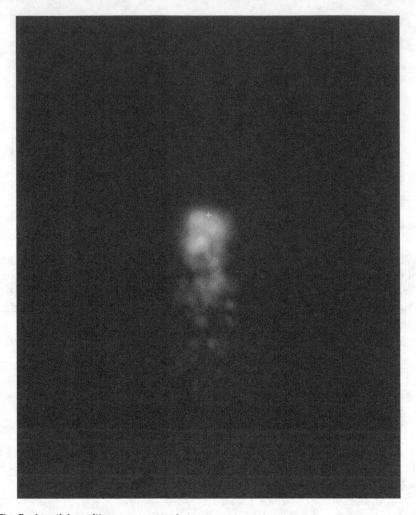

Figure 6-12. *The final particle emitter*

This is exactly what was needed. The fire is being emitted in the correct direction, and the size and Birthrate values will fit nicely attached to the playerNode.

Let's start using the new emitter. If you remember from the previous sections, once you have the emitter looking like you want it to, it is really easy to add to your scene. The first thing you need to do is load the SKEmitterNode using your new SKS file. This is pretty simple and can be accomplished by first adding a constant to hold the new SKEmitterNode instance. To do this, add the engineExhaust constant immediately before the first init() method in the GameScene.

```
let engineExhaust : SKEmitterNode?
```

Now that you have a place to store the emitter, let's load it with the values stored in the EngineExhaust.sks file. The following lines do this:

```
let engineExhaustPath =
    NSBundle.mainBundle().pathForResource("EngineExhaust", ofType: "sks")
engineExhaust =
    NSKeyedUnarchiver.unarchiveObjectWithFile(engineExhaustPath!) as? SKEmitterNode
engineExhaust!.position =
    CGPointMake(0.0, -(playerNode!.size.height / 2))
```

You have seen these lines before, with the exception of the last line. This line sets the position of the emitter to a point at (0.0, -(self.playerNode!.size.height / 2)). I am using this point because the emitter will need to be added to the playerNode, and the playerNode's anchor point is the middle of the player. Using the negative value of half the size of the playerNode will place the emitter at the bottom of the playerNode. Go ahead and add these lines to the end of the GameScene.init(size: CGSize) method.

OK, so far you have the emitter node loaded, and you are ready to add it the playerNode. You can do this with the following two lines:

```
playerNode!.addChild(engineExhaust!)
engineExhaust!.hidden = true;
```

As you look over this change, you will see that the code is pretty straightforward. First the engineExhaust emitter node is added to the playerNode, and then the exhaust is hidden. I am hiding the exhaust here because I want the exhaust emitter to be visible only when the player of the game taps the screen. Add this code right after the line that sets the position of the engineExhaust node.

There is one more thing you need to do, which is to make the engineExhaust visible when the user taps the screen. To do this, add the following line of code to the end of the second if statement in the touchesBegan() method and run the game again:

```
engineExhaust!.hidden = false
```

Notice that when you tap the screen this time, not only does the spaceman fly up through the scene but this time there is an exhaust stream coming out of the bottom of the playerNode.

This looks great, but there is one problem. Even when you are no longer tapping the screen, the exhaust emitter is still visible. The emitter should be removed after a moment so that it emulates a quick burst of force that goes away after a short period of time. This problem can be fixed easily enough with an NSTimer.

To fix this problem, you need to first add a new variable to hold the NSTimer instance. Add this declaration immediately after the declaration of the SKEmitterNode you added earlier:

```
let engineExhaust : SKEmitterNode?
var exhaustTimer : NSTimer?
```

Once you have added the exhaustTimer to the GameScene, then you can modify the touchesBegan() method to start a timer each time the screen is tapped and an impulse is applied. The modified if statement is shown here:

```
if self.impulseCount > 0 {

    playerNode!.physicsBody!.applyImpulse(CGVectorMake(0.0, 40.0))
    impulseCount--

    engineExhaust!.hidden = false

    NSTimer.scheduledTimerWithTimeInterval(0.5,
                                    target: self,
                                    selector: "hideEngineExaust:",
                                    userInfo: nil,
                                    repeats: false)
}
```

As you look over these changes, you will notice at the end of the if statement a new timer is created that will run the hideEngineExhaust() method half a second after the timer is scheduled. The hideEngineExhaust() method that will be invoked is shown here:

```
func hideEngineExaust(timer:NSTimer!) {

    if !engineExhaust!.hidden {

        engineExhaust!.hidden = true
    }
}
```

Examining the hideEngineExhaust() method, you will see that it does exactly what it sounds like it will do. It first checks to see whether the engineExhaust is visible and hides it if it is.

Make these changes to the touchesBegan() method and add the removeEngineExhaust() method to the bottom of the GameScene. Once you have made these changes, run the app again. This time you will notice the exhaust is added to the playerNode each time you tap the screen and will be removed from the playerNode half a second after the last tap. This looks much better. Before closing out this chapter, make sure the final touchesBegan() method looks like the following:

```
override func touchesBegan(touches: NSSet, withEvent event: UIEvent) {

    if !playerNode!.physicsBody!.dynamic {

        playerNode!.physicsBody!.dynamic = true

        coreMotionManager.accelerometerUpdateInterval = 0.3
        coreMotionManager.startAccelerometerUpdatesToQueue(NSOperationQueue(),
            withHandler: {

            (data: CMAccelerometerData!, error: NSError!) in
```

```
        if let constVar = error {

            println("There was an error")
        }
        else {

            self.xAxisAcceleration = CGFloat(data!.acceleration.x)
        }
    })
}

if self.impulseCount > 0 {

    playerNode!.physicsBody!.applyImpulse(CGVectorMake(0.0, 40.0))
    impulseCount--

    engineExhaust!.hidden = false

    NSTimer.scheduledTimerWithTimeInterval(0.5,
        target: self,
        selector: "hideEngineExaust:",
        userInfo: nil,
        repeats: false)
}
}
```

Summary

In this chapter, I briefly introduced you to particle emitters, including a quick look at some of Xcode's template emitters. After that, I showed you how to add a particle emitter to the playerNode so that you could emulate engine exhaust whenever an impulse is applied to the physicsBody.

In the next chapter, you will get your first look at Sprite Kit's SKTextNode when I show you how to add scoring to the SuperSpaceMan game. After that, you will get a look at another use for SKAction when you add sound to the SuperSpaceMan game.

Chapter 7

Adding Points and Sound

In the previous chapter, I briefly introduced you to particle emitters, including a quick look at some of Xcode's template emitters. After that, I showed you how to add a particle emitter to the playerNode so that you could emulate engine exhaust whenever an impulse is applied to the physicsBody.

In this chapter, I will talk about using SKLabelNodes to add labels to your Sprite Kit games. Specifically, I will show you how to add a label that keeps up with the number of impulses remaining for the SuperSpaceMan to use, and then I will show you how to add scoring to the game to keep up with the number of orbs the SuperSpaceMan has collected.

At the end of the chapter, you will get a chance to revisit SKActions when I show you how to use them to play game sounds.

What Are SKLabelNodes?

As I mentioned earlier, Sprite Kit implements text labels using a class named SKLabelNode. The SKLabelNode class, just like all the nodes you have seen so far, is an extension of SKNode. It Is a pretty simple class with only two init() methods and a handful of properties all focused on setting label fonts, colors, and layout.

The simplest way to use an SKLabelNode is shown in the following snippet:

```
let simpleLabel = SKLabelNode(fontNamed: "Copperplate")
simpleLabel.text = "Hello, Sprite Kit!";
simpleLabel.fontSize = 40;
simpleLabel.position = CGPoint(x: size.width / 2.0, y: size.height / 2.0)

addChild(simpleLabel)
```

As you look at this code, you can see that it first creates the SKLabelNode class by passing the init() method the name of the font you want to use. After that, you set the text property of the label. You then set the fontSize and position properties. Finally, you add the label node to the scene.

Let's give this a try in a sample application. Go back to Xcode and create a new Game project using Swift as the language. When you have your new project created, go to the GameScene.swift file and change its body to match Listing 7-1.

Listing 7-1. The New GameScene Class

```
import SpriteKit

class GameScene: SKScene {

    required init?(coder aDecoder: NSCoder) {

        super.init(coder: aDecoder)

        let simpleLabel = SKLabelNode(fontNamed: "Copperplate")
        simpleLabel.text = "Hello, Sprite Kit!"
        simpleLabel.fontSize = 40
        simpleLabel.position = CGPoint(x: size.width / 2.0, y: size.height / 2.0)

        addChild(simpleLabel)
    }
}
```

When you take a look at this listing, you will see it contains a simple init() method that takes an NSCoder. Inside the init() method this super.init() method is called, and then you see the SKLabel-related code.

This code looks exactly like the earlier snippet that added an SKLabelNode. Run the app and take a look at the results. The new app should look like Figure 7-1.

Figure 7-1. A simple SKLabelNode example

As you can see, the SKLabelNode is pretty easy to use. Most of SKLabelNode's properties are straightforward, but there are a couple of properties that you may not have seen. The two SKLabelNode properties are horizontalAlignmentMode and horizontalVerticalMode. Each of these properties is described in the following sections.

Changing the Horizontal Alignment of the Label Node

SKLabelNode's horizontalAlignmentMode is used to set the horizontal position of the text relative to the node's position. There are three horizontal alignment options, all of which are defined by the enum SKLabelHorizontalAlignmentMode. The three options are SKLabelHorizontalAlignmentMode.Left, SKLabelHorizontalAlignmentMode.Center, and SKLabelHorizontalAlignmentMode.Right. To see how this property and these options change the layout of the label node, add the following line of code immediately after the line where you set the position of the label node:

```
simpleLabel.horizontalAlignmentMode = SKLabelHorizontalAlignmentMode.Left
```

Now run the app again. This time you will see that the label has been shifted to the right, as shown in Figure 7-2.

Figure 7-2. A simple SKLabelNode example with its horizontalAlignmentMode set to SKLabelHorizontalAlignmentMode.Right

Setting this alignment to SKLabelHorizontalAlignmentMode.Left tells Sprite Kit to place the left side of the SKLabelNode at the origin of the label node.

The default value for the horizontalAlignmentMode is SKLabelHorizontalAlignmentMode. Center, which places the center of the label at the position property of the label. You saw this mode in Figure 7-1.

Try one more thing before moving on. Change the value of the horizontalAlignmentMode property from SKLabelHorizontalAlignmentMode.Left to SKLabelHorizontalAlignmentMode. Right, as shown here, and run the app again:

```
simpleLabel.horizontalAlignmentMode = SKLabelHorizontalAlignmentMode.Right
```

This time the right side of the label is place at the point of the SKLabelNode's position property, as shown in Figure 7-3.

Figure 7-3. *A simple SKLabelNode example with its horizontalAlignmentMode set to SKLabelHorizontalAlignmentMode.Left*

Changing the Vertical Alignment of the Label Node

In the previous section, you saw how you can change the horizontal alignment of the SKLabelNode using SKLabelNode's horizontalAlignmentMode property. In this section, you will see how you can change SKLabelNode's vertical alignment.

Before getting started, go back to the GameScene.swift file and change it contents so they match Listing 7-2.

Listing 7-2. *The GameScene Class with the Simple Label at the Top of the Scene*

```
import SpriteKit

class GameScene: SKScene {

    required init?(coder aDecoder: NSCoder) {

        super.init(coder: aDecoder)
```

```
let simpleLabel = SKLabelNode(fontNamed: "Copperplate")
simpleLabel.text = "Hello, Sprite Kit!"
simpleLabel.fontSize = 40
simpleLabel.position =
    CGPoint(x: size.width / 2.0,
            y: frame.height - simpleLabel.frame.height)

simpleLabel.horizontalAlignmentMode = SKLabelHorizontalAlignmentMode.Center

addChild(simpleLabel)
    }
}
```

As you look at this code, you will notice it looks like the code you used in the previous section except that the SKLabelNode has been positioned at the top of the scene and horizontalAlignmentMode has been explicitly set to the center. To see how this looks, run the application again. It should now look like Figure 7-4.

Figure 7-4. The simple SKLabelNode at the top center of the scene

The reason I moved the label to the top of the scene was so you can more easily see how changing the vertical alignment affects the node's presentation.

The SKLabelNode property you use to change the vertical alignment is verticalAlignmentMode. There are four values you can set this property to, and they are defined by the SKLabelVerticalAlignmentMode enum.

The first option, SKLabelVerticalAlignmentMode.Baseline, is the default value and positions the text so that the font's baseline is on the node's origin. You already saw an example of this option in Figure 7-4 when verticalAlignmentMode was not set, which resulted in the use of the default value SKLabelVerticalAlignmentMode.Baseline.

The second option is the SKLabelVerticalAlignmentMode enum value SKLabelVerticalAlignmentMode.Center, which is used to center the text vertically on the node's origin. To see how the value changes the text layout, add the following line to the GameScene init() method right before you add the simpleLabel to the scene:

```
simpleLabel.verticalAlignmentMode = SKLabelVerticalAlignmentMode.Center
```

Once you have made this change, run the application again. You will now see that the text has shifted down so that the vertical center of the text is at the simpleLabel's origin, as shown in Figure 7-5.

Figure 7-5. *The simple SKLabelNode example with its verticalAlignmentMode set to SKLabelVerticalAlignmentMode.Center*

The next vertical alignment option is the value SKLabelVerticalAlignmentMode.Top. This value is used to position the text so that the top of the text is on the node's origin. To see how the value changes the text layout, set simpleLabel's verticalAlignmentMode value to SKLabelVerticalAlignmentMode.Top, as shown here:

```
simpleLabel.verticalAlignmentMode = SKLabelVerticalAlignmentMode.Top
```

Once you have made this change, run the application again. You will now see that the text has shifted down even further so that the top of the text is at simpleLabel's origin, as shown in Figure 7-6.

Figure 7-6. The simple SKLabelNode example with its verticalAlignmentMode set to SKLabelVerticalAlignmentMode.Top

The last vertical alignment option is the value SKLabelVerticalAlignmentMode.Bottom. This value is used to position the text so that the bottom of the text is on the node's origin. To see how the value changes the text layout, set simpleLabel's verticalAlignmentMode to SKLabelVerticalAlignmentMode.Bottom, as shown here:

```
simpleLabel.verticalAlignmentMode = SKLabelVerticalAlignmentMode.Bottom
```

Once you have made this change, run the application again. You will now see that the text has shifted up so that the bottom of the text is at simpleLabel's origin, as shown in Figure 7-7.

Figure 7-7. The simple SKLabelNode example with its verticalAlignmentMode set to
SKLabelVerticalAlignmentMode.Bottom

Adding Scoring to the Game

Now that you know how to use SKLabelNode, it is time to put it to some good use. As
mentioned at the beginning of this book, the goal of this game is to collect as many orbs as
you can without colliding with a black hole or running out of impulses.

In this section, you will finally add some scoring to the game. Specifically, you will add an
SKLabelNode to the top right of the scene. The original text will be "SCORE : 0." This numeric
value will increment each time the playerNode comes into contact with an orb node—the
more orbs collected, the higher your score. Let's make this happen.

The first step you need to do to add a scoring label to the GameScene is to create a variable to
hold the score (the number of orbs collected) and an SKLabelNode constant to hold the label.
This can be accomplished with the following two lines of code:

```
var score = 0
let scoreTextNode = SKLabelNode(fontNamed: "Copperplate")
```

This code is pretty straightforward. It creates an integer variable named score and sets it to 0, which makes sense at the beginning of a game, and then it creates an SKLabelNode with a font of Copperplate. I chose Copperplate because I thought it looked good with the images already in place, but you can choose whatever you like. After looking at this code, add it to the end of the GameScene's declaration section immediately before the first init() method:

```
var score = 0
let scoreTextNode = SKLabelNode(fontNamed: "Copperplate")

required init?(coder aDecoder: NSCoder) {

    super.init(coder: aDecoder)
}
```

The next thing you need to do is set all of the SKLabelNode's properties and add it to the GameScene. This is accomplished in the following snippet:

```
scoreTextNode.text = "SCORE : \(score)"
scoreTextNode.fontSize = 20
scoreTextNode.fontColor = SKColor.whiteColor()
scoreTextNode.position =
                    CGPointMake(size.width - 10, size.height - 20)
scoreTextNode.horizontalAlignmentMode = SKLabelHorizontalAlignmentMode.Right

addChild(scoreTextNode)
```

You have seen all of this before, but let's go over it before moving on. The first line sets the text of label to "SCORE :" plus the current value in the variable score. The second and third lines set the font size and font color, respectively.

The fourth and fifth lines in the snippet are important. The fourth line sets the position (origin) of the scoreTextNode to 10 points to the left of the right side of the scene and 20 points from the top of the scene. The fifth line of this snippet sets the node's horizontal alignment to SKLabelHorizontalAlignmentMode.Right, which will result in the label node's right side being set 10 points from the far-right side of the scene.

After that, the scoreTextNode is added to the scene. Once you have taken a look at this code, add it to the bottom of the init(size: CGSize() method and let's move on.

There is one last step you need to complete before you can run the app again and start working on your high score. Find the didBeginContact() method in the GameScene and change the if statement handling contact with the orb nodes to the following:

```
if nodeB.name == "POWER_UP_ORB"  {

    impulseCount++

    score++
    scoreTextNode.text = "SCORE : \(score)"

    nodeB.removeFromParent()
}
```

Once you have saved your changes, take a look at the two lines added before the node is removed. The first of these two lines increments the score by one, and the second of these two lines changes the text of the scoreTextNode to reflect this increment. Make sure you have made all of these changes and run the game again. You will now see the score label in the top-right corner of the scene, as shown in Figure 7-8.

Figure 7-8. The GameScene with a score label

Start tapping the screen and try to collect some orbs. Notice that every time your player comes into contact with an orb, the score is incremented. The game finally has scoring.

Adding an Impulse Counter to the Game

Now that you have scoring in place, it's time to start telling the player how many impulses they have left before they run out and start falling to their demise. This will be much like adding the score label from the previous section. The biggest difference is that you are going to align the impulse label at the top left of the scene. To get started with this, the first thing you need to do is add a constant to hold the impulse count label in the declarations section of the GameScene. This line is shown here:

```
let impulseTextNode = SKLabelNode(fontNamed: "Copperplate")
```

Add this line directly after the definition of the scoreTextNode constant. The next thing you need to do is modify the properties of the impulseTextNode. The code to do this is in the following snippet:

```
impulseTextNode.text = "IMPULSES : \(impulseCount)"
impulseTextNode.fontSize = 20
impulseTextNode.fontColor = SKColor.whiteColor()
impulseTextNode.position = CGPointMake(10.0, size.height - 20)
impulseTextNode.horizontalAlignmentMode = SKLabelHorizontalAlignmentMode.Left

addChild(impulseTextNode)
```

As you examine this snippet, you will notice that you have seen all of this before. This code sets the text of the node to "IMPULSES :" plus the value currently stored in the instance variable impulseCount. It then sets the font size to 20 and the color to white. After that, it sets the position of the label node to 10 points from the left side of the scene and 20 points from the top of the scene. The final property change sets horizontalAlignementMode to SKLabelHorizontalAlignmentMode.Left so that the left side of the text is anchored to the node's origin. After that, the impulseTextNode is added to the scene. Add this snippet to bottom of the GameScene's init(size: CGSize) method and save your work.

There are two more changes you need to make to update the displayed impulse count. The first is to modify the text in the impulseTextNode to reflect each time the player collects an orb, and the second is to modify the impulseTextNode each time the player uses an impulse.

Starting with incrementing the impulse count, you need to modify the didBeginContact() method again. Specifically, you need to modify the if statement that handles contact with orb nodes. Take a look at the following snippet:

```
if nodeB.name == "POWER_UP_ORB"  {

    impulseCount++
    impulseTextNode.text = "IMPULSES : \(impulseCount)"

    score++
    scoreTextNode.text = "SCORE : \(score)"

    nodeB.removeFromParent()
}
```

Everything is the same from the previous section except the line following the increment of the impulse count. This line sets the text of the impulseTextNode to "IMPULSES :" plus the value of the impulseCount variable that was just incremented on the line before. Make these changes to the if statement and save your changes.

The last change you need to make to display the current impulse count is to modify the impulseTextNode each time an impulse is used by the player. To do this, you need to go back the GameScene's touchesBegan() method and modify the if statement that applies the impulse to the playerNode to look like the following snippet:

```
if impulseCount > 0 {

    playerNode!.physicsBody!.applyImpulse(CGVectorMake(0.0, 40.0))

    impulseCount--
    impulseTextNode.text = "IMPULSES : \(impulseCount)"

    engineExhaust!.hidden = false

    NSTimer.scheduledTimerWithTimeInterval(0.5, target: self,
            selector: "hideEngineExaust:", userInfo: nil, repeats: false)
}
```

There is only one change to the body of this if statement, and that is the line following the decrement of the impulseCount instance variable. On this line, the impulseTextNode's text property is being modified just like you did before, except this time the text node will be set to "IMPULSES :" plus the recently decremented impulseCount. When you are finished looking at this snippet, save your changes and run the game again. You will now see the addition of the impulse count label in the top-left corner, as shown in Figure 7-9.

Figure 7-9. The GameScene with an impulse count label

Go ahead and tap the screen a few times. Notice how the impulse count label node decreases each time you tap the screen and increases each time you come into contact with an orb node.

Adding Simple Sounds to the Game

There is one more thing to cover before moving on to the next chapter. As I am sure you have noticed, there is no sound in this game—boring. In this section, you will revisit SKActions so that you can add the functionality to play a sound each time an orb node is collected.

The SKAction method you will use create the action to play a sound is the playSoundFileNamed() method. Its signature is shown here:

```
class func playSoundFileNamed(soundFile: String,
                        waitForCompletion wait: Bool) -> SKAction
```

This method takes the name of an audio file in your application bundle and a `Bool` that indicates whether you want to wait until the sound is finished playing before moving on to the next line of code. The file you pass to this method can be any of these formats and more: MP3, M4A, CAF, WAV. An example usage of this method is shown in the following two lines:

```
let playSoundAction = SKAction.playSoundFileNamed("sound.wav",
                                        waitForCompletion: false)
runAction(playSoundAction)
```

These two lines will create an `SKAction` that will play the file `sound.wav` and move on before the sound has finished playing. Let's add some sound to the SuperSpaceMan game.

Before going any further, find the ZIP file you downloaded in Chapter 1. This file contained all the images you need, plus it has a folder named `sounds`. In this directory you will find a file named `orb_pop.wav`. Copy this file into the `SuperSpaceMan` folder of your project.

Once you have added the sound file to your project, the first step is to create the `SKAction` that will play the sound. The following code does this:

```
let orbPopAction = SKAction.playSoundFileNamed("orb_pop.wav",
                                        waitForCompletion: false)
```

This code creates a constant named `orbPopAction` that holds an `SKAction` that will play the sound file `orb_pop.wav` whenever the action is run. Add this line to the declarations section of the `GameScene` immediately before the first `init()` method:

```
let orbPopAction = SKAction.playSoundFileNamed("orb_pop.wav",
        waitForCompletion: false)

required init?(coder aDecoder: NSCoder) {

    super.init(coder: aDecoder)
}
```

You now have an action that will play the `orb_pop.wav` file. It's now time to add the code to play the sounds. To do this, you need to make one more modification to the `didBeginContact()` method to add the code to run your new action. Take a look at the modified `if` statement that handles orb contact, shown here:

```
if nodeB.name == "POWER_UP_ORB"  {

    self.runAction(orbPopAction)

    self.impulseCount++
    self.impulseTextNode.text = "IMPULSES : \(self.impulseCount)"

    self.score++
    self.scoreTextNode.text = "SCORE : \(self.score)"

    nodeB.removeFromParent()
}
```

Here you can see a new line, at the beginning of the `if` statement, that runs the orbPopAction whenever the contacted node's name is POWER_UP_ORB. Make this change to the `if` statement and run the game again. Now every time the playerNode comes into contact with an orb node, the orb_pop.wav sound is played.

Summary

In this chapter, you saw how you can use SKLabelNodes to add labels to your Sprite Kit games. Specifically, you saw how you can display the remaining number of impulses and how to add scoring to the game to keep up with the number of orbs the spaceman has collected. At the end of the chapter, you got a chance to revisit SKActions when you added sound to the game.

In the next chapter, you will get a chance to add new scenes to the game and do some scene transitions when you add menuing and the ability to start a new game.

Chapter **8**

Transitioning Between Scenes

In the previous chapter, you saw how to use SKLabelNodes to add labels to your Sprite Kit games. Specifically, you saw how to display the remaining number of impulses and how to add scoring to the game to keep up with the number of orbs the SuperSpaceMan has collected. At the end of the chapter, you got a chance to revisit SKActions when you added sound to the game.

In this chapter, you will learn how to implement scene transitions using Sprite Kit's SKTransition class. You will get a look at some of the different types of built-in transitions Sprite Kit makes available to you. You will also see how you can control each scene during a transition. At the end of the chapter, you will take your newfound knowledge and add a menu scene to your SuperSpaceMan game.

Transitioning Between Scenes Using SKTransitions

As you already know, SKScenes are the components you use to present game content to users, and a well-designed game will group related content in individual scenes. For example, you could use different scenes to present different levels of a game, or you could use a scene to present a menu of options to a player.

To provide smooth transitions between scenes, Sprite Kit provides the SKTransition class. Using SKTransitions is accomplished using three steps.

1.   Create the SKScene you want to transition in to.

2.   Use one of the class-level SKTransition methods to create the transition you want to use.

3.   Use the SKView's presentScene(scene: SKScene?, transition: SKTransition?) method to present the new scene.

You can create your own custom transitions using the SKTransition's init() method, but it is more common to use one of the 13 built-in class-level SKTransition methods. Table 8-1 defines each of these methods.

Table 8-1. SKTransition's Class-Level Creation Methods

Template Name	Use
crossFadeWithDuration(_:)	Class-level method that creates a cross-fade transition
doorsCloseHorizontalWithDuration(_:)	Class-level method that creates a transition where the new scene appears like closing horizontal doors
doorsCloseVerticalWithDuration(_:)	Class-level method that creates a transition where the new scene appears like closing vertical doors
doorsOpenHorizontalWithDuration(_:)	Class-level method that creates a transition where the new scene appears like opening horizontal doors
doorsOpenVerticalWithDuration(_:)	Class-level method that creates a transition where the new scene appears like opening vertical doors
doorwayWithDuration(_:)	Class-level method that creates a transition where the previous scene disappears like a pair of opening doors and the new scene starts in the background and moves closer as the doors open
fadeWithColor(_:duration:)	Class-level method that creates a transition that first fades to a constant color and then fades to a new scene
fadeWithDuration(_:)	Class-level method that creates a transition that first fades to black and then fades to a new scene
flipHorizontalWithDuration(_:)	Class-level method that creates a transition where the two scenes are flipped across a horizontal line running through the center of the view
flipVerticalWithDuration(_:)	Class-level method that creates a transition where the two scenes are flipped across a vertical line running through the center of the view
moveInWithDirection(_:duration:)	Class-level method that creates a transition where the new scene moves in on top of the current scene
pushWithDirection(_:duration:)	Class-level method that creates a transition where the new scene moves in, pushing the current scene out of the view
revealWithDirection(_:duration:)	Class-level method that creates a transition where the current scene moves out of the view, revealing the new scene underneath it

As you can see, Sprite Kit provides a pretty complete set of built-in transitions. An example use of one of these transitions is shown in the following snippet:

```
let transition = SKTransition.fadeWithDuration(2.0)
let sceneTwo = SceneTwo(size: self.size)

self.view?.presentScene(sceneTwo, transition: transition)
```

Take a look at this code. The first line of this snippet creates a transition that will fade to black and then fade to a new scene over a two-second duration. The second line creates the scene you will be transitioning in to, and the final line actually presents the scene using the transition.

Pausing Scenes During a Transition

You should be aware of two important SKTransition properties when transitioning between scenes. They are pausesIncomingScene and pausesOutgoingScene. These properties are Bool properties used to pause the animation of the incoming and outgoing scenes, respectively.

If you want a scene's animations to continue during scene transitions, you just set the appropriate property to false before you present the scene. The default value for both of these properties is true.

Detecting When a New Scene Is Presented

Sprite Kit provides two methods in the SKScene class that you can override to detect when a scene is being transitioned away from or transitioned in to. The first method is the SKScene willMoveFromView() method. This method is called on an SKScene when it is about to be removed from a view. To override this method, you add the following code to your SKScene implementation:

```
override func willMoveFromView(view: SKView) {

    // insert code
}
```

The second method is the SKScene didMoveToView() method. This method is called when the scene has just finished being presented by a view. To override this method, you add the following code to your SKScene implementation:

```
override func didMoveToView(view: SKView) {

    // insert code
}
```

Adding a New Scene to SuperSpaceMan

In this section, you will use your newfound knowledge of scene transitions and add a new scene to the SuperSpaceMan game. The purpose of this scene will be to allow the user to see the score of their most recent game and to allow them to start a new game.

Before you do anything, let's add a simple message that tells the game player to tap the screen to start the game. As you know, the game already starts when you tap the screen. This label is just nice to have to start tidying up the user interface. To add this label, go to the GameScene's declaration section and add the following line of code directly before the first init() method:

```
let startGameTextNode = SKLabelNode(fontNamed: "Copperplate")
```

After you have added this line, go to the bottom of the GameScene's init(size: CGSize) method and add the following block of code to the bottom of this method:

```
startGameTextNode.text = "TAP ANYWHERE TO START!"
startGameTextNode.horizontalAlignmentMode = SKLabelHorizontalAlignmentMode.Center
startGameTextNode.verticalAlignmentMode = SKLabelVerticalAlignmentMode.Center
startGameTextNode.fontSize = 20
startGameTextNode.fontColor = SKColor.whiteColor()
startGameTextNode.position =
    CGPoint(x: scene!.size.width / 2, y: scene!.size.height / 2)
addChild(startGameTextNode)
```

As you look at this code, you will notice that you saw code similar to this in the previous chapter. Once you look at the changes, run the game again. You will now see a new label of "TAP ANYWHERE TO START!" in white letters at the center of the scene, as shown in Figure 8-1.

Figure 8-1. The GameScene with the "TAP ANYWHERE TO START!" SKLabelNode

Before moving on, do one more thing: add the code to remove the startGameTextNode label from the scene when the screen is tapped. You can do this by adding the following line to the first if statement in the touchedBegan() method:

```
startGameTextNode.removeFromParent()
```

The new touchesBegan() method's if statement now looks like the following:

```
if !playerNode!.physicsBody!.dynamic {

    startGameTextNode.removeFromParent()

    playerNode!.physicsBody!.dynamic = true

    coreMotionManager.accelerometerUpdateInterval = 0.3
```

```
    coreMotionManager.startAccelerometerUpdatesToQueue(NSOperationQueue(),
        withHandler: {

        (data: CMAccelerometerData!, error: NSError!) in

        if let constVar = error {

            println("There was an error")
        }
        else {

            self.xAxisAcceleration = CGFloat(data!.acceleration.x)
        }
    })
}
```

Ending the Game

Now it's time to add the code that will determine when the SuperSpaceMan game ends. There are really only two ways the game ends; either the player dodges all the black holes and collects orbs until he reaches the top of the scene and wins or he falls off the bottom of the scene and loses. The easiest place to check the player's position as it updates is in the GameScene's update() method. Let's go back to that method and add the necessary code to do this.

Currently, the update() method has a simple if statement that moves the foreground and background nodes according to the playerNode's position as long as the playerNode's y-position is greater than or equal to 180.0. This means the playerNode could leave the backgroundNodes behind and fly off into the black of space. I really don't like the way that looks. To stop this from happening, modify the current if statement to look like the following:

```
if playerNode!.position.y >= 180.0 &&
    playerNode!.position.y < 6400.0 {
```

Save this change and run the game again. Try making it to the top of the game and see what happens. This time, when you reach the top of the scene, the background and foreground will stop moving, and the playerNode will continue out of the viewport. This is a little better.

Winning the Game

At this point, you know that the player is about to fly off the top of the scene, but you need to test to see when the player actually flies off the scene to determine whether he actually wins. To do this, add the following else if to the current if block in the update() method:

```
else if playerNode!.position.y > 7000.0 {

    gameOverWithResult(true)
}
```

This code checks to see whether the playerNode has flown more than 7,000 points up the scene, and if it has, it calls a new instance method gameOverWithResult(), passing true to this method, which indicates that the player won. Make these changes, and let's take a look at the gameOverWithResult() method shown here:

```
func gameOverWithResult(gameResult: Bool) {

    playerNode!.removeFromParent()
    playerNode = nil

    if gameResult {

        println("YOU WON!")
    }
    else {

        println("YOU LOSE!")
    }
}
```

As you look at this method, you will see that it does not do a whole lot at the moment. It first removes the playerNode from the scene, and then it sets node to nil. After that, it tests the gameResult Bool passed to it and prints whether the player won the game.

Don't worry too much about this method at the moment. You will be modifying this code soon enough. For now, add this method to the bottom of the GameScene, and let's get to determining whether the player lost the game.

> **Note**   Numbers like 6400.0 and 7000.0 may seem like crazy numbers when the height of the display is nowhere near either of these numbers. Remember, you added the playerNode to the foregroundNode, and you have been moving the foregroundNode down while the playerNode, virtually, continues up the scene. This is how the player's y-position is so much higher than the height of the device's viewport.

Losing the Game

You now know when the player has won the game. It is now time to test to see whether the player has lost the game. To do this, go back to the update() method and add the following else if to the bottom of the if statement (directly following the else if you just added):

```
else if playerNode!.position.y < 0.0 {

    gameOverWithResult(false)
}
```

This bit of code is pretty easy to understand. If the playerNode's y-position is less than 0.0, then the player has fallen off the bottom of the scene, and the gameOverWithResult() method is called with the value false being passed to it, which indicates that the player has lost the game.

There is one last thing you need to do before transitioning to a new scene. In the gameOverWithResult() method, you removed the playerNode from the parent and then set it to nil. This is perfectly fine, but you need to make sure you do not try to use this property without checking to see whether it is nil first. There are only two places you currently do this.

The first is in the update() method with each time you are checking the playerNode's position. To make sure you don't dereference a nil playerNode, you need to surround the body of the update() method with an if, checking to make sure the playerNode property is not nil. You can see this change in the new update() method shown here:

```
override func update(currentTime: NSTimeInterval) {

    if playerNode != nil {

        if playerNode!.position.y >= 180.0
            && playerNode!.position.y < 6400.0 {

            backgroundNode!.position =
                CGPointMake(self.backgroundNode!.position.x,
                -((playerNode!.position.y - 180.0)/8));

            backgroundStarsNode!.position =
                CGPointMake(self.backgroundStarsNode!.position.x,
                -((playerNode!.position.y - 180.0)/6));

            backgroundPlanetNode!.position =
                CGPointMake(backgroundPlanetNode!.position.x,
                -((playerNode!.position.y - 180.0)/8));

            foregroundNode!.position =
                CGPointMake(self.foregroundNode!.position.x,
                -(playerNode!.position.y - 180.0));
        }
        else if playerNode!.position.y > 7000.0 {

            gameOverWithResult(true)
        }
        else if playerNode!.position.y + playerNode!.size.height < 0.0 {

            gameOverWithResult(false)
        }
    }
}
```

After taking a look at these changes, modify your update() to look like this one and let's move on.

The second place you need to make sure you are not dereferencing a nil `playerNode` is in the `didSimulatePhysics()` method. In this method, you are using the `playerNode`'s `physicsBody` and `position` properties. To prevent the dereferencing of a nil value, you should surround the entire body of the method with an `if` that checks to see whether the `playerNode` is nil. This change is shown here:

```
override func didSimulatePhysics() {

    if playerNode != nil {

        playerNode!.physicsBody!.velocity =
            CGVectorMake(xAxisAcceleration * 380.0,
                playerNode!.physicsBody!.velocity.dy)

        if playerNode!.position.x < -(playerNode!.size.width / 2) {

            playerNode!.position = CGPoint(x: size.width - playerNode!.size.width / 2,
            y: playerNode!.position.y)
        }
        else if playerNode!.position.x > size.width {

            playerNode!.position =
                CGPoint(x: playerNode!.size.width / 2,
                    y: playerNode!.position.y)
        }
    }
}
```

Make these changes, and let's move on to adding the actual transition.

Adding the Transition

Before you can transition to a new scene, you need to have a scene to transition to. The scene this game needs is a scene that tells the player the score they achieved in the most recent game and allows them to play a new game.

To create the new scene, select the File ➤ New ➤ File menu item and then choose iOS ➤ Source ➤ Swift File; click the Next button. Make sure you have the SuperSpaceMan folder selected, name the file MenuScene, and click Create. You will now have an almost empty new file named MenuScene.swift. Replace its contents with the contents of Listing 8-1.

Listing 8-1. MenuScene.swift : The SuperSpaceMan MenuScene

```
import SpriteKit

class MenuScene: SKScene {

    required init?(coder aDecoder: NSCoder) {

        super.init(coder: aDecoder)
    }
```

```
init(size: CGSize, gameResult: Bool, score: Int) {

    super.init(size: size)

    let backgroundNode = SKSpriteNode(imageNamed: "Background")
    backgroundNode.anchorPoint = CGPoint(x: 0.5, y: 0.0)
    backgroundNode.position = CGPoint(x: 160.0, y: 0.0)
    addChild(backgroundNode)

    let gameResultTextNode = SKLabelNode(fontNamed: "Copperplate")
    gameResultTextNode.text = "YOU " + (gameResult ? "WON" : "LOST")
    gameResultTextNode.horizontalAlignmentMode =
        SKLabelHorizontalAlignmentMode.Center
    gameResultTextNode.verticalAlignmentMode =
        SKLabelVerticalAlignmentMode.Center
    gameResultTextNode.fontSize = 20
    gameResultTextNode.fontColor = SKColor.whiteColor()
    gameResultTextNode.position =
        CGPointMake(size.width / 2.0, size.height - 200.0)
    addChild(gameResultTextNode)

    let scoreTextNode = SKLabelNode(fontNamed: "Copperplate")
    scoreTextNode.text = "SCORE :  \(score)"
    scoreTextNode.horizontalAlignmentMode =
        SKLabelHorizontalAlignmentMode.Center
    scoreTextNode.verticalAlignmentMode =
        SKLabelVerticalAlignmentMode.Center
    scoreTextNode.fontSize = 20
    scoreTextNode.fontColor = SKColor.whiteColor()
    scoreTextNode.position = CGPointMake(size.width / 2.0,
        gameResultTextNode.position.y - 40.0)
    addChild(scoreTextNode)

    let tryAgainTextNodeLine1 = SKLabelNode(fontNamed: "Copperplate")
    tryAgainTextNodeLine1.text = "TAP ANYWHERE"
    tryAgainTextNodeLine1.horizontalAlignmentMode =
        SKLabelHorizontalAlignmentMode.Center
    tryAgainTextNodeLine1.verticalAlignmentMode =
        SKLabelVerticalAlignmentMode.Center
    tryAgainTextNodeLine1.fontSize = 20
    tryAgainTextNodeLine1.fontColor = SKColor.whiteColor()
    tryAgainTextNodeLine1.position = CGPointMake(size.width / 2.0, 100.0)
    addChild(tryAgainTextNodeLine1)

    let tryAgainTextNodeLine2 = SKLabelNode(fontNamed: "Copperplate")
    tryAgainTextNodeLine2.text = "TO PLAY AGAIN!"
    tryAgainTextNodeLine2.horizontalAlignmentMode =
        SKLabelHorizontalAlignmentMode.Center
    tryAgainTextNodeLine2.verticalAlignmentMode =
        SKLabelVerticalAlignmentMode.Center
```

```
        tryAgainTextNodeLine2.fontSize = 20
        tryAgainTextNodeLine2.fontColor = SKColor.whiteColor()
        tryAgainTextNodeLine2.position = CGPointMake(size.width / 2.0,
            tryAgainTextNodeLine1.position.y - 40.0)
        addChild(tryAgainTextNodeLine2)
    }
}
```

As you look at this new file, you will see that the second init() method takes three parameters: the size of the scene, the result of the game as a Bool, and the player's score. The size parameter, as you know, is used to set the size of the scene, and the third and fourth parameters will be used to display information about the result of the game to the user.

Inside the init() method, it starts off by adding a background image. The image used is the same image you used in the GameScene. After that, it adds several labels to the scene, including two labels that are added to the middle of the scene. The first tells the user whether they won or lost the game, and the second tells them their score. Next, two labels are added to the bottom of the scene telling the player to tap the screen anywhere to play again. Once you have added the code to the MenuScene.swift file, save your work, and let's go back to the GameScene.swift file.

You now have a scene to transition to, so let's add the code to perform the transition. The code to make this transition is shown in the following snippet:

```
let transition = SKTransition.crossFadeWithDuration(2.0)
let menuScene = MenuScene(size: size,
                    gameResult: gameResult,
                        score: score)

view?.presentScene(menuScene, transition: transition)
```

The first line of this snippet creates a cross-fade transition that will fade in the scene over a two-second duration. The second line creates the MenuScene itself, passing it the size of the current scene followed by the result of the game and the player's score. The third line of this snippet actually presents the MenuScene, which replaces the current scene, using the transition created on the first line. After reading this code, add it to the bottom of the GameScene's gameOverWithResult() method, as shown here:

```
func gameOverWithResult(gameResult: Bool) {

    playerNode!.removeFromParent()
    playerNode = nil

    let transition = SKTransition.crossFadeWithDuration(2.0)
    let menuScene = MenuScene(size: size,
                        gameResult: gameResult,
                            score: score)

    view?.presentScene(menuScene, transition: transition)
}
```

Now run the game and either play to win or play to lose. Either way, you will see the new scene fade in, as shown in Figure 8-2, when the game is over.

Figure 8-2. The MenuScene when the game is over

Awesome. You have now added a simple scene transition that communicates whether the player won or lost the game and what their score was when the game ended.

There is one last change you need to make before moving on to the next chapter, which is to add another transition that will start a new game when the player taps the MenuScene. The code to do this is shown in the following override of the MenuScene's touchesBegan() method:

```
override func touchesBegan(touches: NSSet, withEvent event: UIEvent) {

    let transition = SKTransition.doorsOpenHorizontalWithDuration(2.0)
    let gameScene = GameScene(size: size)

    view?.presentScene(gameScene, transition: transition)
}
```

As you look at this method, you will see that it creates a doorsOpenHorizontalWithDuration transition and a new instance of the GameScene and then presents the new GameScene using the new transition. Add this method to the bottom of the MenuScene class and run the application again. This time, when the game is over and you are presented with the MenuScene, tap the screen, and you will be able to play another game.

Summary

In this chapter, you learned how to implement scene transitions using Sprite Kit's SKTransition class. You looked at some of the different types of built-in transitions Sprite Kit makes available to you. You also saw how you could control each scene during a transition. At the end of the chapter, you took your new knowledge of scene transitions and added a menu scene to your SuperSpaceMan game.

In the next chapter, you will be wrapping up your study of Sprite Kit programming with Swift when you focus on Sprite Kit best practices. At the end of the chapter, you will spend just a little time cleaning up the SuperSpaceMan application when you do some refactoring.

Chapter 9

Chapter

Sprite Kit Best Practices

In the previous chapter, you learned how to implement scene transitions using Sprite Kit's `SKTransition` class. You got a look at some of the different types of built-in transitions Sprite Kit makes available to you. You also saw how to control each scene's animation during a transition. At the end of the chapter, you took your new knowledge and added a menu scene to your SuperSpaceMan game.

In this chapter, you will learn some Sprite Kit best practices; specifically, you will see how you can create your own subclasses of `SKSpriteNode` so that you can better reuse your nodes. You will then move on to changing your game to load all the sprites into a single texture atlas that you can reference when creating all future sprites. After that, you will move on to externalizing some of your game data so that designers and testers can change the game play. Finally, you will close out the chapter when you prune your node tree of all nodes that have fallen off the bottom of the screen.

Creating Your Own Nodes Through Subclassing

The first best practice I want to talk about is refactoring your sprite nodes into their own classes. Doing this will both clean up your scene code and encapsulate each node's specific code to its own class.

The three nodes that can be abstracted to their own classes are the player, orb, and black hole nodes. Before you can start this process, you will need to first create a new file to share constants. The purpose of this file is to hold all of the collision categories that will be used across each of the nodes.

Create this new file and name it `SharedConstants.swift`. Once this file is in place, move all of the collision categories from the `GameScene.swift` file to this file. When you are finished, your new file should look like Listing 9-1.

Listing 9-1. SharedConstants.swift: A File to Hold Constant Used in Multiple Classes

```
let CollisionCategoryPlayer : UInt32 = 0x1 << 1
let CollisionCategoryPowerUpOrbs : UInt32 = 0x1 << 2
let CollisionCategoryBlackHoles : UInt32 = 0x1 << 3
```

After you have the constants set up, create another new file, named `SpaceMan.swift`. This is the file that will hold your refactored `playerNode`'s class. Once you have created the file, copy the code in Listing 9-2 into it and save your work.

Listing 9-2. SpaceMan.swift: The New SpaceMan Class

```
import Foundation
import SpriteKit

class SpaceMan: SKSpriteNode {

    override init() {

        let texture = SKTexture(imageNamed: "Player")
        super.init(texture: texture,
                       color: UIColor.clearColor(),
                        size: texture.size())

        self.physicsBody = SKPhysicsBody(circleOfRadius: self.size.width / 2)
        self.physicsBody!.dynamic = false
        self.physicsBody!.linearDamping = 1.0
        self.physicsBody!.allowsRotation = false

        self.physicsBody!.categoryBitMask = CollisionCategoryPlayer
        self.physicsBody!.contactTestBitMask =
            CollisionCategoryPowerUpOrbs | CollisionCategoryBlackHoles
        self.physicsBody!.collisionBitMask = 0
    }

    required init?(coder aDecoder: NSCoder) {
        fatalError("init(coder:) has not been implemented")
    }
}
```

As you look at the `SpaceMan` class, you will see that it extends `SKSpriteNode`, and all of the code related to setting up the spaceman's texture and `physicsBody` has been moved into the spaceman's `init()` method. This will make it much easier to use in a game scene. Once you have the new `SpaceMan` class, you can replace the following snippet of nine lines of code in the `GameScene` with only two lines of code:

```
playerNode = SKSpriteNode(imageNamed: "Player")
playerNode!.physicsBody = SKPhysicsBody(circleOfRadius: playerNode!.size.width / 2)
playerNode!.physicsBody!.dynamic = false

playerNode!.position = CGPoint(x: 160.0, y: 220.0)
playerNode!.physicsBody!.linearDamping = 1.0
playerNode!.physicsBody!.allowsRotation = false
```

```
playerNode!.physicsBody!.categoryBitMask = CollisionCategoryPlayer

playerNode!.physicsBody!.contactTestBitMask = CollisionCategoryPowerUpOrbs |
CollisionCategoryBlackHoles
playerNode!.physicsBody!.collisionBitMask = 0
```

Remove the previous snippet from GameScene's init(size: CGSize) method and replace it with the following two lines:

```
playerNode = SpaceMan()
playerNode!.position = CGPoint(x: 160.0, y: 220.0)
```

The next class you need to create is a class will encapsulate all of the orb node–related code. To do this, create another file, named Orb.swift, and copy the contents of Listing 9-3 into it.

Listing 9-3. Orb.swift: The New Orb Class

```
import Foundation
import SpriteKit

class Orb: SKSpriteNode {

    override init() {

        let texture = SKTexture(imageNamed: "PowerUp")
        super.init(texture: texture,
                    color: UIColor.clearColor(),
                     size: texture.size())

        physicsBody =
            SKPhysicsBody(circleOfRadius: self.size.width / 2)
        physicsBody!.dynamic = false

        physicsBody!.categoryBitMask = CollisionCategoryPowerUpOrbs
        physicsBody!.collisionBitMask = 0
        name = "POWER_UP_ORB"
    }

    required init?(coder aDecoder: NSCoder) {
        fatalError("init(coder:) has not been implemented")
    }
}
```

This new Orb class, much like the SpaceMan class, contains all the code to set up the node's texture and its physicsBody. Once you have the new Orb class in place, you can then change the addOrbsToForeground() method to look like the following simplified method:

```
func addOrbsToForeground() {

    var orbNodePosition =
        CGPoint(x: playerNode!.position.x, y: playerNode!.position.y + 100)
    var orbXShift : CGFloat = -1.0
```

```
for i in 0...49 {

    // new code to use an orb
    var orbNode = Orb()

    if orbNodePosition.x - (orbNode.size.width * 2) <= 0 {

        orbXShift = 1.0
    }

    if orbNodePosition.x + orbNode.size.width >= self.size.width {

        orbXShift = -1.0
    }

    orbNodePosition.x += 40.0 * orbXShift
    orbNodePosition.y += 120
    orbNode.position = orbNodePosition

    self.foregroundNode!.addChild(orbNode)
    }
}
```

The addOrbsToForeground() method is now much simpler. It performs only three steps.
It creates each of the orb nodes, sets their respective positions, and then adds them to
the scene.

The last node class you are going to create is the BlackHole class. As you can probably
guess, this class will contain all the code related to a black hole. Create another new file
named BlackHole.swift and copy the contents of Listing 9-4 into it.

Listing 9-4. BlackHole.swift: The New BlackHole Class

```
import Foundation
import SpriteKit

class BlackHole: SKSpriteNode {

    override init() {

        let textureAtlas = SKTextureAtlas(named: "sprites.atlas")

        var frame0 = textureAtlas.textureNamed("BlackHole0")
        var frame1 = textureAtlas.textureNamed("BlackHole1")
        var frame2 = textureAtlas.textureNamed("BlackHole2")
        var frame3 = textureAtlas.textureNamed("BlackHole3")
        var frame4 = textureAtlas.textureNamed("BlackHole4")

        var blackHoleTextures = [frame0, frame1, frame2, frame3, frame4]
        var animateAction =
            SKAction.animateWithTextures(blackHoleTextures, timePerFrame: 0.2)
```

```
        var rotateAction = SKAction.repeatActionForever(animateAction)

        super.init(texture: frame0,
                    color: UIColor.clearColor(),
                    size: frame0.size())

        physicsBody = SKPhysicsBody(circleOfRadius: size.width / 2)
        physicsBody!.dynamic = false
        physicsBody!.categoryBitMask = CollisionCategoryBlackHoles
        physicsBody!.collisionBitMask = 0
        name = "BLACK_HOLE"

        runAction(rotateAction)
    }

    required init?(coder aDecoder: NSCoder) {
        fatalError("init(coder:) has not been implemented")
    }
}
```

Once you have the new BlackHole class in place, you can then change the addBlackHolesToForeground() method to look like the following simplified method:

```
func addBlackHolesToForeground() {

    var moveLeftAction = SKAction.moveToX(0.0, duration: 2.0)
    var moveRightAction = SKAction.moveToX(self.size.width, duration: 2.0)
    var actionSequence = SKAction.sequence([moveLeftAction, moveRightAction])
    var moveAction = SKAction.repeatActionForever(actionSequence)

    for i in 1...10 {

        // new black hole usage code
        var blackHoleNode = BlackHole()

        blackHoleNode.position = CGPointMake(self.size.width - 80.0, 600.0 * CGFloat(i))
        blackHoleNode.runAction(moveAction)

        foregroundNode!.addChild(blackHoleNode)
    }
}
```

Moving these nodes into their own classes makes it a lot easier to reuse each of the nodes, and it also cleans up the GameScene.

Reusing Textures

The next best practice you are going to see is how you can use a single instance of an SKTextureAtlas to load all of the sprite images and then just reuse the atlas when setting all of your sprite's textures. The first step to make this happen is to create an SKTextureAtlas and pass it to nodes so they can retrieve their own textures. Add this line of code immediately before the first init() method in the GameScene class:

```
let textureAtlas = SKTextureAtlas(named: "sprites.atlas")
```

After you have created the texture atlas, you need to change the init() method of each of the recently created SKSpriteNodes to take an SKTextureAtlas as a parameter. Once the SKSpriteNode has a reference to the SKTextureAtlas, then you can change the texture-loading code in each node to use this passed-in textureAtlas. The following init() method shows this change made to the SpaceMan class:

```
init(textureAtlas: SKTextureAtlas) {

    let texture = textureAtlas.textureNamed("Player")
    super.init(texture: texture, color: UIColor.clearColor(), size: texture.size())

    physicsBody = SKPhysicsBody(circleOfRadius: size.width / 2)
    physicsBody!.dynamic = false
    physicsBody!.linearDamping = 1.0
    physicsBody!.allowsRotation = false

    physicsBody!.categoryBitMask = CollisionCategoryPlayer
    physicsBody!.contactTestBitMask =
        CollisionCategoryPowerUpOrbs | CollisionCategoryBlackHoles
    physicsBody!.collisionBitMask = 0
}
```

Notice the init() method's parameter list now takes an SKTextureAtlas parameter, and the first line of the init() method uses this SKTextureAtlas to load the Player texture. Also note that the init() method no longer overrides the default init(), and therefore I have removed the override keyword. Make this change to the spaceman's init() method and let's go back to GameScene's init() method. To use the new SpaceMan init() method, you need to change the construction of the SpaceMan to look like the following line:

```
self.playerNode = SpaceMan(textureAtlas: self.textureAtlas)
```

After you have made all of the SpaceMan changes, let's move on to doing the same to both the Orb and BlackHole classes. First change the init() method of the Orb to take an SKTextureAtlas.

```
init(textureAtlas: SKTextureAtlas) {

    let texture = textureAtlas.textureNamed("PowerUp")
    super.init(texture: texture, color: UIColor.clearColor(), size: texture.size())

    physicsBody = SKPhysicsBody(circleOfRadius: size.width / 2)
    physicsBody!.dynamic = false

    physicsBody!.categoryBitMask = CollisionCategoryPowerUpOrbs
    physicsBody!.collisionBitMask = 0
    name = "POWER_UP_ORB"
}
```

After changing the Orb's init() method, change GameScene's addOrbsToForeground() to look like the following:

```
func addOrbsToForeground() {

    var orbNodePosition =
        CGPoint(x: playerNode!.position.x, y: playerNode!.position.y + 100)

    var orbXShift : CGFloat = -1.0

    for i in 0...49 {

        // new code to use an orb
        let orbNode = Orb(textureAtlas: self.textureAtlas)

        if orbNodePosition.x - (orbNode.size.width * 2) <= 0 {

            orbXShift = 1.0
        }

        if orbNodePosition.x + orbNode.size.width >= size.width {

            orbXShift = -1.0
        }

        orbNodePosition.x += 40.0 * orbXShift
        orbNodePosition.y += 120
        orbNode.position = orbNodePosition

        foregroundNode!.addChild(orbNode)
    }
}
```

Next, change the init() method of the BlackHole to take an SKTextureAtlas and then use this texture atlas to load all the textures going forward. This change is shown in the following snippet:

```
init(textureAtlas: SKTextureAtlas) {

    let frame0 = textureAtlas.textureNamed("BlackHole0")
    let frame1 = textureAtlas.textureNamed("BlackHole1")
    let frame2 = textureAtlas.textureNamed("BlackHole2")
    let frame3 = textureAtlas.textureNamed("BlackHole3")
    let frame4 = textureAtlas.textureNamed("BlackHole4")

    let blackHoleTextures = [frame0, frame1, frame2, frame3, frame4];
    let animateAction =
        SKAction.animateWithTextures(blackHoleTextures, timePerFrame: 0.2)
    let rotateAction = SKAction.repeatActionForever(animateAction)

    super.init(texture: frame0, color: UIColor.clearColor(), size: frame0.size())

    physicsBody = SKPhysicsBody(circleOfRadius: size.width / 2)
    physicsBody!.dynamic = false
    physicsBody!.categoryBitMask = CollisionCategoryBlackHoles
    physicsBody!.collisionBitMask = 0
    name = "BLACK_HOLE"

    runAction(rotateAction)
}
```

Finally, change GameScene's addBlackHolesToForeground() so that it passes the SKTextureAtlas to the BlackHole, as shown here:

```
func addBlackHolesToForeground() {

    var moveLeftAction = SKAction.moveToX(0.0, duration: 2.0)
    var moveRightAction = SKAction.moveToX(size.width, duration: 2.0)
    var actionSequence = SKAction.sequence([moveLeftAction, moveRightAction])
    var moveAction = SKAction.repeatActionForever(actionSequence)

    for i in 1...10 {

        // new black hole usage code
        let blackHoleNode = BlackHole(textureAtlas: textureAtlas)

        blackHoleNode.position = CGPoint(x: size.width - 80.0, y: 600.0 * CGFloat(i))
        blackHoleNode.runAction(moveAction)

        foregroundNode!.addChild(blackHoleNode)
    }
}
```

At this point, all of the SKSpriteNodes reuse the same SKTextureAtlas, which will speed up the retrieval of each of your node's textures.

Externalizing Your Game Data

The next best practice I want to talk about will not necessarily improve the performance of your game, but it will help during development and testing. So far, all of the positions of each game node are hard-coded in the SuperSpaceMan Swift code. This is if you are creating a simple game, with you being both the designer and the developer of the game; if you have a team with clearly defined roles, you may want to make it possible for a designer or tester to change the play of the game without changing the Swift code. One way to do this is to externalize the positions of your game nodes.

A simple way to do this in the SuperSpaceMan game is to move the orb and black hole positions to plist files. You can then load the node positions using an NSBundle. This will make it possible for a designer or tester to just change a plist to change the layout of the whole game. An example plist that holds the first three orb node positions is shown here:

```
<?xml version="1.0" encoding="UTF-8"?>
<!DOCTYPE plist PUBLIC "-//Apple//DTD PLIST 1.0//EN" "http://www.apple.com/DTDs/
PropertyList-1.0.dtd">
<plist version="1.0">
<dict>
    <key>positions</key>
    <array>
    <dict>
        <key>x</key>
        <real>120.0</real>
        <key>y</key>
        <real>440.0</real>
    </dict>
    <dict>
        <key>x</key>
        <real>80.0</real>
        <key>y</key>
        <real>560.0</real>
    </dict>
    <dict>
        <key>x</key>
        <real>120.0</real>
        <key>y</key>
        <real>680.0</real>
    </dict>
    ...
    </array>
</dict>
</plist>
```

In this file, you can see an array of dictionaries each containing the x and y positions of the orb nodes. Don't worry about creating this file yourself. You can find an orbs.plist file and a blackholes.plist file in the previously downloaded ZIP file containing the images you used for your sprites. Copy both of these files into the SupportingFiles groups of your project, and let's move on to using each of these files.

Once you have copied both of the plist files into your project, you can then load them using the main bundle. Take a look at the following modified addOrbsToForeground() method:

```
func addOrbsToForeground() {

    let orbPlistPath =
        NSBundle.mainBundle().pathForResource("orbs", ofType: "plist")
    let orbDataDictionary : NSDictionary? =
        NSDictionary(contentsOfFile: orbPlistPath!)

    if let positionDictionary = orbDataDictionary {

        let positions = positionDictionary.objectForKey("positions") as NSArray

        for position in positions {

            let orbNode = Orb(textureAtlas: textureAtlas)
            let x = position.objectForKey("x") as CGFloat
            let y = position.objectForKey("y") as CGFloat
            orbNode.position = CGPointMake(x, y)
            foregroundNode!.addChild(orbNode)
        }
    }
}
```

In the new addOrbsToForeground() method, you can see that it first loads the contents of orbs.plist. After that, it grabs the array of positions out of the dictionary, and finally it iterates over all of the positions, adding each orbNode to the foregroundNode at that position. Now you can change the number and layout of all the orb nodes by simply changing the plist.

Make these changes to the addOrbsToForeground() method, and let's do the same thing with the black holes. You have already copied the blackholes.plist file into your project, so you can skip that step and move on to modifying the addBlackHolesToForeground() method to load the black hole positions from the plist. The new addBlackHolesToForeground() method is shown here:

```
func addBlackHolesToForeground() {

    let moveLeftAction =
        SKAction.moveToX(0.0, duration: 2.0)
    let moveRightAction =
        SKAction.moveToX(size.width, duration: 2.0)
    let actionSequence = SKAction.sequence([moveLeftAction, moveRightAction])
    let moveAction = SKAction.repeatActionForever(actionSequence)

    let blackHolePlistPath =
        NSBundle.mainBundle().pathForResource("blackholes", ofType: "plist")
    let blackHoleDataDictionary : NSDictionary? =
        NSDictionary(contentsOfFile: blackHolePlistPath!)
```

```
if let positionDictionary = blackHoleDataDictionary {

    let positions = positionDictionary.objectForKey("positions") as NSArray

    for position in positions {

        let blackHoleNode = BlackHole(textureAtlas: textureAtlas)

        let x = position.objectForKey("x") as CGFloat
        let y = position.objectForKey("y") as CGFloat
        blackHoleNode.position = CGPointMake(x, y)

        blackHoleNode.runAction(moveAction)

        foregroundNode!.addChild(blackHoleNode)
    }
  }
}
```

As you look over the changes to the addBlackHolesToForeground() method, you will see that it now, just like the addOrbsToForeground() method, reads all of the black hole node positions from the plist and then adds each of the blackHoleNodes at those read-in positions. Make this change and run your game again. You will see no difference, but now people with little to no development experience can completely change the game.

Keeping Your Node Tree Pruned

The final best practice to implement in the SuperSpaceMan game is to remove all SKNodes that have dropped off the bottom of the viewable scene. Removing unnecessary nodes from your games will improve the overall performance of node tree rendering and reduce the amount of memory used to hold all of the nodes in your node tree.

A simple way to remove unnecessary nodes from GameScene is to create a method that will remove all nodes with a given name that are one scene length below the playerNode. Take a look at the following removeOutOfSceneNodesWithName() method:

```
func removeOutOfSceneNodesWithName(name: String) {

    foregroundNode!.enumerateChildNodesWithName(name, usingBlock: {
        node, stop in

        if self.playerNode == nil {

            stop.memory = true
        }
        else if (self.playerNode!.position.y - node.position.y > self.size.height)
        {

            node!.removeFromParent()
        }
    })
}
```

This method takes a single String representing the name of each SKNode you want to test and uses the enumerateChildNodesWithName() method to check to see whether those nodes are positioned one scene length below the playerNode. If the returned node is greater than one scene length, then it is removed from the scene. Notice one thing about this method. Inside the enumerateChildNodesWithName() method it first checks to see whether the playerNode is nil. If the playerNode is nil, then it stops the search for child nodes by setting the stop.memory property to true. Add this method to the bottom of the GameScene.

To use the removeOutOfSceneNodesWithName(), you need to add a call to this method, for each node that can be removed from the scene, to the bottom of GameScene's update() method. In this instance, the two nodes that can fall out of the scene are the BLACK_HOLE and POWER_UP_ORB nodes. Take a look at the modified update() method with these two calls added to the end of the method, shown here:

```
override func update(currentTime: NSTimeInterval) {

    if self.playerNode != nil {

        if self.playerNode!.position.y >= 180.0 &&
            self.playerNode!.position.y < 6400.0 {

            self.backgroundNode!.position =
                CGPointMake(self.backgroundNode!.position.x,
                            -((self.playerNode!.position.y - 180.0)/8));

            self.backgroundStarsNode!.position =
                CGPointMake(self.backgroundStarsNode!.position.x,
                            -((self.playerNode!.position.y - 180.0)/6));

            self.backgroundPlanetNode!.position =
                CGPointMake(self.backgroundPlanetNode!.position.x,
                            -((self.playerNode!.position.y - 180.0)/8));

            self.foregroundNode!.position =
                CGPointMake(self.foregroundNode!.position.x,
                            -(self.playerNode!.position.y - 180.0));
        }
        else if self.playerNode!.position.y > 7000.0 {

            self.gameOverWithResult(true)
        }
        else if self.playerNode!.position.y + self.playerNode!.size.height < 0.0 {

            self.gameOverWithResult(false)
        }

        removeOutOfSceneNodesWithName("BLACK_HOLE")
        removeOutOfSceneNodesWithName("POWER_UP_ORB")
    }
}
```

The new `update()` method now calls the `removeOutOfSceneNodesWithName()` method at the end of every scene rendering, removing all unnecessary nodes. Make this change to the `update()` method and run the SuperSpaceMan game one last time. When you play the game this time, tap the screen until you are about to win the game and then stop tapping so that the `playerNode` starts to fall. Notice this time that as you fall, the passed-up orb and black hole nodes have been removed from the scene.

Summary

In this chapter, you learned some Sprite Kit best practices, including how to create your own subclasses of `SKSpriteNode` so that you can better reuse your nodes. You then moved on to changing your game to load all the sprites into a single texture. After that, you moved on to externalizing your game data. Finally, you pruned your node tree of all nodes that had fallen off the bottom of the screen.

In the next chapter, you will begin your journey into Scene Kit. Have fun.

Part II

Swift and Scene Kit

In this section of the book we are going cover the basics of Scene Kit, including how you render, animate, and manipulate the scene graph, add collision detection, and control your game play with the accelerometer. We will cover all the basics you need to create your own Scene Kit game.

Chapter 10

Creating Your First Scene Kit Project

In this chapter, you will dive right in and create your own game. For this game you will continue with the SuperSpaceMan theme and create a hide-and-seek style of game. You will start with some basic 3D code for a portrait-only game. By the end of the chapter, you will have a complete landscape-only 3D game with your hero in the middle of the scene.

Scene Kit Primer

Scene Kit is Apple's powerful 3D graphics framework that makes creating casual 3D games simple. By using the Scene Kit API, you can create fully immersive 3D games without having knowledge of OpenGL. Scene Kit was first released for OS X Mountain Lion, but now with the release of iOS 8, developers can create amazing casual 3D games.

Scene Kit is used to create a *scene graph*, which contains a scene and a hierarchy of nodes, as shown in Figure 10-1. Scene Kit uses these nodes to display scenes in a view and processes the scene graph using the graphics processing unit (GPU). This improves the performance of rendering the frames on the device.

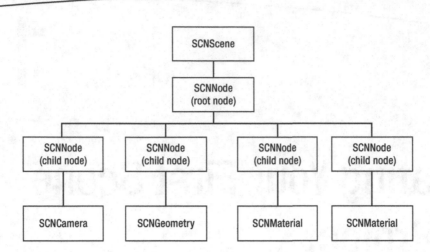

Figure 10-1. Scene graph

Apple has integrated Sprite Kit with in the Scene Kit technology. This integration will allow you to use your Sprite Kit knowledge to create your casual 3D game. Table 10-1 gives you an overview of the various classes and describes each of these Scene Kit classes.

Table 10-1. Scene Kit Classes

Class	Description
SCNView	This view is used to display Scene Kit objects.
SCNScene	A scene can be created programmatically or by using a 3D file from graphic tools.
SCNNode	This is the starting point to create a scene.
SCNCamera	This is the point of view for the scene.
SCNGeometry	This is a 3D object used to attach to a node. This also can use 3D files from graphic tools.
SCNMaterial	Material is used to describe how the surface of the node will be rendered.
SCNLight	This is a light source attached to a node to provide shading and lighting of the scene.

Scene Kit Animation

Scene Kit is integrated with ImageKit and CoreAnimation, so you will not need to have advanced knowledge of 3D programming knowledge. When you create scenes, you can create animations that transition elegantly between different values of the scene's properties.

Scene Kit uses the SCNTransaction class to create an atomic run loop to combine all your implicit animation changes. These types of changes are ideally small atomic changes that occur almost immediately, and you are able to increase the duration. These types of animated properties automatically animate.

Since Scene Kit is based on CoreAnimation, you can explicitly create animation objects and attach them to the animated scene. For this more complex animation, you subclass

CAAnimation. After creating this subclass using key-value coding, set the animation parameters and attach them to the node or elements in the scene. The CAAnimation class is also able to use objects from third-party graphic authoring tools.

What You Need to Know

Scene Kit is a 3D-based API, so you should have a basic understanding of graphing concepts such as coordinate systems and 3D geometry.

- *Points*: In this context, a point is a position in a three-dimensional space.

- *Vectors*: You will use vectors for mostly directions.

- *Cartesian coordinate system*: This comprises two axes: the x-axis that extends along the horizontal plane and the y-axis that extends perpendicular to the x-axis.

- *Euclidean space*: This is simply the 3D coordinate system, with the addition of the z-axis that represents the depth of view.

- *Transformations*: There are many operations that do transformations; however, for now you will be dealing with operators that will be used for points and rotations. Think of this as transforming a point to a different point or applying a vector (direction) to the rotation of the object.

If you want to get more information on computer graphics programming, I suggest looking at *Geometric Algebra for Computer Graphics* by John Vince (www.apress.com/9781846289965). By default the camera, or user view angle, is along the z-axis (Figure 10-2).

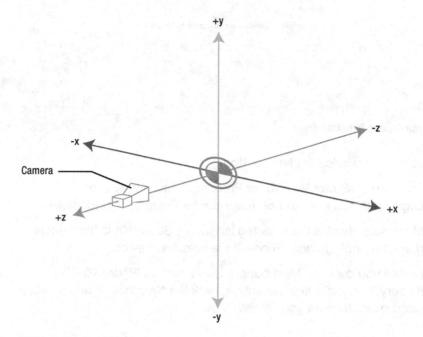

Figure 10-2. Scene Kit coordinate system

Creating the Scene Kit Project

The best way to learn this is to simply dive in and start from scratch. You will create a game project using Swift as the language and Scene Kit as the game technology. After you have this project created, you will then add a new type of file used by Scene Kit: the Collada type. To create the project, open Xcode and complete the following steps:

1. Select File ➤ New Project.

2. Select Application from the iOS group.

3. Select the Game icon. The Choose Template dialog should now look like Figure 10-3.

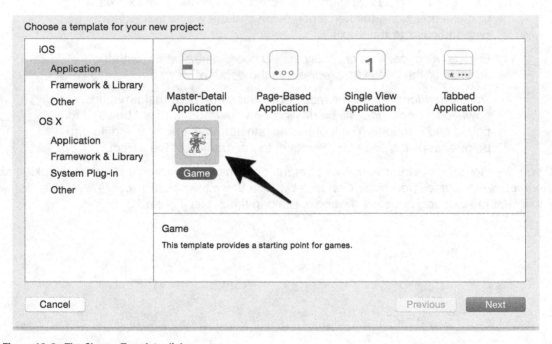

Figure 10-3. The Choose Template dialog

4. To move on, click the Next button.

5. Enter **SuperSpaceMan3D** for Product Name, **Apress** for Organization Name, and **com.apress** for Organization Identifier.

6. Make sure Swift is the selected language, Scene Kit is the selected game technology, and iPhone is the selected device.

7. Before you click the Next button, take a look at Figure 10-4. If everything looks like this image, click the Next button and select a good place to store your project files.

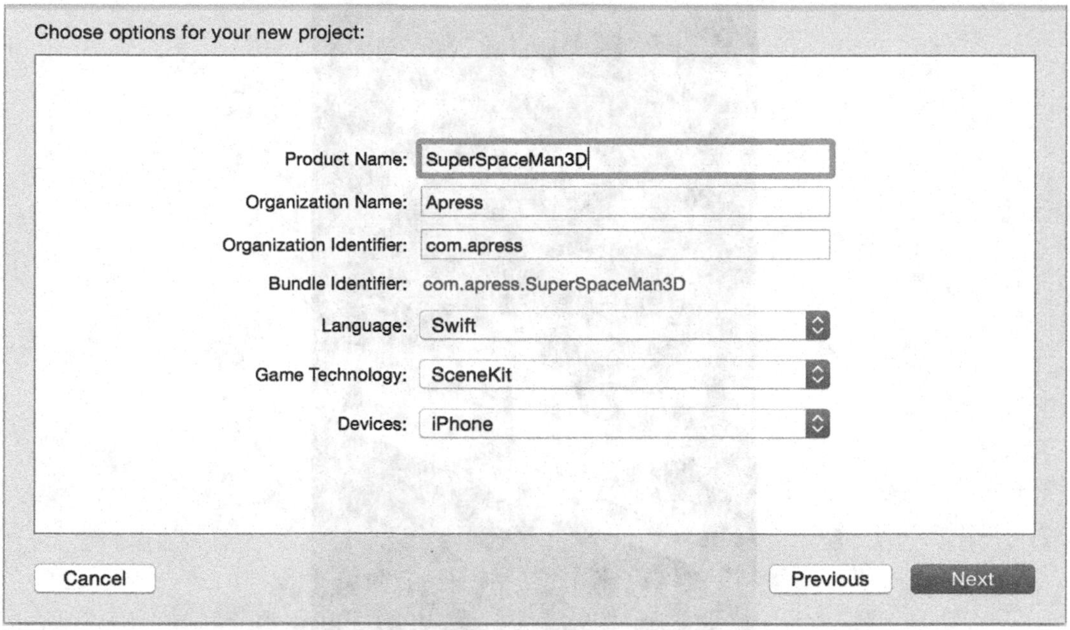

Choose options for your new project:

Product Name:	SuperSpaceMan3D
Organization Name:	Apress
Organization Identifier:	com.apress
Bundle Identifier:	com.apress.SuperSpaceMan3D
Language:	Swift
Game Technology:	SceneKit
Devices:	iPhone

Cancel   Previous   Next

Figure 10-4. Choosing options for your project

Note You will notice you are creating an iPhone-only game. This is because the game you are creating lends itself better to the iPhone. Everything I will cover in this book translates to any iOS device.

You now have a working Scene Kit project. Click the Play button to see what you have created. If everything went OK, you will see your new app running in the simulator. It does not do a whole lot yet, but there is more to it than displaying a spinning 3D rendition of a jet plane, similar to Figure 10-5.

Figure 10-5. The Scene Kit sample application

Wiring Up and Building a Scene

Now that you have a basic project and an understanding of Scene Kit, it is time to actually learn how to put these classes together and create a game. Right now you have a project that is running the default Apple sample code. In this section, you will remove that code and create a floor and the spaceman in his new environment.

SuperSpaceMan3D

Before you move on, let's get the project fully cleaned out so that you can start from scratch. Unlike the previous game that was in portrait orientation only, this time you will go with landscape orientation only, so you will need to change your target settings so they look like Figure 10-6.

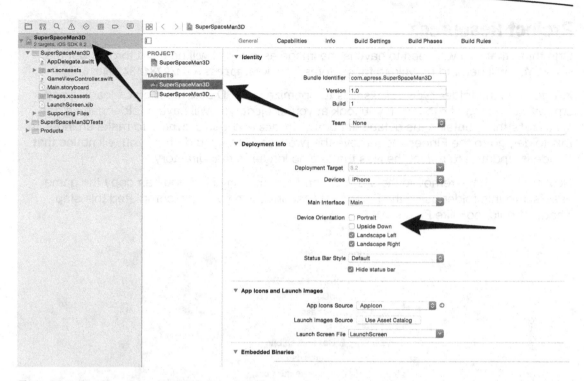

Figure 10-6. *The SuperSpaceMan3D device orientation*

The next thing to do is to replace the GameViewController.swift file's contents with the class in Listing 10-1. You want to override the viewDidLoad() method and create an empty SCNScene.

Listing 10-1. *GameViewController.swift: The GameViewController*

```swift
import UIKit
import QuartzCore
import SceneKit

class GameViewController: UIViewController {

    override func viewDidLoad() {
        super.viewDidLoad()
        self.view = SCNView()
    }
}
```

Now if you run the game, you will see a blank screen, which is a great place for you to start the game.

Project Resources

One thing that you will need to have is the image assets that will be used throughout the book. You will need to download these items from www.apress.com/9781484204016.

Xcode uses the folder type.scnassests to optimize your 3D assets for quick loading and smooth rendering at runtime. If you look at your project, you will have a folder named art. scnassets that contains the default images ship.dea and texture.png. To make changes to this folder, go to the Finder and remove the two files. Once you do this, you will notice that Xcode is updated to reflect the files that are no longer in that directory.

Now that you have removed the ship.dea and texture.png files, you can copy the game assets into this folder using the Finder application. Once you have completed this step, Xcode should look like Figure 10-7.

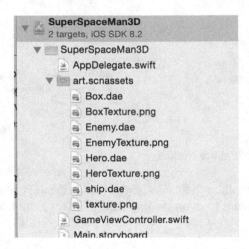

Figure 10-7. Art assets

Now that you have these files in the project, you will need to add the static images to the project. This time you can simply drag the image from your folder in the Finder to the Xcode project and drop them into Xcode's image asset catalog: Images.xcassets. All of the images that you will be using for this game will be added at this time.

Building the Scene

A good place to start is in the GameViewController class. You will need to remove the temporary code in the viewDidLoad() method where you were creating an empty SCNScene.

```
override func viewDidLoad() {
  super.viewDidLoad()

}
```

You now have an overridden method that will call the superclasses' `viewDidLoad` method to allow UIKit to finish completing anything it needs to do when the view loads. After this call, you will create a variable.

```
let mainScene = createMainScene()
```

You will use separate methods to create the nodes. This will allow you to understand what is going on and make it easier to refactor later if you want. So, now there is an error you need to fix: the unresolved identifier.

```
func createMainScene() -> SCNScene {

    var mainScene = SCNScene(named: "art.scnassets/hero.dae")
    return mainScene!
}
```

This method is small but powerful; this is where Scene Kit's power starts to be shown. As you can see, you are loading a Collada file (`.dae`) that a 3D artist has provided you. Once you finish coding the scene, with just a few more lines of code you will have the spaceman in his glorious 3D-ness.

Now let's add the scene that is being created to your view. In the `viewDidLoad()` method, after your created scene, add the following code:

```
let sceneView = self.view as SCNView
sceneView.scene = mainScene

 // Optional, but nice to be turned on during developement
sceneView.showsStatistics = true
 sceneView.allowsCameraControl = true
```

This code will get the view, and then you add the scene to the view's scene. Since you are here, why not add `showStatistics` so you can see how well Scene Kit handles 3D objects? You can also add `allowsCameraControl = true` so that you can manipulate the view using gestures. Pinching and zooming will zoom into the scene, and panning will allow you to pan around the scene.

Now you should be able to run the project and see the spaceman in full 3D, as shown in Figure 10-8.

+ ⬤▭▭▭▭▭ 60fps   ◆1 ▲1.48K ✱4.43K ▮

Figure 10-8. Spaceman in 3D

Before moving on, your GameViewController should look similar to Listing 10-2.

Listing 10-2. GameViewController Class Setup

```
class GameViewController: UIViewController {

    override func viewDidLoad() {

        super.viewDidLoad
        // Create the scene
        let mainScene = createMainScene()

        // Get the games main view
        let sceneView = self.view as SCNView

         sceneView.scene = scene

        // Optional, but nice to be turned on during developement
        sceneView. showsStatistics = true
        sceneView.allowsCameraControl = true

    }

    func createMainScene() -> SCNScene {

        var mainScene = SCNScene(named: "art.scnassets/hero.dae")
        return mainScene!
    }

}
```

Next you will create a floor for the spaceman to walk on. In the `GameViewController` class, you will create a new method that will create the floor node.

In the function declaration, you can see you will return an `SCNNode` to the caller. This allows you to easily refactor the code if you choose to at a later date.

```
func createFloorNode() -> SCNNode {

}
```

Next you create two variables, one that will be used as the return `SCNNode` and an `SCNFloor` to create the geometry for the `SCNNode`.

```
    let floorNode = SCNNode()
    let floor =  SCNFloor()
```

The `SCNFloor` is a special Scene Kit class that creates an infinite plane. It is important to know that this plane will extend along the x- and z-coordinates, with the y-coordinate is set to zero.

```
floorNode.geometry = floor
floorNode.geometry?.firstMaterial?.diffuse.contents = "Floor"
```

```
return floorNode
```

In this section of code, you will set up the geometry for the `floorNode`. A node can have only one geometry assigned to it, so to create animated geometries, you would create an empty node and add child nodes to it. For the `floorNode`, you won't be creating animated geometries, but that's something I will touch on later in creating the game.

You now have a method that will create a new `SCNNode` for the floor. Next you need to add it to your main scene so that you will be able to see and interact with this node. Head back up to the `viewDidLoad` method, and after you create the main scene, add the following:

```
mainScenerootNode.addChildNode( createFloorNode() )
```

Run the game now, and you will notice that the spaceman is standing on a floor instead of in the middle of nowhere, as shown in Figure 10-9.

Figure 10-9. Spaceman standing on the floor

This isn't that much fun and really doesn't show what Scene Kit is providing for you. So, in the viewDidLoad() method, add the following line of code at the end of the method:

```
sceneView.allowsCameraControl = true
```

Run the game now, and you will be able to move the view's perspective, in other words, a camera, around the object and see that you do have a 3D scene. You can do this because you set the camera control to true. Use the pinch-zoom and panning gestures to move around the scene. If you are running this in the simulator, notice the frames per second (fps) and see that it is never near 60fps. On my simulator, it never gets above 20fps. This time, run the game on your iPhone that has iOS 8 installed on it. Now when you move the camera around, you should see the fps stays closer to 60fps. Does this mean your little iPhone is more powerful than your Mac? Probably not. The simulator is simply simulating the different devices to allow you as a developer to quickly test your code. However, when you run the game on an actual device, you can see the power of Scene Kit. Scene Kit is using the GPU to render the scene and nodes. This one reason why Apple recommends you always run the application on a device before submitting it to the App Store for approval. Before Scene Kit was available, you had to use other third-party libraries or OpenGL in order to accomplish this. This could take more than several thousand lines of code to accomplish what you have done in less than 50 lines.

Summary

Congratulations! You now have a simple 3D scene running. In this chapter, you learned some of the power that Scene Kit provides. You created a project in which you will build upon. In the next chapter, you will examine what a scene graph is and how Scene Kit works with a scene graph. You will also start using some of Scene Kit's built-in classes that will allow you to create the obstacles that will be used within the game.

Building the Scene

In the previous chapter, you learned some of the basics of Scene Kit. I covered how a scene is created using SCNNodes and showed a basic tree structure of those nodes.

In this chapter, you will learn how Scene Kit uses the scene graph to render the objects in the scene. Once you have an understanding of the scene graph, you will then see how to use the built-in models from Scene Kit. You will use the models to make obstacles in your game for the hero to avoid and for the enemy to hide behind.

Scene Graph

Basically, the scene graph is just a collection of data structures used to manage and organize the scene data. The SCNScene is the base for a tree structure of the scene graph, as shown in Figure 11-1. In the early days of graphic programming, the scene graph was modeled with scene data, and its behavior was created procedurally, which usually led to a mess of code. Developers were unable to easily reuse your nodes or other objects through the application. A separation of concerns allows you to have a clean boundary between your scenes and how they're rendered. Figure 11-1 shows an example of how this looks.

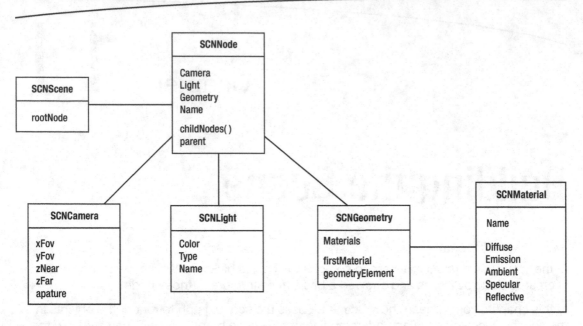

Figure 11-1. Scene graph example

Every node in a scene has a parent except the topmost node, in other words, the root node. See Figure 11-2.

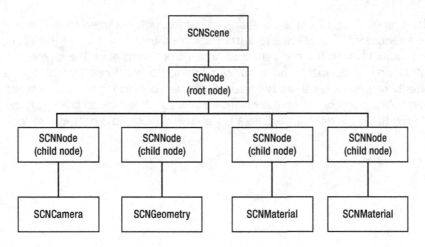

Figure 11-2. Scene nodes

Nodes that contain other child nodes are considered *group nodes*. In Figure 11-2, you can see a parent node and several child nodes.

- Node trees (group nodes) are what appear in the scene. Node positions are defined in the coordinate system defined by its parent node.

- Leaf nodes are the ones that are actually rendered. These execute the animation and specify the material and lighting for the node tree.

Scene Kit Editor

Xcode provides a special editor similar to Interface Builder that is used to edit your Collada files by manipulating the scene graph, as shown in Figure 11-3.

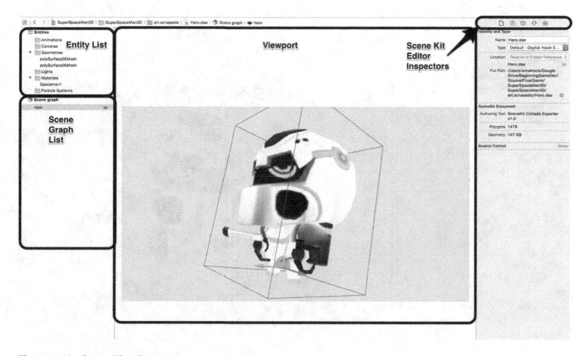

Figure 11-3. Scene Kit editor

What is a Collada file, and why is it important to Scene Kit? Collada is a COLLAborative Design Activity file, formatted for interactive 3D applications. This file is an example of how the separation of concerns is implemented. A 3D graphic artist has the ability to create objects in their own tool set and provide this exported file to you, the developer. This technique allows the graphic artist to create complex and sophisticated scenes that produce an immersive experience for your players.

If you look at your spaceman, you can see how you used the scene graph for him.

As shown in Figure 11-4, the scene was loaded when you loaded the Collada file, which was exported for use as a Data Asset Exchange (.dae) file. The Collada file specifies the following:

a.   The camera node to view him

b.   The geometry

c.   The material

d.   The light node for the spotlight around him

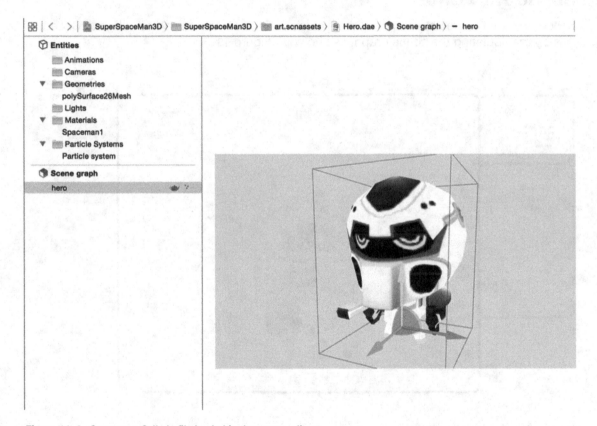

Figure 11-4. *Spaceman Collada file loaded in the scene editor*

Figure 11-5 shows the Scene Kit editor for the materials node. Here you can experiment with different properties and see how they affect your hero. For example, change the Diffuse property to a different image. Notice the viewport reflects your changes in real time. Change the Reflective property, and you will see how the lighting is reflected from the hero. Before you move on, make sure you set Diffuse back to the heroTexture.png image so that your hero will have his modeled skin.

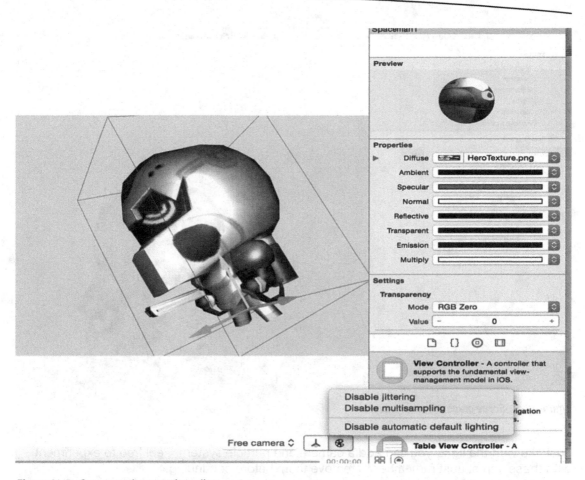

Figure 11-5. *Scene graph properties editor*

In Figure 11-6, you can see how you can adjust the scene graph in the scene graph editor. Right-click the scene graph and select Add Light. When you do this, you will add a light to the Entities section. Select it, and you will be able to change the type, color, and other properties in the properties editor.

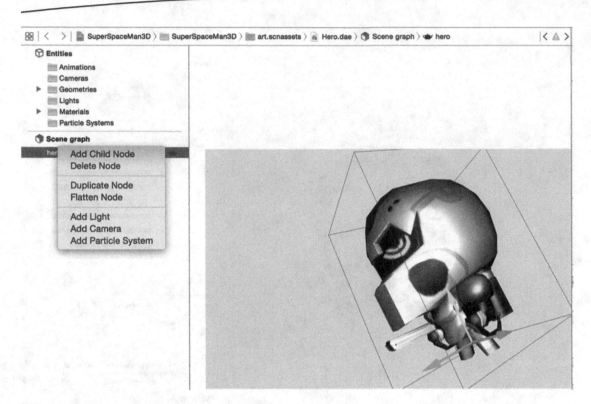

Figure 11-6. Scene graph submenu example

Just like with the light, you can add a camera and particle system. Feel free to experiment with these items. Just remember to remove them before continuing.

Now that you have a good understanding of the scene graph, let's look at the render cycle that is used by Scene Kit.

Render Cycle

It is important to have a basic understanding of Scene Kit's render cycle because this will allow you make changes to your game as the scene is being drawn. You will use the callbacks provided by Scene Kit to execute your code (see Figure 11-7).

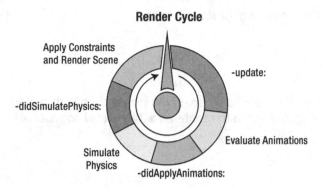

Figure 11-7. Scene graph render cycle

In your game you will use the render delegate method for your game logic.

```
func renderer(aRenderer: SCNSceneRenderer, didSimulatePhysicsAtTime time: NSTimeInterval)
```

As you can see in Figure 11-5, this is one of the last callbacks that you can use, and it appears after the physics and animations are applied. You will want to use this delegate so that you can check for collisions within the scene.

The update delegate is a common method that is used frequently in Scene Kit development. This delegate allows you to make changes to the scene before the animations or physics run. You can use it when you are changing the lighting or want to transform an object.

```
renderer(aRenderer: SCNSceneRenderer!, updateAtTime time: NSTimeInterval)
```

The didApplyAnimation callback is called after the animation has completed.

Scene Kit's Built-in Model Classes

Scene Kit provides almost all the primitive geometries that you will need in order to create immersive games.

SCNGeometry Objects

In this section, you will use Scene Kit geometries to create some of the obstacles. There are several geometries that are provided by Scene Kit. When you create any of these geometries, the center is around its local coordinate system. In other words, if you create an SCNBox with the width, length, and height of 20.0, these will be along the x-, y-, and z-axes at 10.0 and -10.0.

Here is a list of the Scene Kit primitive geometries types:

- SCNBox: This is a basic six-sided polyhedron with rectangles for faces. You will also be able to create an SCNMaterial for each of these sides if you want.

- SCNCapsule: This is a cylinder that is capped at both ends by a hemisphere. You can define the hemisphere radius and the height.

- SCNCone: This is a geometric feature that has a circular base, and its sides taper at the center of the circle. You create an SCNCone by giving it a radius for the bottom and a height for the sides.

- SCNCylinder: To create an SCNCylinder, you give it a radius and a height.

- SCNFloor: This is an infinitely expanded plane along the x- and z-axes.

- SCNPlane: This is a one-sided surface that expands along the x- and y-axes.

- SCNPyramid: This is a geometric feature of right triangles. When initializing an SCNPyramid, you give the height, width, and length for the pyramid.

- SCNSphere: This is a geometric shape of a globe. When instantiating an SCNSphere, you provide the radius to be used for the SCNSphere.

- SCNTorus: A torus is simply a circle around a coplanar axis. You provide an inner radius and an outer radius for its circles.

- SCNTube: This is a tube or pipe. You give it an inner radius, an outer radius, and the height for the tube.

- SCNShape: This geometric shape is created from a Bezier path. SCNShape gives you the most control over the shape of your 3D object.

- SCNText: You provide an NSString or NSAttributedString that is used to create a 3D object from this string.

As you can see, Apple has provided you with most of the shapes you will need. You can combine these primitive shapes to create complex objects. However, for this game, you will stick to the basic primitives for now. Let's get back into the code and start adding some obstacles for the spaceman to maneuver around in order to find the enemy.

Adding Obstacles

Create a new Swift file and name it Obstacles.swift. In the newly created file, you first want to import the Scene Kit framework so that you can use the Scene Kit library.

You will do a few things differently in this class, in that you will create class-level methods. If you are familiar with other languages, this is similar to static methods.

For your first obstacle, create a pyramid (Listing 11-1).

Listing 11-1. PyramidNode

```
class func PyramidNode() -> SCNNode {

    let pyramid = SCNPyramid(width: 10.0, height: 20.0, length: 10.0)
    let pyramidNode = SCNNode(geometry: pyramid)
    pyramidNode.name = "pyramid"

    let position = SCNVector3Make(30, 0, -40)
    pyramidNode.position = position
    pyramidNode.geometry?.firstMaterial?.diffuse.contents = UIColor.blueColor()
    pyramidNode.geometry?.firstMaterial?.shininess = 1.0

    return pyramidNode
}
```

In this bit of code, you create a geometric object using the SCNPyramid Next you create an SCNNode, and this time you are creating it using the geometry. This allows you to easily manipulate the pyramid as you would any SCNNode. As with any node, you need to give it a position. Don't worry too much about the pyramidNode.geometry?.firstMaterial?.diffuse.contents = UIColor.blueColor() part because you will learn more about materials in the next chapter. At this time, you are just giving the pyramid some color so that you will be able to see it.

Now that you have the code to create your new pyramid obstacle, you can go back to the GameViewController.swift file and add the code so that when you run the game, the pyramid node is added to your scene. In the viewDidLoad() method, you add the pyramid to the scene's rootNode as a child node.

```
// Create the scene
let mainScene = createMainScene()
mainScene.rootNode.addChildNode(createFloorNode())
mainScene.rootNode.addChildNode(Obstacles.PyramidNode())

// Get the games main view
let sceneView = self.view as SCNView
sceneView.scene = scene
```

After adding the line of code, run the game. Now you see a pyramid near the spaceman, as shown in Figure 11-8.

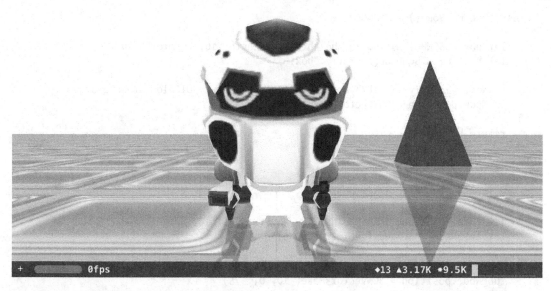

Figure 11-8. Spaceman scene with pyramid node

You now have some basic knowledge of how to create a primitive Scene Kit geometric object. Why don't you go back to the `Obstacle.swift` file and use this pattern to create four or five different objects? See Listing 11-2.

Listing 11-2. Obstacles Class

```
class Obstacles {

    class func PyramidNode() -> SCNNode {

        let pyramid = SCNPyramid(width: 10.0, height: 20.0, length: 10.0)
        let pyramidNode = SCNNode(geometry: pyramid)

        let position = SCNVector3Make(0, 0, -100)
        pyramidNode.position = position
        pyramidNode.geometry?.firstMaterial?.diffuse.contents = UIColor.blueColor()

        return pyramidNode
    }

    class func GlobeNode() -> SCNNode {

        let globe = SCNSphere(radius: 15.0)
        let globeNode = SCNNode(geometry: globe)
        globeNode.position = SCNVector3Make(20, 40, -50)
        globeNode.geometry?.firstMaterial?.diffuse.contents = UIColor.redColor()

        return globeNode
    }
```

```
class func BoxNode() -> SCNNode {

    let box = SCNBox(width: 10, height: 10, length: 10, chamferRadius: 0)
    let boxNode = SCNNode(geometry: box)

    boxNode.geometry?.firstMaterial?.diffuse.contents = UIColor.brownColor()
    boxNode.position = SCNVector3Make(0, 10, -20)

    return boxNode

}

class func TubeNode() -> SCNNode {

    let tube = SCNTube(innerRadius: 10, outerRadius: 14, height: 20)
    let tubeNode = SCNNode(geometry: tube)

    tubeNode.geometry?.firstMaterial?.diffuse.contents = UIColor.yellowColor()
    tubeNode.position = SCNVector3Make(-10, 0, -75)

    return tubeNode
}

class func CylinderNode() -> SCNNode {

    let cylinderNode = SCNNode(geometry:SCNCylinder(radius: 3, height: 12))
    cylinderNode.geometry?.firstMaterial?.diffuse.contents = UIColor.greenColor()
    cylinderNode.position = SCNVector3Make(14, 0, -25)

    return cylinderNode

}

class func TorusNode() -> SCNNode {

    let torus = SCNTorus(ringRadius: 12, pipeRadius: 5)
    let torusNode = SCNNode(geometry: torus)

    torusNode.geometry?.firstMaterial?.diffuse.contents = UIColor.orangeColor()
    torusNode.position = SCNVector3Make(50, 10, -50)

    return torusNode

}

}
```

This code is used to create almost all the Scene Kit primitives that you can use within a scene. Right now they don't do much, and they are not all that interesting to see. Remember, if you want to see these obstacles, you will need to add them to the scene in the GameViewController. Feel free to adjust the sizes and locations so that you can get a better understanding of how these variables change the object.

Using SCNText

Adding text in Scene Kit is straightforward because the kit has an SCNText object that is derived from SCNGeometry. There are two ways to provide the text that is used by the geometry object: either NSString or NSAttributedString.

Starting Screen

For this game, you will use the SCNText to create an open start node and then a "game over" node. You need to go into the GameViewController.swift file and create a new function called createStartingText() -> SCNNode.

In this function, you will do a few things in order to create the text and be able to use it within the main scene.

```
func createStartingText() -> SCNNode {

  let startText = SCNText(string: "Start!", extrusionDepth: 5)
  startText.chamferRadius = 0.5
  startText.flatness = 0.3
  startText.font = UIFont(name: "Copperplate", size: 30)
  startText.firstMaterial?.specular.contents = UIColor.blueColor()
  startText.firstMaterial?.shininess = 0.4

  let textNode = SCNNode(geometry: startText)
  textNode.scale = SCNVector3Make(0.75, 0.75, 0.75)
  textNode.position = SCNVector3Make(200, 0, 1000);

  return textNode
}
```

Most of what you did here is similar to what you have been doing for all SCNNode object types.

- First you create an SCNText object by using the convenience init function. extrusionDepth refers to the depth of the letters.

- chamferRadius is defaulted to 0.0. You change this to give a slight edge to the letters in the text. Note that the maximum chamfer you can do is half of the extrusionDepth value. If you exceed that amount, Scene Kit may reduce the amount; it will also reduce the value if you use a thin stroke for the text.

- The flatness for the text refers to the accuracy of the text geometry. This is how smooth the line looks to the user. By default this is set to 0.6.

- The rest of the function contains everything already covered in previous chapters of the book.

In the viewDidLoad() function, simply add the textNode as a child node to the scene's root node, after the createMainScene() function call: scene.rootNode.addChildNode (createStartingText()).

Summary

In this chapter, you learned more about how Scene Kit uses the tried-and-true scene graph to render objects. You also dove into the primitive objects that are provided to you in the Scene Kit library. You will expand on these primitives to create a simple yet interesting game as you progress through the book.

In the next chapter, you will learn how to manipulate the camera, which allows you to manipulate the point of view of the user. Another important item that you will examine closer is how lighting is used and how it can totally change the look and feel of your game.

Chapter 12

Lighting, Camera, and Material Effects in Scene Kit

In the previous chapter, you gained an understanding of how Scene Kit uses the scene graph to render the objects for the user. You also now have an Xcode project that is just waiting to have more done to it.

In this chapter, you will explore how the lighting of a scene works and the different type of lights that are available in Scene Kit. Along with the lighting, you will learn about how the object's material plays an important role in how the object is lit up and displayed to your user. After you have the object lit up and looking nice, you will see how the camera, in other words, the point of view, can be controlled to give the user a new perspective of the scene.

Lighting Up the Scene

Ask any director or photographer, and one of the most important items to a scene is lighting. You are in luck because Scene Kit provides several types of lighting that you can manipulate to make your scene pop.

In Scene Kit, you will use the SCNLight object to create a light source in your scene. You will set the light type to one of four different light types provided to you from Scene Kit.

- SCNLightTypeAmbient: This light will illuminate your scene from all directions; the light's position or direction has no effect on the lighting of the scene.

Ambient

- ■ `SCNLightTypeOmni`: This light will illuminate your scene from a certain point.

Omni

- ■ `SCNLightTypeDirectional`: This light will illuminate all objects in your scene uniformly from the same direction.

Directional

- ■ `SCNLightTypeSpot`: This light will illuminate your scene like a rock star!

Spot

So, these are the light types that you will be able to use in your games. Some items of note are that the material of the object influences how the object is illuminated. Also, you will have full control of the color of the light.

Scene Kit does have some "rules" it uses when updating a scene with lighting to make the scene display efficiently.

- ■ Lighting affects only moving objects in your scene.

- ■ Scene Kit uses only up to eight light sources per node, so making more than this will be a waste. In fact, Apple recommends using no more than three lighting effects and a single ambient light.

I'm sure you are ready to jump into some code. So, for SuperSpaceMan, you will create a nice ambient light for the scene, and you will create a spotlight so he is never in the dark.

To make things easy for you, you will control all the lighting in the `GameViewController` for now. If you don't have the `GameViewController` open, open it up, and you will need to create a new class variable for the spotlight. At the top of the class, go ahead and create your new variable: `var spotLight: SCNNode!`. After you have created this variable, you can now create the `setupLighting()` method, as in Listing 12-1.

Listing 12-1. setupLighting() Method

```
func setupLighting(scene:SCNScene) {

    var ambientLight = SCNNode()
    ambientLight.light = SCNLight()
    ambientLight.light!.type = SCNLightTypeAmbient
    ambientLight.light!.color = UIColor(white: 0.3, alpha: 1.0)
    scene.rootNode.addChildNode(ambientLight)

    var lightNode = SCNNode()
    lightNode.light = SCNLight()
    lightNode.light!.type = SCNLightTypeSpot
    lightNode.light!.castsShadow = true
    lightNode.light!.color = UIColor(white: 0.8, alpha: 1.0)
    lightNode.position = SCNVector3Make(0, 80, 30)
    lightNode.rotation = SCNVector4Make(1, 0, 0, Float(-M_PI/2.8))
    lightNode.light!.spotInnerAngle = 0
    lightNode.light!.spotOuterAngle = 50
    lightNode.light!.shadowColor = UIColor.blackColor()
    lightNode.light!.zFar = 500
    lightNode.light!.zNear = 50
    scene.rootNode.addChildNode(lightNode)

    spotLight = lightNode
}
```

First you create SCNLight and SCNNode objects. As you can see, you will set the type of light to the light object. A light type of SCNLightTypeAmbient does not need to set a direction, position, attenuation, spotlight angle, or shadows since an ambient light is for the entire scene.

Don't forget to call this method in the createMainScene() method, similar to setupLighting(mainScene).

Materials

Now you will dive into how Scene Kit manages the visual attributes of your objects. Scene Kit uses the SCNMaterial class to control the lighting and shading attributes for the geometry of your SCNNode.

Scene Kit provides eight different properties you can use to set these attributes.

- *Diffuse*: Diffuse shading is the amount of light and color reflected in all directions.

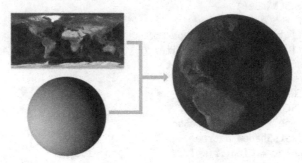

- *Ambient*: Ambient light is reflected in all points from the surface at a fixed intensity and fixed color. If there is no ambient light object in the scene, this attribute has no effect on the node.

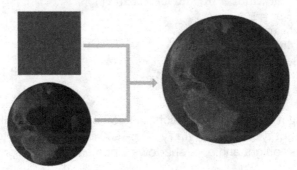

- *Specular*: Specular is the light that is reflected straight to the user similar to how a mirror reflects light. This is the bright spot of light that appears shiny on an object. This property is defaulted to black, which will cause the material to appear dull.

■   *Normal*: Normal lighting is a technique used to create lighting out of the surface of the material. Basically it tries to figure out the bumps and dents of the material to give more realistic lighting.

■   *Reflective*: Reflective lighting is a mirrored surface from the reflective environment. The surface will not actually reflect other objects in the scene.

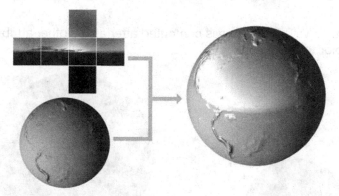

■   *Emission*: Emission is the color that is emitted by the surface. By default this property is set to black, which means no light is reflected. If you provide a color, that color will be reflected, and if you really want to get fancy, you can provide an image. Scene Kit will use this image to provide the "glowing" effect based on the material.

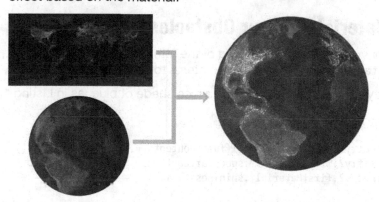

- *Transparent*: Transparent is the opacity of the material. This attribute is basically used to make parts of the material invisible.

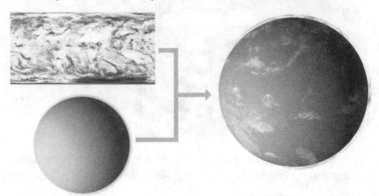

- *Multiply*: This attribute is computed after all the other attributes and adds a color to the material.

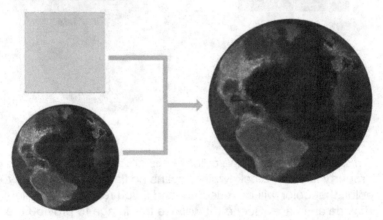

Appling Materials to Your Obstacles

Now that you have a basic understanding of the attributes to the SCNMaterial, let's head over to the Obstacle class and add some material to your obstacles.

First why don't you make the PyramidNode a nice shade of blue, as in Listing 12-2?

Listing 12-2. PyramidNode Material

```
pyramidNode.geometry?.firstMaterial?.diffuse.contents = UIColor.blueColor()
pyramidNode.geometry?.firstMaterial?.specular.contents = UIColor.blueColor()
pyramidNode.geometry?.firstMaterial?.shininess = 1.0
```

In this game you are going to keep it simple and work with just one material. Scene Kit provides easy access to this via the firstMaterial object. You set the diffuse contents to the color blue. You also want this object to be shiny, so you add another blue color object to the specular attribute and increase the shininess to 1. You can experiment with different colors and shininess to see how these attributes affect your PyramidNode.

Next up is your GlobeNode. Listing 12-3 shows you how to add some items to make it look more like Earth.

Listing 12-3. GlobeNode Lightening Enhancements

```
globeNode.geometry?.firstMaterial?.diffuse.contents = UIImage(named: "earthDiffuse.jpg")
globeNode.geometry?.firstMaterial?.ambient.contents = UIImage(named: "earthAmbient.jpg")
globeNode.geometry?.firstMaterial?.specular.contents = UIImage(named: "earthSpecular.jpg")
globeNode.geometry?.firstMaterial?.normal.contents = UIImage(named: "earthNormal.jpg")
globeNode.geometry?.firstMaterial?.diffuse.mipFilter = SCNFilterMode.Linear
```

With the GlobeNode you are expanding on the NSMaterial and creating a more lifelike Earth. If you look at each of the JPG files, you will see how these files affect the output from Scene Kit and NSMaterial. You will notice you added a mipFilter to the diffuse property. Scene Kit uses this property to improve the performance when rendering a texture image as a smaller size.

You will now add some materials to the BoxNode. Scene Kit allows you to apply an array to the materials, and it will apply this to the geometry. With the BoxNode, you will apply six different materials, so you have six different sides, as you can see in Listing 12-4.

Listing 12-4. BoxNode Materials

```
var materials = [SCNMaterial]()
let boxImage = "boxSide"
for i in 1...6 {
    let material = SCNMaterial()
    material.diffuse.contents = UIImage(named: boxImage + String(i))
    materials.append(material)
}

boxNode.geometry?.materials = materials
```

For the other obstacle types, add a color similar to how you did the PyramidNode. Listing 12-5 is the rest of the obstacles, so feel free to use different colors and images if you happen to have some images available.

Listing 12-5. Remaining Obstacle Materials

```
class func TubeNode() -> SCNNode {

    let tube = SCNTube(innerRadius: 10, outerRadius: 14, height: 20)
    let tubeNode = SCNNode(geometry: tube)
    tubeNode.position = SCNVector3Make(-10, 0, -75)

    tubeNode.geometry?.firstMaterial?.diffuse.contents = UIColor.redColor()


    return tubeNode
}
```

```
class func CylinderNode() -> SCNNode {

    let cylinderNode = SCNNode(geometry:SCNCylinder(radius: 3, height: 12))
    cylinderNode.position = SCNVector3Make(14, 0, -25)

    cylinderNode.geometry?.firstMaterial?.diffuse.contents = UIColor.yellowColor()
    cylinderNode.geometry?.firstMaterial?.specular.contents = UIColor.yellowColor()
    cylinderNode.geometry?.firstMaterial?.shininess = 0.5

    return cylinderNode

}

class func TorusNode() -> SCNNode {

    let torus = SCNTorus(ringRadius: 12, pipeRadius: 5)
    let torusNode = SCNNode(geometry: torus)
    torusNode.position = SCNVector3Make(50, 10, -50)

    torusNode.geometry?.firstMaterial?.diffuse.contents = UIColor.redColor()
    torusNode.geometry?.firstMaterial?.specular.contents = UIColor.blackColor()
    torusNode.geometry?.firstMaterial?.shininess = 0.75

    return torusNode

}
```

Adding Textures to Collada Files

You can change the materials of a Collada file using Xcode's scene editor. As you are aware, you or your friendly 3D designer using a 3D modeling program create a Collada file. If you have been using Xcode for any amount of time, you will see by Figure 12-1 that the scene editor is similar to Interface Builder.

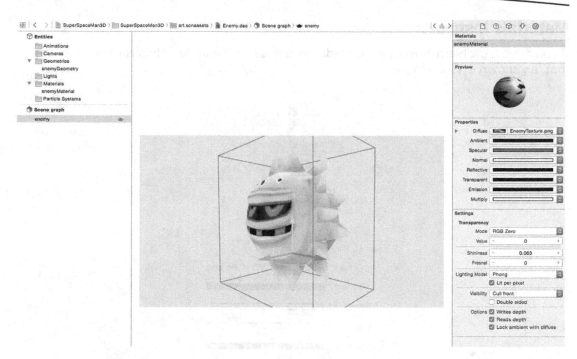

Figure 12-1. Scene Editor

Examining the Scene Editor

The first section you will see on the left side is the Entities List. Your Enemy.dae scene has only two entity attributes: Geometry and a Material. In the center you have a visual representation of your enemy that will be used in the game. You can use your mouse to move the object around and see it from all sides.

On the right side you have your inspectors.

- *File Inspector*: This shows basic information about the Collada file.

- *Quick Help*: This is more for Interface Builder and most likely doesn't have any help for your Collada file.

- *Node Inspector*: Once you have selected an element from the scene graph list on the left, you will have some attributes you can adjust.

- *Attributes Inspector*: The attributes you will see here are dependent on which entity you select from the Entities section.

- *Materials Inspector*: Here is where you will be able to adjust the material attributes for the Collada file.

Materials Inspector

If you have a problem where your Collada file is missing the texture, this is where you can fix that, as shown in Figure 12-2.

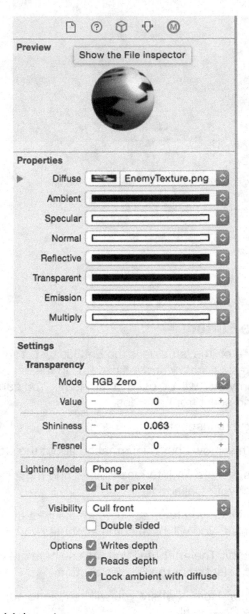

Figure 12-2. Scene Editor Materials inspector

As you can see, your enemy has a diffuse attribute that is set to EnemyTexture.png. If for some reason yours is not, use the drop-down picker and select it. You can also change this to something else if you want. You can change all the attributes that I have already gone over here. You will not be able to see some of the changes until you apply a lighting node to it.

Feel free to adjust anything here or on any of the other Collada files.

Scene Kit Camera Usage

Lights are great, but they are better when you interact with the camera and a light. Previously you created an ambient light that was used to light the scene. You already have allowed the player to move the camera around. This time you will attach a spotlight to the camera node to light up your hero.

The camera object is used to present scenes to the user from their point of view. You can use the camera object to set and adjust the field of view, near and distant visibility limits, and the focal length of the camera. Figure 12-3 shows you the main parameters of the field of view. These variables are as follows:

- xFOV: This is the angle at which the x-axis will be seen.

- yFOV: This is the angle at which the y-axis will be seen.

- zNear: This parameter is the minimal distance between the camera and the surface. Any object that is closer to the camera is not shown.

- zFar: This parameter is the maximum distance between the camera and the surface. Any object that is beyond this distance does not appear.

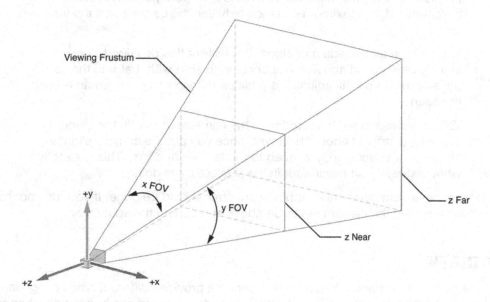

Figure 12-3. Camera field of view diagram

Now it is time to create the camera node that you will use to view the game. In the GameViewController, you will add the class-level variable that will be used to follow the spaceman around the scene: var cameraNode: SCNNode!.

The next piece of the code puzzle is to find the `createMainScene()` method. In this method, you will add a call to `setupCameras(mainScene)`. You need to add this method call anywhere after the `mainScene` variable is initialized. You should have an unresolved error at this time; now you will create the missing `setupCameras()` method, as shown in Listing 12-6.

Listing 12-6. setupCameras() Method

```
func setupCameras(scene:SCNScene) {

    cameraNode = SCNNode()
    cameraNode.camera = SCNCamera()
    cameraNode.camera!.zFar = 500
    cameraNode.position = SCNVector3(x: 0.0, y: 30.0, z: 200.0)
    cameraNode.rotation = SCNVector4(x: 1.0, y: 0.0, z: 0.0, w: Float(-M_PI_4*0.75))
    scene.rootNode.addChildNode(cameraNode)
}
```

Let's go over this bit of code.

- You first initialize the `cameraNode` as a scene node (`SCNNode()`).

- After you have the node initialized, you initialize the camera parameter for the node.

- For this camera, you will need to set the `zFar` parameter. The `zFar` parameter is the maximum distance between the camera and the visible surface.

- The camera also needs a position; you will set this position to be slightly behind and above the spaceman to start with. Later in the game development you will adjust this position to follow the spaceman around the scene.

- You now need to set the rotation of the camera. Currently the camera is pointing straight ahead; however, since you put the camera slightly above your spaceman, you need to rotate it slight down. This is exactly what setting the `w:` parameter in the `SCNVector4` is doing.

Now that you have completed this method, your error should be gone. If you run your game now, you will now see the camera set to be above and behind the spaceman.

Summary

There was a lot in this chapter. You learned Scene Kit provides different types of lighting. You should spend some time experimenting with your code base and see how subtle changes in lighting can affect the playability of your game. Another learning experience was how Scene Kit uses materials to make your objects more realistic or futuristic. Then there was the scene editor, which is helpful to see your changes immediately without having to run your game.

In the next chapter, you will examine how Scene Kit moves objects around, via animations.

Chapter 13

Animating Your Models

In the previous chapter, you set up your objects with lighting and materials. You also found out how the camera interacts within the scene. In this chapter, you will see how Scene Kit and your objects are able to move around using animation.

If you have done any work using CoreAnimation, you will be happy to know that Scene Kit is fully integrated with it. In Scene Kit, just about everything can be animated by adding an animation to the node. In the first part of the chapter, you will do some code cleanup. You will then take a look at animating your obstacles using a simple animation, and finally you will look at a couple of advanced ways to animate your objects.

CoreAnimation is not covered as part of this book, so if you want to learn more about the framework, you can look at the Apple documentation, available here:

```
https://developer.apple.com/library/ios/documentation/Cocoa/Conceptual/CoreAnimation_guide/
Introduction/Introduction.html
```

Refactoring the Project

You will need to do some cleanup in order to make this a little easier. Go through both Obstacle and GameViewController, and give each SCNNode that you created a unique name. This will allow you to find these items later within the scene graph.

```
let pyramid = SCNPyramid(width: 10.0, height: 20.0, length: 10.0)
let pyramidNode = SCNNode(geometry: pyramid)
pyramidNode.name = "pyramid"
```

Scene Kit is able to animate your 3D scenes and objects using the CoreAnimation API that has been in the iOS toolkit for years. This proven API will give you the power and flexibility to create simple and complex animations for your game or application.

Scene Kit also allows you to mix some OpenGL code into your scenes; however, I will not address any of these items since they are more advanced topics.

Starting Animations

You'll start with the `Obstacle` class; for each obstacle, you will do something slightly different. To keep things simple, you will use CoreAnimation's `CABasicAnimation` class to rotate these first few obstacles.

PyramidNode

In the following code, you rotate the `PyramidNode` around the x-axis. When you do this animation, the pyramid node will rotate below the floor from the base of the pyramid.

```
let rotation = CABasicAnimation(keyPath: "rotation")
rotation.fromValue = NSValue(SCNVector4:SCNVector4Make(0, 0, 0, 0))
rotation.toValue =  NSValue(SCNVector4:SCNVector4Make(1, 0, 0, Float(2.0*M_PI)))
rotation.duration = 5
rotation.repeatCount = .infinity
pyramidNode.addAnimation(rotation, forKey: "rotation")
```

In this code, you are doing a few things. First you use the `CABasicAnimation` class to do basic animations.

- The `.fromValue` property is where you define a starting vector or current location of the object. For this animation, you simply set everything to 0 as the starting point.

- The `.toValue` property is where you want the object to end up when the animation is complete.

- The `.duration` property is how long in seconds it takes to complete the animation. You can adjust this as you see fit.

- The `.repeatCount` property is how many times your animation will run. For this movement, you set it to infinity. Again, this is another setting you can adjust for some of your animations.

The final line adds the animation to the node. When the node is created, the animation runs immediately.

When you run the game, you will be able to see the pyramid node rotating along the x-axis, similar to Figure 13-1. You may need to move your camera around to see it; you can do this via the pinch-zoom gestures if need be.

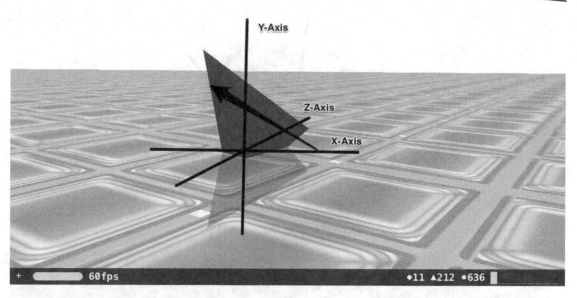

Figure 13-1. Pyramid node x-axis rotation

GlobeNode

In the GlobeNode you will rotate the globe around the y-axis so that it looks similar to the earth's rotation.

```
// Spin around the Y-Axis
let rotation = CABasicAnimation(keyPath: "rotation")
rotation.fromValue = NSValue(SCNVector4:SCNVector4Make(0, 0, 0, 0))
rotation.toValue =  NSValue(SCNVector4:SCNVector4Make(0, 1, 0, Float(2.0*M_PI)))
rotation.duration = 10
rotation.repeatCount = .infinity
globeNode.addAnimation(rotation, forKey: "rotation")
```

This is similar to the PyramidNode; you are just adjusting the rotation in the .toValuevalue property around the y-axis.

Run the game now, and you will see the globe rotating slowly around the y-axis similar to Figure 13-2. If you want to give the world a real turn, change the duration to something fast like one second.

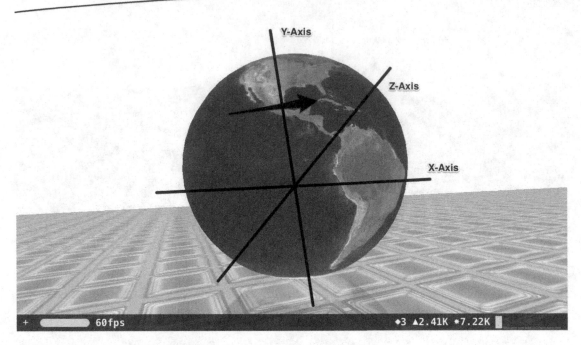

Figure 13-2. Globe node y-axis rotation

TubeNode

For the TubeNode, how about rotating it around the z-axis?

```
// Spin around the Z-Axis
let rotation = CABasicAnimation(keyPath: "rotation")
rotation.fromValue = NSValue(SCNVector4:SCNVector4Make(0, 0, 0, 0))
rotation.toValue =  NSValue(SCNVector4:SCNVector4Make(0, 0, 1, Float(2.0*M_PI)))
rotation.duration = 10
rotation.repeatCount = .infinity
tubeNode.addAnimation(rotation, forKey: "rotation")
```

Again, you are creating the same animation but just changing the z-axis.

Now when you run the game, you will see the tube rotating along the z-axis, similar to Figure 13-3.

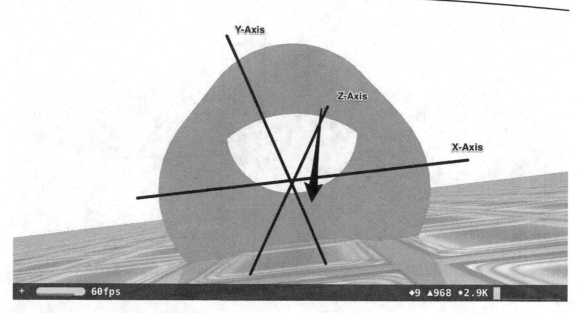

Figure 13-3. Tube node z-axis rotation

BoxNode

Next you will animate the BoxNode to rotate along all three axes.

```
let rotation = CABasicAnimation(keyPath: "rotation")
rotation.fromValue = NSValue(SCNVector4:SCNVector4Make(0, 0, 0, 0))
rotation.toValue =  NSValue(SCNVector4:SCNVector4Make(1, 1, 1, Float(2.0*M_PI)))
rotation.duration = 10
rotation.repeatCount = .infinity
boxNode.addAnimation(rotation, forKey: "rotation")
```

Once you have all three axes moving, the animation should look similar to Figure 13-4.

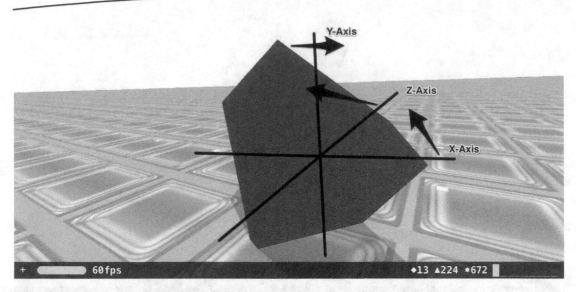

Figure 13-4. Box node x-, y-, z-axis rotation

Now you have some obstacles that are moving around and looking good in the scene.

When you start the game, look around—you will see all the objects animating. If you are running the game in the simulator, you will notice that it is performing terribly. However, if you run the game on a device, you'll see it is animating at a minimum of 35 frames per second, if not closer to 60, depending on which device you are running the game on. I suggest running it in the simulator if you haven't so that you can see how the hardware affects the frame rate.

More Animations

Like with Sprite Kit, you can use actions to animate your Scene Kit nodes. Next you will add some of the actions to the nodes. This way, you will have some CoreAnimation actions as well as the SCNAction taking place at the same time.

Using the SCNAction on a node will allow you to change the structure and content of the node. These actions are animated over more than one frame of animation rendered by the scene.

For your first type of action, go to the Obstacle class. Here you will make the globe bounce up and down as it rotates around its axis. Find the function where you created the globe, and do the following before returning the node:

```
let moveGlobeUp = SCNAction.moveByX(0.0, y: 10.0, z: 0.0, duration: 1.0)
let moveGlobeDown = SCNAction.moveByX(0.0, y: -10.0, z: 0.0, duration: 1.0)
let sequence = SCNAction.sequence([moveGlobeUp, moveGlobeDown])
let repeatSequence = SCNAction.repeatActionForever(sequence)
globeNode.runAction(repeatSequence)
```

In this code segment, you have animated the position of the globeNode. First you created a new SCNAction using the constructor moveByX:y:z:duration, which moves a node to a new position. After this, you created another SCNAction that moves the globeNode back to the original position. In this action, you simply reversed the y-axis the same amount as you moved it.

Just like with Sprite Kit, creating a sequence can create Scene Kit actions. When the code executes, the actions are run in the order in which the sequence was created, and the sequence duration is the sum of all the durations of the actions.

Since you are animating the globeNode, you want the sequence to repeat, and there is an action that will repeat another action forever. For this you will use the SCNAction.repeateActionForever: class initializer. Then the final step is to call the runAction function on the globeNode.

Now when you run your game, you will notice the globe is bouncing as well as rotating around the y-axis, as shown in Figure 13-5.

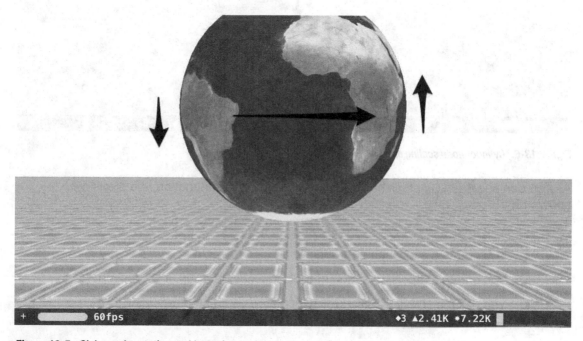

Figure 13-5. *Globe node rotating and bouncing*

For the next animation, you will animate the cylinder so that you change the scale.

For the cylinder, you will animate its scale so that it will appear as though the cylinder is growing and then starting over. However, this time, instead of repeating forever, you will repeat it only ten times.

```
let scaleToZero = SCNAction.scaleTo(0.0, duration: 0)
let scaleUp = SCNAction.scaleTo(1.0, duration: 5)
let opacityToZero = SCNAction.fadeOutWithDuration(5)

let sequence = SCNAction.sequence([scaleToZero, scaleUp])
let repeatSequence = SCNAction.repeatAction(sequence, count: 10)
cylinderNode.runAction(repeatSequence)
```

In this bit of code, you immediately set the scale for `cylinderNode` to 0.0 with a duration of 0.0. This way, when you scale up the `cylinderNode`, it will appear as though it is growing. Like before, you will need to create the sequence so that these actions can run in order. Now you repeat this action ten times instead of repeating forever. Figure 13-6 shows you how the cylinder should look as it's scaling up.

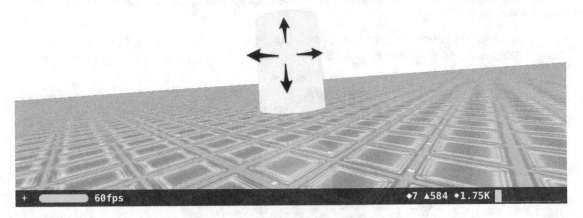

Figure 13-6. Cylinder node scaling up

As you can see, the `SCNAction` has a pattern similar to CoreAnimation; the steps are shown here:

1. You create several types of actions.

2. You create a sequence or grouping.

3. You create a repeating action of the sequence or group, if so desired.

4. You call the `SCNode`'s `runAction` with the newly created repeating sequence.

Summary

You now have your obstacles doing various animations. You learned that there are several ways in which you can animate your `SCNodes`, by either using your CoreAnimation knowledge or using `SCNActions`. You can go back and experiment with different types of `SCNActions` and various durations. Make sure you run the game both in the simulator and on your device to see how Scene Kit leverages the hardware in order to render the 3D images proficiently.

In the next chapter, you will learn about hit testing and collision detection. You will also get the enemy and hero moving around.

Chapter 14

Hit Testing and Collision Detection

So far in the game you have not moved the hero, and now you need to get him up on his feet and moving around. You are going to keep this simple and use a one-finger touch to move forward and two fingers to move back. To move left and right, you will use the accelerometer.

GameView: Moving the Hero

Start by creating a new Swift file in the project and name it `GameView.swift`. Once the file is created, you will create a subclass from `SCNView` called `GameView`. This view will be used in order to capture the touches from the user. If you look at Listing 14-1, you can see that you are overriding the `touchesBegan` method and the `touchesEnded` method.

Listing 14-1. GameView.swift

```swift
import SceneKit

class GameView : SCNView {

    var touchCount:Int?

    required init(coder aDecoder: NSCoder) {
        super.init(coder: aDecoder)

    }
```

```swift
    override func touchesBegan(touches: NSSet, withEvent event: UIEvent) {
        var taps = event.allTouches()
        touchCount = taps?.count
    }

    override func touchesEnded(touches: NSSet, withEvent event: UIEvent) {
        touchCount = 0
    }
}
```

Here you are overriding the base function touchesBegan. You will capture the touches that
occur and assign them to the class variable, touchCount. After the user releases the touch,
you have to set the count to zero; otherwise, your poor hero would always be running. You
will use the render method in the GameViewController to read the touchCount variable in order
to move the hero a direction based on how many touches occur during that render cycle.

For this class to be used by your game, you will need to set it in the Main.storyboard file
for the view. Open Main.storyboard and in the scene select the view below the Game View
Controller section. After that is selected, head on over to the Identity Inspector and set the
class to your newly created GameView, as shown in Figure 14-1.

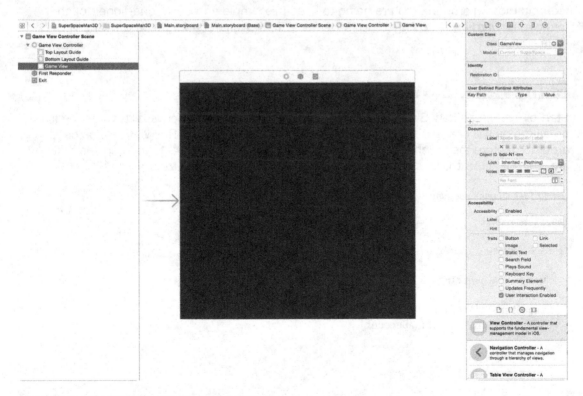

Figure 14-1. GameView change in Interface Builder

Now that you have the code in place to capture a touch, you need to put it somewhere you can get the update from the scene. To do this, you will use SCNSceneRendererDelegate and put your game logic into renderer.didSimulatePhysicsAtTime. In Figure 14-2, you can see this is one of the last times before the scene is drawn for you to make adjustments to the scene on a per-frame basis.

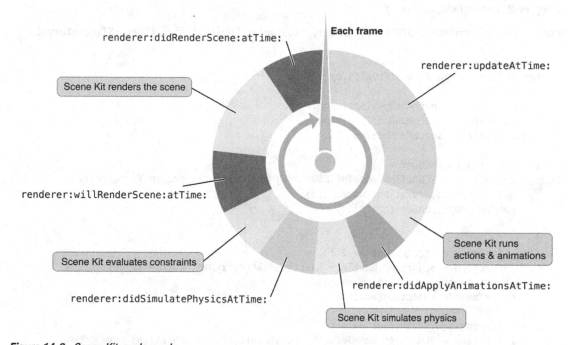

Figure 14-2. Scene Kit render cycle

For you to receive these delegate notifications, you will need to add SCNSceneRendererDelegate to your class declaration.

```
class GameViewController: UIViewController, SCNSceneRendererDelegate {
```

Now that you have the delegate, you need to assign it to an object that will handle the functions. In this case, you will use the GameViewController self as the delegate. Add the following line of code in the viewDidLoad() function after the sceneView is declared:

```
sceneView.delegate = self
```

You need to create some class-level variables that you will use throughout the GameViewController class. Add these variables right after the class declaration line, as shown here:

```
var spotLight: SCNNode!
var cameraNode: SCNNode!
var spaceManNode: SCNNode!
```

Writing the Callback Delegate Function

Now you will create the delegate function to get the callback from the Scene Kit framework for every frame. Listing 14-2 shows the code you need in order to get this callback, and then you will get the touchCount from the GameView in order to move the hero in one direction.

Listing 14-2. Render Delegate Method

```
func renderer(aRenderer: SCNSceneRenderer, didSimulatePhysicsAtTime time: NSTimeInterval) {

    let moveDistance = Float(10.0)
    let moveSpeed = NSTimeInterval(1.0)

    let currentX =  spaceManNode.position.x
    let currentY =  spaceManNode.position.y
    let currentZ =  spaceManNode.position.z

    if sceneView.touchCount == 1 {
        let action = SCNAction.moveTo(SCNVector3Make(currentX, currentY, currentZ -
        moveDistance), duration: moveSpeed);
        spaceManNode.runAction(action)

    }
    else if sceneView.touchCount == 2 {
        let action = SCNAction.moveTo(SCNVector3Make(currentX, currentY, currentZ +
        moveDistance), duration: moveSpeed)
        spaceManNode.runAction(action)
    }
    else if sceneView.touchCount == 4 {
        let action = SCNAction.moveTo(SCNVector3Make(0, 0, 0), duration: moveSpeed)
        spaceManNode.runAction(action)
    }

    positionCameraWithSpaceman()

}
```

That was a lot of code, but you are doing several things in this function. You are also getting an error about a missing method positionCameraWithSpaceman; don't worry about that right now because you will add that method soon.

- The first part of this code is to create a few convenience variables to hold the current location of your spaceman as well as a couple of variables to control the speed and distance in which the spaceman will move during a render cycle.

- Based on the touch count, you move him either forward the moveDistance value or backward the moveDistance value. Feel free to add some "Easter eggs" for your user to find, like that 11-touch gesture.

Moving the Camera

Now that you have your spaceman moving, you will need to move the camera with him to keep him in the frame. Now you will create the missing method positionCameraWithSpaceman, as in Listing 14-3.

Listing 14-3. positionCameraWithSpaceman()

```
func positionCameraWithSpaceman() {
    let spaceman =  spaceManNode.presentationNode()
    var spacemanPosition = spaceman.position
    let cameraDamping:Float = 0.3

    var targetPosition = SCNVector3Make(spacemanPosition.x, 30.0, spacemanPosition.z + 20.0)
    var cameraPosition =  cameraNode.position

    var cameraXPos = cameraPosition.x * (1.0 - cameraDamping) + targetPosition.x *
    cameraDamping
    var cameraYPos = cameraPosition.y * (1.0 - cameraDamping) + targetPosition.y *
    cameraDamping
    var cameraZPos = cameraPosition.z * (1.0 - cameraDamping) + targetPosition.z *
    cameraDamping
    cameraPosition = SCNVector3(x: cameraXPos, y: cameraYPos, z: cameraZPos)

    cameraNode.position = cameraPosition

    spotLight.position = SCNVector3(x: spacemanPosition.x, y: 90, z: spacemanPosition.z +
    40.0)
    spotLight.rotation = SCNVector4(x: 1, y: 0, z: 0, w: Float(-M_PI/2.8))
}
```

- You get the spaceman node using the presentationNode() method so you can get the current position of him.

- Next, using a little math and SCNVector3 initializer, you position the camera above and behind the spaceman.

- While you are here, you light him up so that he is the star of the game.

Now would be a good time to start up the game and check your progress. Once the game starts, notice that when you touch the screen, your hero moves forward some distance. Next, when you touch with two fingers, your hero moves backward a certain distance. This is great, but now you need to have your hero move left and right as well. For this you will use the accelerometer to capture the tilting of the device.

Since this book is for beginners and Scene Kit, I will not go into too much detail about the CoreMotion framework; however, you will use that framework in order to access the device's accelerometer. If you want to learn more about the CoreMotion framework, the Apple documents are a good place to start.

CoreMotion Framework Introduction

The step is to import the CoreMotion framework into your `GameViewController` class using `import CoreMotion`.

With `CoreMotion` imported, you can create another class-level variable that will store the CoreMotion manager. The reason you do this is because once you set up the CoreMotion manager, you will create an `NSOperationQueue` that will run in the background and detect the movements from the accelerometer. After you have the class declaration, add `var motionManager: CMMotionManager`.

Now you can create a method that will set up the accelerometer and capture the input from the accelerometer, similar to Listing 14-4.

Listing 14-4. setupAccelerometer Function

```
func setupAccelerometer() {

// Create the motion manager to receive the input
    motionManager = CMMotionManager()
    if  motionManager.accelerometerAvailable {

        motionManager.accelerometerUpdateInterval = 1/60.0
        motionManager.startAccelerometerUpdatesToQueue(NSOperationQueue()) {
            (data, error) in

            // Get the current location.
            let currentX =  self.spaceManNode.position.x
            let currentY =  self.spaceManNode.position.y
            let currentZ =  self.spaceManNode.position.z
            let threshold = 0.20
            // Moving right
            if data.acceleration.y < -threshold {

                var destinationX = (Float(data.acceleration.y) * Float( self.spacemanSpeed) +
                Float(currentX))
                var destinationY = Float(currentY)
                var destinationZ = Float(currentZ)

                self.motionManager.accelerometerActive == true
                let action = SCNAction.moveTo(SCNVector3Make(destinationX, destinationY,
                destinationZ), duration: 1)
                self.spaceManNode.runAction(action)

            }
            else if data.acceleration.y > threshold {
                var destinationX = (Float(data.acceleration.y) * Float(self.spacemanSpeed) +
                Float(currentX))
                var destinationY = Float(currentY)
                var destinationZ = Float(currentZ)
```

```
        self.motionManager.accelerometerActive == true
        let action = SCNAction.moveTo(SCNVector3Make(destinationX, destinationY,
        destinationZ), duration: 1)
        self.spaceManNode.runAction(action)

            }
        }
    }
}
```

Now that you have created this function, you can take a closer look at what is happening here.

The first thing you do is create a `CMMotionManager`. This is one of the entry points into the CoreMotion framework. Then you check to make sure you have an accelerometer. If you don't do this and run this code without the check, you will get a crash whenever you try to use the manager. Also, some devices such as older iPods don't have accelerometers. Remember, your games and applications can run on just about any iOS device.

Now that you know there is an accelerometer, you will want to set the update interval to be used. In some games, you may want to have the interval be slower or faster. For this game, you are going to get an update every 1/60th of a second.

Since you are getting updated every 1/60th of a second, you don't want to tie up the main cycle of the game, so you will create an update queue. This queue will take a closure and run this function every time the accelerometer update is called.

When the function is called, you create a few variables to store the current location of your hero. To keep things simple, you will check to see whether the y-axis has changed a certain amount. A negative change indicates the user has tilted the device right, so you need to move the hero to the right; a positive change indicates the user has tilted the device left. Here you are using 0.20; however, if you want a fine-grained adjustment, you can decrease that number.

Using this information, you simply create an animation for the hero to move a certain distance.

The only thing left now is to add the `setupAccelerometer()` call to your `viewDidLoad()` method in the `GameViewController`. Once you have added all that, it is another good time to run the game and see what you have accomplished.

When you have your hero moving by touching the device, tilt it to the left or right, and you will see him move in that direction. There are some variables that you can adjust to have him move faster or slower. You should go back and modify the `moveDistance` in the render function to see how this affects the movement. Also, adjust the threshold in the `setupAccelerometer` function to see how the device response changes.

Enemy Node

The one item you now need to add is the enemy node, which is created just like the spacemen node. Open the `GameViewController` class and create a variable for the `enemyNode` right after `spacemanNode`: `var enemyNode: SCNNode`.

You will follow the same pattern as the spacemanNode, so now you need to create an SCNNode to assign to this class-level variable. In the createMainScene() method, you will call the setupEnemy() method, enemyNode = setupEnemy(mainScene). You will create this method next, so don't worry about the error at this time.

It is now time to get rid of that error about a missing method. Right after your setupSpaceMan(), you will create the new setupEnemy(), as Listing 14-5 shows.

Listing 14-5. setupEnemy()

```
func setupEnemy(scene:SCNScene) -> SCNNode {

    var enemyScene = SCNScene(named: "art.scnassets/Enemy.dae")
    var enemyNode = enemyScene!.rootNode.childNodeWithName("enemy", recursively: false)
    enemyNode!.name = "enemy"
    enemyNode!.position = SCNVector3(x: 40, y: 10, z: 30)
    enemyNode!.rotation = SCNVector4(x: 0, y: 1, z: 0, w: Float(M_PI))

    scene.rootNode.addChildNode(enemyNode!)

    return enemyNode!
}
```

Now you have the enemy out in the playing floor, so you can dive into the collision detection of the various items.

Collision Detection

Now that you have the hero moving around an assortment of moving objects, you need to determine when your hero runs into something.

Scene Kit uses the SCNPhysicsBody object to add physics simulations to a node. During the render of a scene, Scene Kit prepares the frame in which it will perform physics calculations. These calculations include gravity, friction, and collisions with other nodes.

The SCNPhysicsBody class has a couple of properties that you will need to set for each of your SCNNodes in order to detect the collisions.

```
spaceManNode!.physicsBody = SCNPhysicsBody(type: .Dynamic, shape: nil)
```

As you can see, the first item we are setting is the type. Scene Kit has three different types of physics bodies.

- *Static*: This type of physic body is unaffected by forces or collisions. You will use this for the floor, obstacles, and walls since they will collide with objects, but they themselves will not move.

- *Dynamic*: This type of physic bodies is affected by forces or collisions. You will use this type for the spaceman and enemy.

- *Kinematic*: This type is unaffected by forces or collisions but can cause collisions to occur within the physic world. You will not use this type, but it could be used for an invisible node that would represent the user's finger when touching an object.

Shape is the next parameter in the initializer. The shape defines the body for collision detection. In your calls you will set this to `nil`, which will allow Scene Kit to automatically create a physics shape based on the node's geometric property. If you want to have more control over the actual shape Scene Kit uses for collision detection, then you can set it to a different shape. For your purpose, allowing Scene Kit to define the shape will be enough for you. Listing 14-6 gives you the `physicsBody` you will need to set on all of your nodes. So, take your time and set each of the nodes at each of their locations. Note that since you are using the clone method for each of the walls, you will need to add the new method call only the first time you create the wall node.

Listing 14-6. SCNPhysicsBody Class Initialization

```
//Add the following line to the GameViewController setupSpaceMan():
spaceManNode!.physicsBody = SCNPhysicsBody(type: .Dynamic, shape: nil)

//Add the following line to the GameViewController setupEnemy():
enemyNode!.physicsBody = SCNPhysicsBody(type: .Dynamic, shape: nil)

//Add the following line to the GameViewController setupFloor():
floorNode.physicsBody = SCNPhysicsBody(type: .Static, shape: nil)

//Add the following line to the GameViewController setupWalls():
wall.physicsBody = SCNPhysicsBody(type: .Static, shape: nil)

//Add the following line to the Obstacle PyramidNode():
pyramidNode.physicsBody = SCNPhysicsBody(type: .Static, shape: nil)

//Add the following line to the Obstacle GlobeNode():
globeNode.physicsBody = SCNPhysicsBody(type: .Static, shape: nil)

//Add the following line to the Obstacle BoxNode():
boxNode.physicsBody = SCNPhysicsBody(type: .Static, shape: nil)

//Add the following line to the Obstacle TubeNode():
tubeNode.physicsBody = SCNPhysicsBody(type: .Static, shape: nil)

//Add the following line to the Obstacle CylinderNode():
cylinderNode.physicsBody = SCNPhysicsBody(type: .Static, shape: nil)

//Add the following line to the Obstacle TorusNode():
torusNode.physicsBody = SCNPhysicsBody(type: .Static, shape: nil)
```

The next part of getting the collision detection working is to create the bit masks that will be used to determine when and if an object actually touches another one. Collision detection is based on using a bit mask that creates a table in order to determine whether two objects should collide. For this you will create a new file called `SharedConstants.swift`, and you will use this file to create the bit mask variables that will be used for all of your objects. Listing 14-7 is the code that you will need to add to this newly created file.

Listing 14-7. SharedConstants.swift Contents for the Bit Mask

```
let CollisionCategorySpaceMan = 2
let CollisionCategoryObstecles = 4
let CollisionCategoryWalls = 6
let CollisionCategoryEnemy = 8
let CollisionCategoryFloor = 10
```

If you completed the first section of the book for Sprite Kit, this code should look familiar. However, while Sprite Kit's collision bit masks use UInt32 variables, Scene Kit uses Int variables. This is just one of the subtle differences between the two frameworks.

Now that you have the variables that you will use for the bit mask, you will need to again update all of your nodes. As mentioned, these variables will be used to create a table to determine whether an object should collide with another.

SCNPhysicsBody has a couple of parameters that you will set in order for the collision detection to work. The first of the two parameters is the category bitmask.

```
spaceManNode!.physicsBody!.categoryBitMask = CollisionCategorySpaceMan
```

The second parameter to set is the collisionBitMask.

```
spaceManNode!.physicsBody!.collisionBitMask = CollisionCategoryObstacles |
CollisionCategoryWalls | CollisionCategoryEnemy
```

So, basically what you are doing is as follows: this node is a SpaceMan, and it will interact with the Obstacle, Wall, and Enemy nodes. Then, for the other nodes, it will be an Obstacle or Enemy, and it will interact with the spaceman.

Listing 14-8 shows all of the categoryBitMask and collisionBitMask values that you have to set on each of the nodes. Make sure you do this after the SCNPhysicsBody has been initialized and set on the node. Otherwise, setting this on an optional parameter will have no effect on the node. It is also important that you initialize the physicsBody of the SCNode before it is added as a child to your scene.

Listing 14-8. SCNPhysicsBody categoryBitMask and collisionBitMask

```
// Add the following line to the GameViewController setupSpaceMan() after the physicsBody
initialization:
spaceManNode!.physicsBody!.categoryBitMask = CollisionCategorySpaceMan
spaceManNode!.physicsBody!.collisionBitMask = CollisionCategoryObstacles |
CollisionCategoryWalls | CollisionCategoryEnemy

//Add the following line to the GameViewController setupEnemy() after the physicsBody
initialization:
enemyNode!.physicsBody!.categoryBitMask = CollisionCategoryEnemy
enemyNode!.physicsBody!.collisionBitMask = CollisionCategorySpaceMan

//Add the following line to the GameViewController setupFloor() after the physicsBody
initialization:
floorNode.physicsBody?.categoryBitMask = CollisionCategoryFloor
floorNode.physicsBody?.collisionBitMask = CollisionCategorySpaceMan | CollisionCategoryEnemy
```

```
//Add the following line to the GameViewController setupWalls() after the physicsBody
initialization:
wall.physicsBody!.categoryBitMask = CollisionCategoryWalls
wall.physicsBody!.collisionBitMask = CollisionCategorySpaceMan

//Add the following line to the Obstacle PyramidNode() after the physicsBody initialization:
pyramidNode.physicsBody?.categoryBitMask = CollisionCategoryObstacles
pyramidNode.physicsBody?.collisionBitMask = CollisionCategorySpaceMan

//Add the following line to the Obstacle GlobeNode() after the physicsBody initialization:
globeNode.physicsBody?.categoryBitMask = CollisionCategoryObstacles
globeNode.physicsBody?.collisionBitMask = CollisionCategorySpaceMan

//Add the following line to the Obstacle BoxNode() after the physicsBody initialization:
boxNode.physicsBody?.categoryBitMask = CollisionCategoryObstacles
boxNode.physicsBody?.collisionBitMask = CollisionCategorySpaceMan

//Add the following line to the Obstacle TubeNode() after the physicsBody initialization:
tubeNode.physicsBody?.categoryBitMask = CollisionCategoryObstacles
tubeNode.physicsBody?.collisionBitMask = CollisionCategorySpaceMan

//Add the following line to the Obstacle CylinderNode() after the physicsBody
initialization:
cylinderNode.physicsBody?.categoryBitMask = CollisionCategoryObstacles
cylinderNode.physicsBody?.collisionBitMask = CollisionCategorySpaceMan

//Add the following line to the Obstacle torusNode() after the physicsBody initialization:
torusNode.physicsBody?.categoryBitMask = CollisionCategoryObstacles
torusNode.physicsBody?.collisionBitMask = CollisionCategorySpaceMan
```

Now it's time to check your work. Build and run the game and you should be able to move the spaceman around; only this time you should notice that he can go through the nodes in the scene, he can go over some objects and he is stopped by the walls.

While this is great, you need a way for him to react to these collisions. Since you are making a hide-and-seek game, you will want to know when you have found the enemy. In finding the enemy, you will have to catch or collide with him. This is accomplished by using SCNPhysicsContactDelegate.

The first thing you will need to do is tell your class that you want to receive the SCNPhysicsContactDelegate.

```
class GameViewController: UIViewController, SCNSceneRendererDelegate,
SCNPhysicsContactDelegate {
```

In conjunction with this, you will also need to set the delegate to a class that will respond to these collisions. In this case, you will set the mainScene's contactDelegate to self so that the GameViewController can react to the collisions.

```
mainScene.physicsWorld.contactDelegate = self
```

The SCNPhysicsContactDelegate has three protocols that you can use, as shown in Listing 14-9.

Listing 14-9. SCNPhsicsContact Protocols

```
func physicsWorld(world: SCNPhysicsWorld, didBeginContact contact: SCNPhysicsContact) {
      println("didBeginContact")
}

func physicsWorld(world: SCNPhysicsWorld, didEndContact contact: SCNPhysicsContact) {
      println("didEndContact")
}

func physicsWorld(world: SCNPhysicsWorld, didUpdateContact contact: SCNPhysicsContact) {
      println("didUpdateContact")
}
```

You should add Listing 14-9 to your GameViewController. This time when you run your game, you will get the notifications when your spaceman moves around and interacts with the environment. For this game, however, you will be using only the didBeginContact protocol. It will be at this time you check to see whether the contact object has the node for the spaceman and the node for the enemy. To do this, you will keep things simple and check nodeB for what type of contact was made in Listing 14-10.

Listing 14-10. SCNPhysicsWorld didBeginContact Protocol

```
func physicsWorld(world: SCNPhysicsWorld, didBeginContact contact: SCNPhysicsContact) {

    if contact.nodeB.physicsBody!.categoryBitMask == CollisionCategoryEnemy {
        println("Enemy HIT!--------")
    }

    if contact.nodeB.physicsBody!.categoryBitMask == CollisionCategoryObstacles {
        println("OUCH HIT Obstacle!-------")
    }
}
```

At this time you are just going to print a line when you hit either the enemy or an obstacle. So, run your game at this time and move the spaceman around the playing field. As you keep an eye on the console logs, notice that when you run into an obstacle or the enemy, the appropriate line is output.

Summary

In this chapter, you have done a lot to get the spaceman moving. You also have the spaceman colliding with objects instead of going through them. At this point, you are almost finished with the hide-and-seek game.

In the next chapter, you will use this collision protocol to update the score. This scoreboard that you will create will be in a Sprite Kit view. This way, you can see how to combine a Sprite Kit view with in a Scene Kit scene.

Chapter 15

Using Sprite Kit with a Scene Kit Scene

In the previous chapters, you worked within the Scene Kit paradigm; however, Apple has created a way for you to add a 2D scene to overlay on your 3D scenes. In this chapter, you will add a 2D scene that will be used for your timer so it can track how long it will take you and your friends to find and capture the enemy.

Sprite Kit Integration

Scene Kit gives you a property to add a Sprite Kit scene.

```
var overlaySKScene: SKScene! { get set }
```

This property can render a 2D scene that overlays the Scene Kit scene. To provide better performance, Scene Kit and Sprite Kit use the same OpenGL context and resources to render the scene.

For this game, you will add a scoreboard to the top of the scene, as well as the amount of "lives" the user has left. To get started, create a new Swift file and name it GameOverlay.swift.

Now that you have the file created, you will need to import both Scene Kit and Sprite Kit.

```
import SceneKit
import SpriteKit

class GameOverlay: SKScene {

}
```

Your class should look similar to this code snippet. Your GameOverlay class is a subclass from the SKScene, which should look familiar from previous chapters. For this class you will add a node for the score and another one to keep track of the player's lives.

The first part you will need to do is to make one variable to hold the SKLabelNode object. Since you will be using the time interval from NSDate, you will need to create an NSNumberFormatter.

```
var timeNode: SKLabelNode!
var livesLeftNode: SKLabelNode!
var lives:Int = 3
var timerFormat: NSNumberFormatter!
```

Now that you have some variables, you will need to initialize them before you use them. Listing 15-1 shows you the overridden init(size: CGSize) function.

Listing 15-1. GameView.init

```
override init(size: CGSize) {
    super.init(size: size)

    self.anchorPoint = CGPointMake(0.5, 0.5)
    self.scaleMode = .ResizeFill

    self.timeNode = SKLabelNode(fontNamed: "AvenirNext-Bold")
    self.timeNode.text =  "Time: 0.0"
    self.timeNode.fontColor = SKColor.redColor()
    self.timeNode.horizontalAlignmentMode = .Left
    self.timeNode.verticalAlignmentMode = .Bottom
    self.timeNode.position = CGPointMake(-size.width/2 + 20, size.height/2 - 40)
    self.timeNode.name = "timer"
    self.addChild(timeNode)

    self.timerFormat = NSNumberFormatter()
    self.timerFormat.numberStyle = .DecimalStyle
    self.timerFormat.minimumFractionDigits = 1
    self.timerFormat.maximumFractionDigits = 1
}
```

In this initializer function, you will do a few things that you should stop and look at before moving on. This first part is creating the SKLabelNode that will be used to show the timer counting up. You can change the font and color if you want something that would suit your needs better; however, the red with Copperplate looks pretty decent in this game.

Following the SKLabelNode setup is the NSNumberFomatter setup section. The NSNumberForatter allows you to use numbers to be represented as string text. You will have a maximum and minimum of one fraction digit. This will allow you to show the timer within a tenth of a second. Don't forget you will also need to override the required initializer, as in Listing 15-2.

Listing 15-2. Required Initializer

```
required init?(coder aDecoder: NSCoder) {
      super.init(coder: aDecoder)
}
```

When your game starts, you will need start the timer so the user knows how fast he gets to the enemy. To do this, you will create a function that will start the timer, and it will update your SKLabelNode for the player. Listing 15-3 shows the startTimer() for this purpose.

Listing 15-3. GameOverlay.startTimer()

```
func startTimer() {
    var startTime = NSDate.timeIntervalSinceReferenceDate()
    var timerNode = self.childNodeWithName("timer") as SKLabelNode

    var timerAction = SKAction.runBlock({ () -> Void in
        var now = NSDate.timeIntervalSinceReferenceDate()
        var elapsedTime = NSTimeInterval( now - startTime )
        var tempString = String(format: "%@", self.timerFormat.stringFromNumber(elapsedTime)!)
        timerNode.text = "Time: " + tempString
    })
    var startDelay = SKAction.waitForDuration(0.5)
    var timerDelay = SKAction.sequence([timerAction, startDelay])
    var timer = SKAction.repeatActionForever(timerDelay)
    self.timeNode.runAction(timer, withKey: "timerAction")
}
```

The next function you will need to add to the GameOverlay class is to stop the timer when you have found the enemy. If you look at Listing 15-4, you will see it is pretty simple. You will get the node that you named timer in the start function and then stop the action timerAction.

Listing 15-4. GameOverlay.stopTimer

```
func stopTimer() {
    var timerNode =  childNodeWithName("timer") as SKLabelNode
    timerNode.removeActionForKey("timerAction")
}
```

You have your GameOverlay class completed, so now you will need to update the GameViewController to use this class and place it over your 3D Scene Kit scene.

Hooking Up the Controller to the Overlay

You have the GameOverlay class complete, so now it's time to connect it to the GameViewController. First you will want to create a class-level variable that you will use to get access to the GameOverlay class. Doing this, you will easily be able to call the methods to start the timer.

```
var gameOverlay: GameOverlay!
```

In the `GameViewController viewDidLoad` function, you will need to add this `GameOverlay` to the `SCNScene`. Doing this will allow the Scene Kit framework to overlay your `GameOverlay` onto the current scene.

```
sceneView.overlaySKScene = GameOverlay(size:view.frame.size)
gameOverlay =  sceneView.overlaySKScene as GameOverlay
```

Right now is a good time to run your game and see the overlay timer on top of the scene you have been working on. Once you run the game, you should have a scene similar to Figure 15-1.

Figure 15-1. Overlay scene with a timer

Now that you have the overlay, you need to start the timer when the user starts to move the spaceman. Since you will be using the `touchCount` in the `sceneView` to start the timer, you will want to also make sure your player hasn't already started the game; otherwise, the timer will always reset itself with every touch. After the `GameViewController` class definition, you will add another variable that will be used as a flag for when the game starts, and you will initialize it to false: `var gameStarted = false`.

Now when your player starts the game, you will set this to true and then back to false at the end of the game. To accomplish this, you will need to add some logic into the `didSimulatePhysicsAtTime` function in the `GameViewController`.

```
func renderer(aRenderer: SCNSceneRenderer, didSimulatePhysicsAtTime time: NSTimeInterval) {
```

In this function, you will add Listing 15-5 at the top of the function. This will check to see whether the user has touched the screen and, if so, start the timer and set the gameStarted flag. You will use this flag later in the code.

Listing 15-5. Start the Timer in the didSimulatePhysicsAtTime Protocol

```
if sceneView.touchCount > 0 && !gameStarted {
    gameOverlay.startTimer()
    gameStarted = true
}
```

This time when you run the game, you will notice the timer start running when you touch the device, as in Figure 15-2.

Figure 15-2. Timer running

The last thing you need to do for the timer is to call the stopTimer() method when you find the enemy. The best place for this will be in the SCNPhysicsWorld didBeginContact protocol. Find the section in your GameViewController class and replace the println("Enemy found") with the following:

```
gameOverlay.stopTImer()
```

This time when you run the game and maneuver the spaceman to the enemy, the timer will stop, and you will have the time it took you to find him.

"Game Over" Screen

You have a working game now, but wouldn't it be nice to have a "game over" screen to show your time and be able to restart the game? You will create another view that will update the sceneView.overlaySKScene when the spaceman finds the enemy.

Create a new Swift file called GameOverView.swift just like you have created in the past. The GameOverView will look familiar; Listing 15-6 has the code you need to put into the GameOverView class.

Listing 15-6. GameOverView

```
import SpriteKit

class GameOverView: SKScene {

    required init?(coder aDecoder: NSCoder) {
        super.init(coder: aDecoder)
    }

    init(size: CGSize, score: String) {
        super.init(size: size)

        backgroundColor = UIColor.redColor()
        let backgroundNode = SKSpriteNode(imageNamed: "GameOverBackground")
        backgroundNode.anchorPoint = CGPoint(x: 0.5, y: 0.0)
        backgroundNode.position = CGPoint(x: 160.0, y: 0.0)
        addChild(backgroundNode)

        let scoreTextNode = SKLabelNode(fontNamed: "Copperplate")
        scoreTextNode.text = "SCORE :  \(score)"
        scoreTextNode.horizontalAlignmentMode = SKLabelHorizontalAlignmentMode.Center
        scoreTextNode.verticalAlignmentMode = SKLabelVerticalAlignmentMode.Center
        scoreTextNode.fontSize = 20
        scoreTextNode.fontColor = SKColor.whiteColor()
        scoreTextNode.position = CGPointMake(size.width / 2.0, size.height - 75.0)
        addChild(scoreTextNode)

        let tryAgainTextNodeLine1 = SKLabelNode(fontNamed: "Copperplate")
        tryAgainTextNodeLine1.text = "TAP ANYWHERE TO PLAY AGAIN!"
        tryAgainTextNodeLine1.horizontalAlignmentMode = SKLabelHorizontalAlignmentMode.Center
        tryAgainTextNodeLine1.verticalAlignmentMode = SKLabelVerticalAlignmentMode.Center
        tryAgainTextNodeLine1.fontSize = 20
        tryAgainTextNodeLine1.fontColor = SKColor.whiteColor()
        tryAgainTextNodeLine1.position = CGPointMake(size.width / 2.0,size.height - 200)
        addChild(tryAgainTextNodeLine1)
    }
}
```

Listing 15-7 shows the updated didBeginContact method. This method will do one of two things depending on if you run into the enemy or an obstacle.

■ The player makes contact with the enemy. Stop the timer and set the gameStarted to false. Then transition to the "game over" scene.

■ The player makes contact with an obstacle; reset the spaceman to the starting point.

Listing 15-7. Contact with Enemy Node Enhancement

```
func physicsWorld(world: SCNPhysicsWorld, didBeginContact contact: SCNPhysicsContact) {

            if contact.nodeB.physicsBody!.categoryBitMask == CollisionCategoryEnemy {
                    gameOverlay.stopTimer()
                    gameStarted = false
                    sceneView.overlaySKScene = GameOverView(size:
                    view.bounds.size, score: gameOverlay.timeNode.text)
            }

            if contact.nodeB.physicsBody!.categoryBitMask == CollisionCategoryObstecles {
                    resetSpaceman()
            }
}
```

Now when you run your game and you get to the enemy, the player will be shown a "game over" view and their time. There is one other item you need to deal with, and that is to update the sceneView.overlaySKScene to the original timer screen.

In func renderer(aRenderer: SCNSceneRenderer, didSimulatePhysicsAtTime time: NSTimeInterval), you update the if statement where you are checking for the touchCount and whether the game is not started, as shown in Listing 15-8. You will reset the spaceman to his starting location and then change the overlay back to the timer.

Listing 15-8. Update the overlaySKScene Parameter

```
if sceneView.touchCount > 0 && !gameStarted {

        resetSpaceman()
    sceneView.overlaySKScene = gameOverlay

    gameOverlay.startTimer()
    gameStarted = true
}
```

To restart the player, just touch anywhere on the screen in order to restart the game, as shown in Figure 15-3.

Figure 15-3. "Game over" screen

Bonus Section

To make the game a bit more dynamic, it would be great if you had your obstacles and enemy randomly placed in the playing field. To do that, you need to create some methods that will give you a random position. A good place to put these methods is the SharedConstants.swift file. Open the SharedConstants.swift file to add a couple of imports.

```
import UIKIt
import SceneKit
```

With these imports in place, you will be able to add the methods you will use to create the random position, as in Listing 15-9.

Listing 15-9. Random Position Methods in the SharedConstants.swift File

```
func randomSign() -> Float {
    if arc4random_uniform(2) == 0 {
        return 1.0
    }else {
        return -1.0
    }
}
```

```
func randomFloat() -> Float {
    return Float(arc4random_uniform(100))
}

func randomPosition() -> SCNVector3 {

    return SCNVector3Make(randomSign()*randomFloat(), 0.0, randomSign()*randomFloat())
}
```

The first method you created, randomSign(), is a helper function to give you a negative or positive number. You are using the arc4random_uniform() method, which is used to generate a random number between 0 and n-1. In the randomSign() method, you are asking for a number between 0 and 1; then based on the number, you return a positive or negative 1 that will be used to change the sign for one of your axis points.

The next helper method is used to generate a number between 0 and 99. Again, you are using the arc4random method and supplying it with the highest number you want to generate a random number. The extra item is a Float object that you will use in the next method.

The randomPosition() method is the main method that you will use in order create a random position. You are setting the y-axis to 0.0 so that the items are all on the floor. As you can see, it uses the two help methods in order to create an SCNVector3 for any object you want to place in the game scene.

The only thing left to do now is to update all your nodes to use this new method to place the objects in random places. Now when you run the game, everything will be randomly placed and make it that much more difficult and fun to find the enemy.

Summary

Now you have an overlay Sprite Kit scene that has a timer, and you are randomly placing the objects in the scene. You can expand on this overlay scene and add more Sprite Kit features as you choose to for your games.

You now have a simple game that has explored Apple's Scene Kit library. You have learned what a scene graph is and how Scene Kit uses this graph to display 3D objects while using the GPU on the device. Try running this game in the simulator instead of on the device, and you will see how much the GPU improves performance.

The next and final chapter will explore some advanced topics with 3D programming. This will include doing some math and some tips on using Xcode.

Chapter

16

Advanced Topics and Tips

3D graphic programming is sometimes difficult to do. Scene Kit allows you to easily create an immersive world for your imagination to explore. So far, you have used Scene Kit and 3D graphics in a basic way because this is a beginner-level book. As you explore deeper into the Scene Kit world, you might want to learn more, so this chapter covers some advanced topics for you to get started in the right direction. You will also gain some tips on Xcode that I hope help you in your programming experience.

Normal Mapping

Normal mapping is basically using the bumps and dents of an image to create lighting effects. These mappings are usually grayscale images that use the varying shades of gray to show depth and height; these vectors have points that are perpendicular to the surface. By using a normal map, you can provide a greater amount of detail to your objects.

Vectors and Various Math Operations

Graphics programming relies heavily on vectors to represent almost all objects in some shape or form. This includes but is not limited to object positions, normals, colors, and even data structures.

Throughout this book you have used vectors and some of the operations for them. One important concept to remember is that a vector can represent different items based on context.

You create a vector by using one of two functions or using the respective initializer. Throughout this game you used both and saw that both ways work. Swift best practices would be to use the initializer over the make functions, listed here:

- `func SCNVector3( x:Float, y:Float, z:Float) -> SCNVector3`
- `func SCNVector3Make( x:Float, y:Float, z:Float) -> SCNVector3`
    - This is usually used to describe node positions; however, you should be aware of the context in which it is being used.

- `func SCNVector4(x:Float, y:Float, z:Float, w:Float) -> SCNVector4`
- `func SCNVector4Make(x:Float, y:Float, z:Float, w:Float) -> SCNVector4`
    - This data structure can be used to represent a color value or as a way to rotate an object.

Creating matrices is relatively straightforward, and they allow you to transform (move, rotate, and so on) an object within the 3D space.

- `func SCNMatrix4MakeTranslation(x:Float, y:Float, z:Float) -> SCNMatrix4`
    - The variables are distances you want the object to be moved along the associated axis.
- `func SCNMatrix4MakeRotation(angle:Float, x:Float, y:Float, z:Float) -> SCNMatrix4`
    - The angle in this function is in radians and counterclockwise around the rotation axis (which is the x-, y-, z-coordinates you supply).
- `func SCNMatrix4MakeScale( sx:Float, sy:Float, sz:Float) -> SCNMatrix4`
    - The variables represent the scale factor you want to change the object along that axis.

Now that I have reviewed the ways in which you create these elements, Scene Kit provides you with some ways to perform operations on them.

- `func SCNMatrix4Translate(mat:SCNMatrix4, x:Float, y:Float, z:Float) -> SCNMatrix4`
    - This is used to add a matrix to a specified matrix with a transformation.
    - mat is combined with the translation (x, y, z) directions.
- `func SCNMatrix4Rotate(mat:SCNMatrix4, angle:Float, x:Float, y:Float, z:Float) -> SCNMatrix4`
    - You are probably getting used to what this means; mat is the matrix that you want to rotate.
    - angle is the angle in which the rotation will occur.
    - Then specify the x-, y-, z-axes of the rotation axis.
- `func SCNMatrix4Scale(mat:SCNMatrix4, x:Float, y:Float, z:Float) -> SCNMatrix4`
    - This is the matrix that is scaled by the x-, y-, and z-axes.
- `func SCNMatrix4Invert(mat:SCNMatrix4) -> SCNMatrix4`
    - This returns the mat value (the matrix) inverted; however, if the matrix is unable to be inverted, the original matrix is returned.

■ ```
func SCNMatrix4Mult(matA:SCNMatrix4, matB:SCNMatrix4) ->
SCNMatrix4
```

■ Note that this is actually transforming the result of matA by matB.

# Tips

The most important tips you can have is for how to use your tools well, so here are some Xcode tips that you may or may not know. Let's start with your workspace (Figure 16-1).

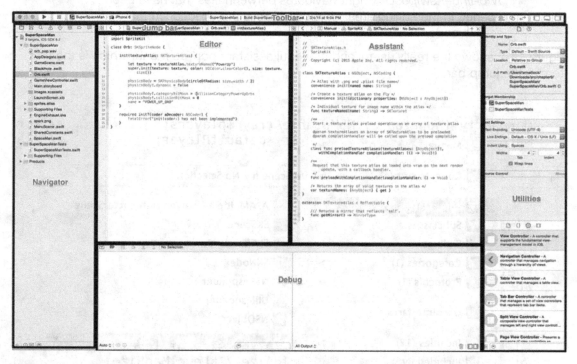

*Figure 16-1. Xcode editor*

Using hotkeys to navigate your workspace will elevate you from a novice to an expert in no time.

■ The Command key is used for the navigation area.

■ The Alt key is for the Assistant Editor and the Utility editor.

■ The Control key is used with the jump bar and the editing area.

■ Here are some hotkey combinations that you will use on a regular basis:

■ *Command+Shift+O*: Open File

■ *Command+R*: Run

■ *Command+B*: Build
```

- *Command+Shift+F*: Find in Project

- *Command+Shift+K*: Clean the projects build directories

In conjunction with hotkeys, Xcode has some gestures that will help you navigate.

- *Three-finger swipe*: This switches you between your `.m` and `.h` files. Though you don't have these files with Swift, if you are doing any Objective-C coding, you will use this action often.

- *Two-finger tap*: This opens the context menu.

- *Two-finger swipe*: Left/right navigates between files that have been opened in the editing area. Up/down scrolls the direction in the source code.

Figure 16-2 shows the really useful and powerful assistant pop-up menu, which is the first item in the jump bar.

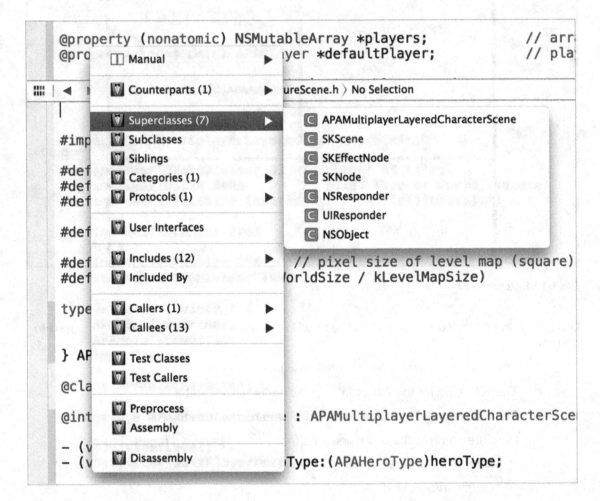

Figure 16-2. *Assistant pop-up menu*

Using this menu, you can navigate around to see the counterparts of your class and to find out what superclasses your class is from. This is really helpful when trying to see what classes are calling your function.

Another interesting feature in Xcode is behaviors (Figure 16-3).

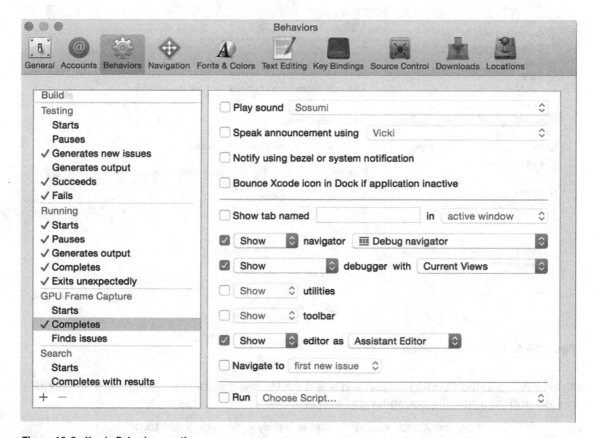

Figure 16-3. Xcode Behaviors section

Behaviors allow you to customize your views based on an action. For example, if you don't want to see the debugger when there are no errors, you can make that happen.

- *Make a sound when the application pauses*: Sometimes when working with several windows, it can get confusing when the application pauses. Figure 16-4 shows you how to add a sound when this happens.

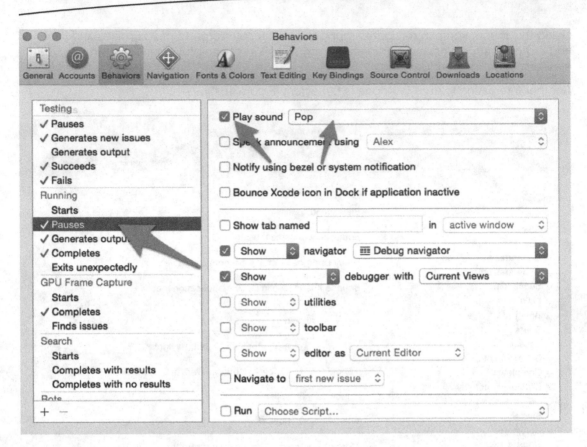

Figure 16-4. *Behavior setting sound*

To do this, go to the Running section and select the Pauses action. Then select the "Play sound" option and your favorite sound for this action.

- *Clean up the Xcode IDE*: This one is handy when you want to get back to a simple editing mode. Sometimes after running your application and the debugger appears, if your application crashes, you have yet another tab appear. This behavior is a new one that will simply clear the screen and get you back to a mode where you can write code. Figure 16-5 shows you this important new behavior.

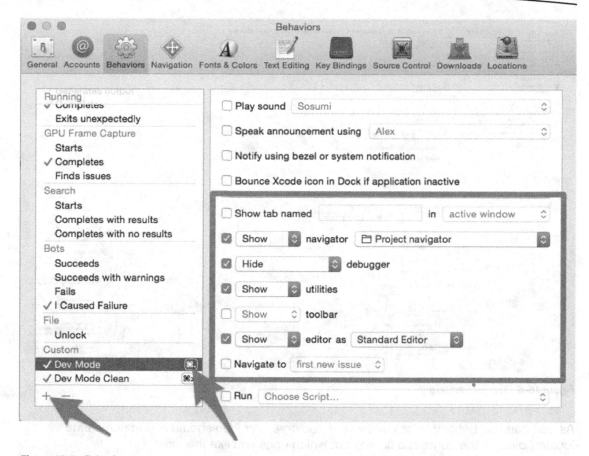

Figure 16-5. Behavior new type

For this behavior, you press the plug (+) on the bottom of the Behaviors section. Once you do this, you can give your action a name as well as a hotkey. Then you can adjust the screen the way you would like. The highlighted box has the clean layout, and now when you hit the hotkey, the Xcode IDE will change its layout to look like Figure 16-6.

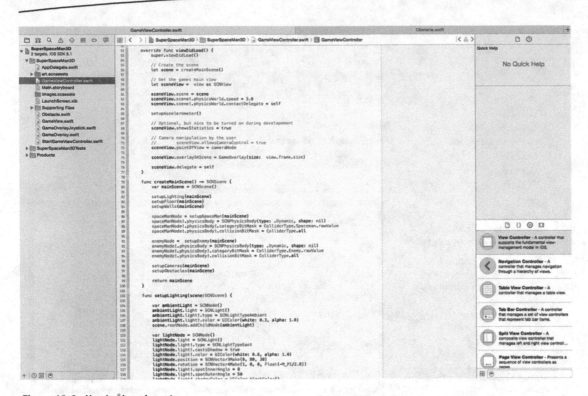

Figure 16-6. Xcode clean layout

As you can tell, behaviors can make your coding easier. You should spend some time looking over all the items and finding out which ones you like the most.

Summary

In this chapter, you looked at how normal mapping can help you create a detailed 3D object.

You examined some of the 3D math functions that you will use in creating more complex 3D games.

Finally, you found out some tips on using Xcode along with how to use behaviors to customize the IDE to your individual preferences.

Appendix **A**

The Swift Programming Language

Swift is Apple's new programming language intended to be the future replacement of Objective-C for Mac and iOS development. Some people are referring to it as a functional programming language, but it is actually an object-oriented programming language with a healthy dose of generic programming.

One of the most important facts about Swift is that it uses the same LLVM compiler and runtime as Objective-C, which means Swift and Objective-C code can live side-by-side. It also has access to all of the Cocoa and Cocoa Touch features you have in Objective-C applications.

Here are some notable features of Swift:

- Closures (similar to Objective-C blocks)
- Tuples that return values
- Generics
- Fast iterators
- Structs and enums that support methods, protocols, and extensions
- The ability to pass, nest, and return functions
- A more advanced `switch` statement

In this chapter, you will take a quick (you might say a *swift*) look at each of the features in the Swift programming language. I will start by describing each feature and then cement your knowledge through consecutive examples. I will not cover every aspect of Swift, but I will cover enough to make sure you can complete all of the examples in this book.

Before you can continue, you will need to create a Swift project. Here are the necessary steps:

1. Open Xcode.

2. Select File ➤ New Project.

3. Select an application from the OS X group.

4. Select Command Line Tool and click the Next button.

5. Enter SwiftConsoleApp for the product name.

6. Enter Apress for the organization name and **com.apress** for the organization identifier.

7. Make sure Swift is the selected language, click the Next button, and select a good place to store your project files.

I chose an OS X command-line tool so you can focus on Swift and not concern yourself with other distractions. You are now ready to go, but before moving on, let's examine what you just created.

Let's start with the file `main.swift`. As you will notice, there's not a whole lot to this file. It contains a single `import` statement used to make all of the Foundation classes available to this Swift file. After this statement is where you will be adding all of your code in the following sections.

> **Note**   Throughout this chapter you will be running different examples. When you run each example, you will need to replace the body of `main.swift` with the new code.

Variables and Constants

The first things I will talk about are variables and constants. Their syntax is similar except to declare a variable, you use the keyword `var`, and to declare a constant, you use the keyword `let`. Take a look at the following two declarations:

```
var color = "Blue"
let city = "Denver"
```

The first line of code declares a variable named `color`, and the second line of code declares a constant named `city`. Notice how neither of these declarations explicitly defines the type. Swift will derive the type based upon what you store in either the variable or the constant. If you want to define the type, then you do so using the following syntax:

```
var color : String
```

If you want to both declare a variable or constant's type and initialize it at the same time, you use this:

```
var color : String = "Blue"
let city : String = "Denver"
```

To print values to the console in Swift, you use the `print()` or `println()` function. Their syntax is pretty straightforward. When you want to print something to the console, you call either of these functions, passing them a `String` value. The only difference between these two functions is that the `println()` function adds a new line after the `String` value.

Let's take a look at these functions in action. Copy the following snippet into `main.swift` and run the application:

```
println("Hi, I live in")
```

You will see output similar to this:

```
Hi, I live in
```

This is pretty simple, but notice there is no semicolon at the end of the line. Semicolons are optional in Swift. You need them only if you put multiple statements on a single line. Let's get back to the `print()` and `println()` functions. Your first question is probably, "How do I print the values in variables and such?" There are a couple of ways to do this. The first is to use the + operator, as shown here:

```
var home = "Denver"
println("Hi, I live in " + home + ".")
```

This will print the following:

```
Hi, I live in Denver.
```

The second way to do this is to embed the variable in the `String` and surround it with \().

```
println("Hi, I live in \(home).")
```

This is much simpler and will result in the same output.

Flow of Control

Swift provides the most common methods to control the flow of a program, including the `if` and `switch` statements to support branching and the `for` and `while` statements to support looping. They are all similar to their Objective-C counterparts, but there are a few differences.

if

The Swift `if` statement is much like Objective-C's `if` statement, with the exception that the parentheses surrounding the Boolean expression is optional. You can include them if you like, but they are not required. To Swift, the following two `if` statements are identical:

```
var count = 10

if (count < 7){

    println("less than 7")
}
else if (count > 7) {

    println("greater than 7")
}
else {

    println("equals 7")
}

if count < 7 {

    println("less than 7")
}
else if count > 7 {

    println("greater than 7")
}
else {

    println("equals 7")
}
```

switch

The Swift `switch` statement is powerful. Unlike with Objective-C, you can test any type of value in a `switch` statement. The Swift `switch` statement has another difference from the Objective-C `switch` statement. It does not require break statements. The `case` ends at the next `case` or default statement. Take a look at this Swift `switch` statement:

```
var food = "broccoli"

switch food {

case "cheeseburger":
    println("YUM")

case "broccoli":
    println("YUCK")
```

```
default:
    println("UKNOWN FOOD")
}
```

In this switch you are testing `String` values. Notice there are no breaks. Go ahead and copy this snippet into your `main.swift` file and run the code. You will get exactly what you would expect—"YUCK."

Try one more thing. Go back to this code in Xcode and remove the default section of the `switch`. You will see the following error:

```
Switch must be exhaustive, consider adding a dafault clause
```

Every `switch` statement must be exhaustive, which means that every possibility of the type being tested must have a matching case. In this case of a `String`, this is impossible, which is why you need the default clause at the end of the `switch`.

There is one last thing I need to discuss: optionals. Optionals are Swift variables that can have a value or have no value and are set to `nil`. The syntax of an optional is the same as a normal variable declaration, except you add a question mark (?) after the type of the variable.

```
var optionalAddress : String?
```

This variable `optionalAddress` can either have an `Address` value or have no value. You can use an `if` to see whether the variable has a value.

```
if optionalAddress {

    println("The number is \(optionalAddress!.number())")
}
```

Optionals are useful when there is a possibility that a variable will not contain a value. One way this can happen is when you are searching for something in a collection and the value is not found—an address in this instance. Note the exclamation mark (!) after the variable in `println()`. You use this operator to unwrap the optional. If you do not unwrap the optional, the compiler will not recognize the type of your variable.

There is another way to unwrap an optional. Take the previous address instance. You can use an `if` or `case` statement to store an optional's unwrapped value in a constant.

```
if let address = optionalAddress {

    println("The number is \(address.number())")
}
```

Using the `if` like this automatically unwraps the optional and stores it in the constant `address`.

for Loops

Swift provides two different implementations of the `for` loop: `for-conditional-increment` looping and `for-in` looping.

for-conditional-increment

The `for-conditional-increment` implementation of the `for` loop is the implementation you have probably used for years. This version of the `for` loop is the traditional C-style loop that uses an initializer, a condition, and an incrementer separated by semicolons. Take a look at this loop:

```
var colors = ["red", "blue", "green", "black", "blue", "orange"]

for var index = 0; index < colors.count; index++ {

    println("The color is : \(colors[index])")
}
```

In this example, you create an array of strings representing different colors. You then use an `Int` value named `index` to iterate over the array and print its values. We have all seen this type of loop a million times.

for-in

The `for-in` version of the `for` loop is most useful when you are iterating over a complete collection of values or when you want to iterate over a range of values in a collection. Take a look at the following loop:

```
var colors = ["red", "blue", "green", "black", "blue", "orange"]

for color in colors {

    println("The color is : \(color)")
}
```

This loop does exactly what the previous `for` loop did, but look at how much simpler this version is. This loop iterates over the `colors` array assigning each element to the `color` variable and then prints the value in color. You are iterating over the entire collection, which means you don't care about a conditional.

If you want to iterate over only part of this array, you can use a range. You represent a range in Swift using three dots (`...`) following the `in` part of the `for` loop.

```
var colors = ["red", "blue", "green", "black", "blue", "orange"]

for index in 2...4 {

    println("The color is : \(colors[index])")
}
```

This loop will print the values only in the third, fourth, and fifth positions of the `colors` array.

The `for-in` loop has a really cool feature for iterating over dictionaries.

```swift
var states = ["CO":"Colorado", "UT":"Utah", "NM":"New Mexico"]

for (abbreviation, state) in states {

    println("The abbreviation for \(state) is \(abbreviation)")
}
```

This code begins by creating a dictionary with state abbreviations as the keys and the state names as the values. Then the `for-in` loop iterates over the dictionary assigning the two variables surrounded by parentheses each key-value pair found in each element of the dictionary. Drop this code into the body of your `main.swift` file and run it. You will see the following output:

```
The abbreviation for New Mexico is NM
The abbreviation for Utah is UT
The abbreviation for Colorado is CO
```

This is a handy method of iterating over dictionaries.

while Loops

Swift's `while` loop implementations are, for the most part, just like Objective-C's. There are two `while` loop implementations: the standard `while`, with the condition at the beginning of the loop, and the do-while loop, with the condition at the end. The only real difference in these loops and the Objective-C equivalents is the optional parentheses.

while

The `while` loop first tests its condition, and if the result is true, then it executes the code block until the condition is false. This code will check to see whether the index variable is less than the number of elements in the `colors` array. If the result is true, then the code in the braces is executed. This behavior will repeat until the index is no longer less than the number of elements in the array.

```swift
var colors = ["red", "blue", "green", "black", "blue", "orange"]

var index = 0

while index < colors.count {

    println("The color is : \(colors[index])")
    index++
}
```

do-while

The do-while loop has its conditional at the end of the loop. This means its code block will be executed one time before the condition is checked. If the variable index equaled 10000, the code would still be executed at least once. The program would crash because there are only six elements in the array, but the while would still try to run that first time.

```
var colors = ["red", "blue", "green", "black", "blue", "orange"]

var index = 0

do {

    println("The color is : \(colors[index])")
    index++
} while index < colors.count
```

Functions

Swift and Objective-C functions have a very different syntax. The basic syntax of a Swift function is as follows:

```
func catTwoWords(word1: String, word2: String) ->String {

    return "\(word1)\(word2)"
}

println(catTwoWords("Hello", "World"))
```

You start the function declaration with the keyword func followed by the function name. After this, you have a named list of parameters with their respective types followed by the return arrow (->) and the return type of the function. The body of the function is represented by opening and closing braces ({}) just like Objective-C.

This function is named catTwoWords(). It takes two String parameters named word1 and word2. And it returns a String. Calling a Swift function is much like calling a C function. You use the name of the function with your parameter list surrounded by parentheses.

Replace the body of your main.swift file with this code and run it. You will see this output:

```
HelloWorld
```

If you want to create a function that has no parameters or return types, you simply omit them.

```
func thisFunctionDoesNothing() {
}
```

Variadic Parameters

You can also pass a variable number of arguments to a single parameter in a Swift function. This parameter is called a *variadic* parameter. When defining a variadic parameter, you follow the type with three dots (...).

```
func catWords(words: String...) ->String {

    var cattedWords = ""

    for word in words {

        cattedWords+=word
    }
    return cattedWords
}
```

This function takes a variable number of String values and stores them in an array named words. It then iterates over the array appending each String to the variable cattedWords and then returns a single String representing all the words as one String.

To call the function, you simple invoke it, like you did before, passing it any number of String values.

```
println(catWords("Hello", "World", "I", "Am", "Swift"))
```

Go ahead and run this code. You will see all the words as one. Then change the number of String values you pass to this function and play around with it while watching the results.

You can add other parameters to a function that has a variadic parameter, but there can be only one variadic parameter, and it must be the last parameter in the function definition.

Tuples

Swift functions can also return multiple values called *tuples*. A function that returns a tuple will have its return types defined in parentheses separated by commas.

```
func getGasPrices() ->(Double, Double, Double) {

    return (3.50, 3.73, 3.87)
}
var prices = getGasPrices()
println(prices)
```

Take a look at the previous snippet. You first define a function named getGasPrices() that takes no parameters and returns three Double values. Following the function, you are invoking it and storing the results in a variable named prices, and finally you are printing that value. To see the tuple value, use this code to replace the body of `main.swift` and run it again. The output will look like the following:

```
(3.5, 3.73, 3.87)
```

This might look a little strange, but this is what a tuple looks like. If you want to reference each of the values in the tuple, you can do so by using its numeric position in the tuple.

```
println(prices.0)
println(prices.1)
println(prices.2)
```

Replace `println()` in the previous snippet and rerun it. Now you will see each value printed on a different line. This seems OK, but it would be much easier to reference each value using a unique name as opposed to keeping up with its position in the tuple. You can do this by naming each of the returned values.

```
func getGasPrices() ->(unleaded : Double, premium : Double, diesel : Double) {

    return (3.50, 3.73, 3.87)
}
```

Now you can invoke the function and reference the results as follows:

```
var prices = getGasPrices()

println(prices.unleaded)
println(prices.premium)
println(prices.diesel)
```

Nested Functions

So far all of the functions you have seen defined have been global. Swift makes it possible to hide functions by nesting them in other functions. Take a look at this function definition:

```
func divideAndPrint(num1: Int, num2:Int) {

    func divide(num1: Int, num2:Int) ->(quotient : Int, remainder : Int) {

        var quotient = num1 / num2
        var remainder = num1 % num2

        return (quotient,remainder)
    }
  var r = divide(num1, num2)
  println("\(r.quotient) with a remainder of : \(r.remainder)")
}
```

This function, named `divideAndPrint()`, has another function defined in it named `divide()` that takes two Int values and returns a tuple with two labeled Int values. `divide()` is visible only inside its encompassing parent, `divideAndPrint()`. It cannot be used by any other functions.

To invoke `divideAndPrint()`, you pass it two `Int`s. It then invokes the nested `divide()` function and returns the tuple to the caller. And then the outer function stores the result in the `r` variable and prints the tuple values showing the whole-number result of dividing the two numbers. Replace the body of `main.swift` with this code and add a call to `divideAndPrint()`, passing values of your choice, directly after the function definition. You invoked the function with the following call:

```
divideAndPrint(5, 3)
```

This invocation resulted in 1, with a remainder of 2.

```
1 with a remainder of : 2
```

Functions Returning Functions

In the previous section, I said a nested function was visible only inside its outer function. This is correct, but there is a way you can access a nested function. Swift gives you the ability return a nested function just like any other type. The syntax is just a little different.

When defining a function that returns another function, you have to change the return type of the returning function to match the parameter list and return the type of the returned function. This may sound like a mouthful, but it really is pretty straightforward. Take a look at this function definition:

```
func getMathFunction(operator: Character) ->(Int, Int) ->Int {

}
```

This function looks pretty normal to a point. It takes a single `Character` parameter, but the return looks a little different. It starts with a normal `->`, but after that you see the parameter list, `(Int, Int)`, of the function to be returned followed by the return type of the function to be returned, `Int`.

It may be easier to understand this syntax if you put an imaginary function name in the return definition.

```
func getMathFunction(operator: Character) ->imaginaryFunctionName(Int, Int) ->Int {

}
```

Notice the text `imaginaryFunctionName()`. If you think about it like this, it looks like any other function definition.

> **Note**   The previous syntax, using a function name in a return type, is only for clarity purposes. You cannot do this in a real Swift function.

Let's take a look at a real function that returns another function. The function you are going to create will take a single character representing a simple math operator (+, -, *, /) and match the operator to a nested function. When it has a match, it will return the nested function, and you can use it to perform a math operation. Here is the function:

```swift
func getMathFunction(op: Character) ->(Int, Int) ->Int {

    func add(num1: Int, num2 :Int) ->Int {

        return num1 + num2
    }

    func subtract(num1: Int, num2 :Int) ->Int {

        return num1 - num2
    }

    func multiply(num1: Int, num2 :Int) ->Int {

        return num1 * num2
    }

    func divide(num1: Int, num2 :Int) ->Int {

        return num1 / num2
    }

    switch (op) {

        case "+" : return add
        case "-" : return subtract
        case "*" : return multiply
        default : return divide
    }
}
```

This function has the same definition you saw earlier, but it has an implementation now. As you look over the implementation, you will see four nested functions matching the return type of getMathFunction(). They each take two Int parameters, and they all return a single Int.

After the nested functions, you will see a simple switch statement that tests the passed-in character and returns a nested function based upon the test results.

To invoke and use this function, you do the following:

```swift
var mathFunction = getMathFunction("-")
println(mathFunction(5,5))
```

You start by invoking the outer function, passing it a minus sign (-), and storing the results in the mathFunction variable. The resulting function is the subtract() function. Once you have a reference to the returned function, you can execute it just like any other function. Replace the body of main.swift with this function and the invocation code shown previously and run the new code. You will see a 0 printed to the console.

To see the other functions in action, add the following calls to the bottom of main.swift and run it once more:

```
mathFunction = getMathFunction("+")
println(mathFunction(5,5))

mathFunction = getMathFunction("*")
println(mathFunction(5,5))

mathFunction = getMathFunction("/")
println(mathFunction(5,5))
```

Passing Functions As Parameters

Swift also gives you the ability to pass functions to other functions. It uses a similar syntax as you would use when you return a function. The following function definition takes three parameters including two Int parameters and a function named mathFunction and returns a single Int:

```
func performOperation(num1: Int, num2: Int, mathFunction: (Int, Int) ->Int) ->Int {
}
```

Notice the third parameter. It looks just like the return type you defined when you returned a math function. The difference this time is you have to name the parameter that will hold the passed-in function. In this case, you are storing the function in the mathFunction parameter. Let's implement and use this function.

```
func performOperation(num1: Int, num2: Int, mathFunction: (Int, Int) ->Int) ->Int{

    return mathFunction(num1, num2)
}

func multiply(num1: Int, num2 :Int) ->Int {

    return num1 * num2
}

println(performOperation(100, 6, multiply))
```

The implementation of the performOperation() function is simple. It takes the two Ints passed to it, passes those values to the passed-in function, and returns the result.

After the `performOperation()` function, you define another function that multiplies two `Int`s and returns the result. To invoke the `performOperation()` function, you pass it a 100 and a 6 along with the `multiply()` function. Go ahead and try it. Replace the current body of `main.swift` with this code and run it. You will see 600 printed to the console.

inout Parameters

In all of the previous examples, you have never tried to change the value of a passed-in variable while you were in the body of the function. You probably think you could just set the parameter's value to something else and all would be fine. This is not the case. When you pass a parameter like you have been doing so far, you are actually passing a copy of the value to the function, and the parameter is treated as a constant.

If you need to change the value of a parameter in the body of a function, you have to pass a reference to the variable you are passing in. This is done using a Swift `inout` parameter. Take a look at the `swapWords()` function:

```
func swapWords(inout param1: String, inout param2: String) {

    var tmp: String = param1
    param1 = param2
    param2 = tmp
}

var word1 = "Hello"
var word2 = "Goodbye"

swapWords(&word1, &word2)

println(word1)
println(word2)
```

Here you have a simple function the takes two `String`s and swaps their values. To use the function, you create two `String` variables and pass them to `swapWords()`. After the function is executed, you print the words.

Notice the two parameters with the keyword inout in front of them. This is how you tell the Swift compiler that this function is expecting a `reference` to a variable and not a copy of a variable. Now look at the invocation of this function. You have prepended an ampersand (&) to each of the variables being passed to the function. This indicates you are passing a reference to the variable.

When you run the program, you will see that the values have been swapped. When you pass parameters using this method, you are said to be passing them *by reference*.

Closures

Closures in Swift are self-contained blocks of functionality that can be passed to other functions or closures to be executed by the receiver. They are similar to Objective-C blocks. The syntax is just a little easier to read. You can think of closures as functions with no name. Closures have the following syntax:

```
{(parameters) - > return type in

    // implementation
}
```

A closure starts with an opening brace ({) followed by a list of parameters in parentheses. After the parameter list you see the return type symbol (->) with the return type followed by the keyword in. After the in, you have the implementation of the closure and finally a closing brace (}). The following code shows an example of a closure:

```
{ (num1: Int, num2: Int) -> Int in

        return num1 + num2
}
```

This code will look familiar. It is the add() function from earlier converted to a closure. It takes two Ints and returns an Int. To use a closure, you can pass it as a parameter to another function.

```
func performOperation(num1: Int, num2: Int,
                mathClosure: (Int, Int) ->Int) ->Int{

    return mathClosure(num1, num2)
}

var result = performOperation(5, 6, {

        (num1: Int, num2: Int) -> Int in

        return num1 + num2
    }
)
println("The result is : \(result)")
```

Here you have the performOperation() function from the previous section. The only thing different about this function is the last parameter has been renamed to mathClosure. Next you invoke this function, passing it two numbers and the closure, and store the results in the variable results. Finally, you print the results to the console.

If you run the new code, you will see 11 printed to the console.

Classes

Classes in Swift are the main ingredients of most applications. They are reusable pieces of code that encapsulate both state and functionality. The components of a class are its methods and properties. When speaking in relation to classes, we refer to functions as *methods* and variables as *properties*. The basic syntax of a class follows:

```
class MyClass {

    // insert class definition here
}
```

While this class does not do anything, it is a complete class. This is one of the really nice features of Swift. Unlike Objective-C, you don't need an interface file (.h). In Swift, the interface and implementation are in a single file, and the external interface is automatically made available to all other consumers. Let's see some examples.

Go back to your Xcode project, create a new Swift file named Vehicle.swift, copy the following code into it, and save the file:

```
import Foundation

class Vehicle {

    var engine : String = "gas"
    var horsePower : Int = 500

    func info() -> String {

        return "I am a \(engine) powered vehicle with \(horsePower) horse power"
    }
}
```

Here you have defined a simple class named Vehicle that has two properties, engine and horsepower, and a single method named info(). To create a class, you invoke its default initializer by referencing the class's name followed by an empty set of parentheses.

```
var vehicle = Vehicle()
println("engine type : \(vehicle.engine)")
println("horse power : \(vehicle.horsePower)")
println(vehicle.info())
```

Once you have an instance of your class, you can access its properties and invoke its methods using the dot (.) operator. Go back to your main.swift file, replace its body with this snippet, and run it. Notice how the compiler did not complain about the Vehicle class not being imported. In Swift, you have to import only frameworks.

Open your `Vehicle.swift` file, change the declaration of `engine` to the following, and save your changes:

```
var engine : String
```

Swift does not like this. You should see an error message saying "Class Vehicle has no initializers." Swift requires you to initialize each variable before you can use an instance of a class. To do this, you use an `init()` method. Take a look at the new Vehicle class:

```
import Foundation

class Vehicle {

    var engine : String
    var horsePower : Int

    init(engine : String, horsePower : Int) {

        self.engine = engine
        self.horsePower = horsePower
    }

    func info() -> String {

        return "I am \(engine) powered with \(horsePower) horse power"
    }
}
```

As you can see, you have added an `init()` method that takes two parameters matching the two properties of the class. Inside the `init()`, you use the keyword `self` with a dot followed by the property names to set them to their initial values. `self`, like in Objective-C, refers to the current instance of the class. Another thing to note about an `init()` method is that it is not prepended by the keyword `func`.

To create an instance of your modified class, you have to change how you pass parameters to the `init()`. The following shows this change:

```
var vehicle = Vehicle(engine: "gas", horsePower: 500)
```

The first thing to take note of is you are not explicitly calling `init()`. This is because when you create a class using its name, it implicitly calls the matching `init()`. Another thing to look at is you are now using labels when passing values to a method. This is a requirement of Swift. When you are invoking a method on an object that contains a parameter list, you must label the values being passed. As you saw earlier, this is not required when calling functions.

Extending Classes

To extend a class in Swift, you follow the class name with a colon (:) and the name of the class you are extending. The following class defines a new class named Car that extends the original Vehicle:

```
import Foundation

class Car : Vehicle {

    init(engine : String, horsePower : Int) {

        super.init(engine : engine, horsePower : horsePower)
    }
}
```

Notice the init() method. It has the same parameter list as its parent, and it calls its parent, passing the required values to ensure the parent is properly initialized. Before you run the code again, let's add some functionality to the new class.

The car has an upgrade and includes a navigation system and therefore will have two new properties, lat and long, that represent the location of the car. Let's add these properties now. Here is the new Car:

```
class Car : Vehicle {

    var latitude : String
    var longitude : String

    init(engine: String, horsePower : Int, latitude: String, longitude: String) {

        self.latitude = latitude
        self.longitude = longitude
        super.init(engine : engine, horsePower : horsePower)
    }

    override func info() -> String {

        return "\(super.info()) and I am at (\(latitude),\(longitude))"
    }
}
```

As you look over these changes, you will see that you modify init() to include the two new properties, and you add a new method with the keyword override prepended to the method declaration. override tells the compiler you want to replace the parent method with this one.

To see the new Car in action, go back to Xcode, create a new Swift file named Car.swift, and copy this code into its body. After you have done this, go back to main.swift, add the following lines, and rerun the program:

```
var car = Car(engine: "gas",
        horsePower: 500,
          latitude: "39.7392 N",
          longitude: "104.9847 W")
println(car.info())
```

When you run the program this time, you will see the output from the new info() method.

```
I am gas powered with 500 horse power and I am at (39.7392 N,104.9847 W)
```

Computed Properties

You have already seen Swift's simple properties, but it also has the ability to use explicit getters and setters for more complex operations. To see how you can use computed properties, let's go back to the original Vehicle class and add two new properties, mpg and gallonsInTank, and a getter and setter for a third property, distanceTillEmpty(). Here are the changes:

```
import Foundation

class Vehicle {

    var engine : String
    var horsePower : Int
    var mpg : Int
    var gallonsInTank : Int

    init(engine : String, horsePower : Int, mpg : Int, gallonsInTank : Int) {

        self.engine = engine
        self.horsePower = horsePower
        self.mpg = mpg
        self.gallonsInTank = gallonsInTank
    }

    var distanceTillEmpty : Int {

    get {

        return self.mpg * self.gallonsInTank
    }
    set {

        gallonsInTank = newValue / self.mpg
    }
    }
}
```

The mpg and gallonsInTank properties are not very exciting; it's the third property that is interesting. Starting with the bold text, you can see you have a new variable named distanceTillEmpty that is of type Int. Following the type definition, you see a set of braces. This is where the getter and setter of the new property are placed.

You start with the getter in this case. Here you are multiplying mpg and gallonsInTank and returning the result. Notice you are not even using the property distanceTillEmpty. This is why it is called a *computed* property. Its value is determined inside the getter using other properties of the object.

After the getter, you see the setter. In the setter, you are dividing a variable named newValue by the property of mpg. Where did this variable, newValue, come from? When using a computed property, the value being passed in to the setter is stored in a constant with the implicit name of newValue. Also note that the variable distanceToEmpty is not being set. When using a computed property's set, you are not setting the property's value but modifying the properties that will be used to compute its value when the getter is called.

Before moving on, go ahead and delete both the Car.swift and Vehicle.swift files from your project.

Structures

Swift structures are similar to classes. Like classes, they can have initializers, properties, and methods, and you must use labeled parameters when you pass values to their methods and initializers. The biggest difference is that when you pass a structure to another method or function, it is copied as opposed to being passed by reference like classes.

To implement a structure, you use the keyword struct followed by a set of braces and then its implementation.

```
struct LatLong {

    var lat : String
    var long : String

    func stringValue() ->String {

        return "My location is \(lat) : \(long)"
    }
}
```

In this structure you are defining a simple representation for a location based on a latitude and a longitude. It has two properties, lat and long, and one method, stringValue(), that returns a String representing the LatLong. To use this structure, you can call it using the following two lines of code:

```
let location = LatLong(lat: "39.7392 N", long: "104.9847 W")
println(location.stringValue())
```

As you can see, it looks like how you use a class. You might have noticed there is another difference between classes and structures. All structures have an automatically generated memberwise initializer, but classes do not. You can pass values to the initializer of a structure without creating the initializer.

Enumerations

To implement a Swift enumeration, you use the keyword enum followed by its type and a set of braces with a case or collection of case statements defining the members of the enum. Take a look at this enum defining an enumeration containing each day of the week:

```
enum DaysOfTheWeek: Int {
    case Sunday = 0, Monday, Tuesday, Wednesday, Thursday, Friday, Saturday
}
```

You define each member of an enum using a case. Notice the way you are defining your members. You have a comma-separated list with only the first member being set. If the type of the enum is an Int raw value (raw values are the values you assign to an enum member), then you have to set only the first value and Swift will determine the remaining values. To see how this enum is used, copy it and the following snippet into your main.swift and run it:

```
var today = DaysOfTheWeek.Friday
println("Today is \(today.rawValue).")
```

You will see the following output.

```
Today is 5.
```

Notice println() in the second line. You are invoking the toRaw() method on the enum. This function is a built-in function of every enum that will return whatever the raw value of each member of the enum has stored as its value.

You can use other raw values such as Strings and Floats, but you will have to explicitly set each value.

```
enum RGBColors : String {
    case Red = "Red", Green = "Green", Blue = "Blue"
}
```

If an enumeration does not have a meaningful raw value, then you don't have to assign it a value at all. Each member of the enum will have a value assigned to it by Swift.

```
enum RGBColors {
    case Red, Green, Blue
}
```

Another nice thing about Swift enumerations is that they can have methods associated with them. Take a look at the new DaysOfTheWeek enumeration:

```swift
enum DaysOfTheWeek: Int {
    case Sunday = 0, Monday, Tuesday, Wednesday, Thursday, Friday, Saturday

    func name() -> String {
        switch self {
        case .Sunday:
            return "Sunday"
        case .Monday:
            return "Monday"
        case .Tuesday:
            return "Tuesday"
        case .Wednesday:
            return "Wednesday"
        case .Thursday:
            return "Thursday"
        case .Friday:
            return "Friday"
        case .Saturday:
            return "Saturday"
        default:
            return String(self.rawValue)
        }
    }
}

var today = DaysOfTheWeek.Friday
println("Today is \(today.name()).")
```

In the new version of the enumeration, you add a new method called name() that returns a String representation of each member. It does this using a simple case statement that tests self, the current instance of an enum, and returns its matching String. Notice the test in the case statement. You are using a dot (.) followed by the member. You can do this because you already know the value of self is a DaysOfTheWeek enumeration. If you want to see the new changes in action, add the new code to main.swift and try running it again.

Protocols

Protocols in Swift are used to define the contract of properties and methods that classes, enumerations, or structures guarantee to implement when extending a protocol. Swift protocols are very much like Objective-C protocols, but with a little different syntax and a lot more flexibility. They basic syntax of a protocol is simple.

```swift
protocol EngineProtocol {

    var type : String {get set}
    func start()
    func stop()
}
```

Here you have a protocol named EngineProtocol that defines two functions, start and stop, and one property type. Take note of the {get set} following the definition of the type property. This part of the property requirement indicates that any implementer of this protocol must provide a getter and a setter for this property. Let's take a look at a class that implements this protocol:

```
class GasPowerEngine : EngineProtocol {

    var type : String = "gas"

    func start() {

        println("I am starting.")
    }

    func stop() {

        println("I am stopping.")
    }
}
```

This class satisfies all the requirements of the protocol and can now be used just like any other class. You may wonder how you satisfied the property requirement of {get set}. By default a property has both a getter and a setter. If a class implements this protocol and implements only a getter, like the following, it will not compile:

```
class GasPowerEngine : EngineProtocol {

    var type : String {

        return "gas"
    }

    func start() {

        println("I am starting.")
    }

    func stop() {

        println("I am stopping.")
    }
}
```

So far you have seen only instance methods defined in your protocols. If you want to add a class method, also known as a *static*, requirement to a protocol, you simply prefix the function definition with the keyword class. Here is a short example doing just this:

```
protocol TypeProtocol {

    class func type() -> String
}

class MyClass: TypeProtocol {

    class func type() -> String {

        return "MyClass"
    }
}
println("The class type is \(MyClass.type())")
```

Extensions

Extensions in Swift allow you to add functionality to an existing class, structure, or enumeration. They are much like Objective-C categories but do not have names, which makes for a much more readable syntax.

The syntax of a Swift protocol is straightforward and looks like a Swift class or structure, but using the keyword extension as opposed to class or structure. To see how they work, let's create an extension to the String class that adds a reverse function.

```
extension String {

    func reverse() -> String {

        var s = ""

        for char in self {

            s = String(char) + s
        }
        return s
    }
}

var reversableString = "esrever"
println("The String is now \(reversableString.reverse())")
```

As you examine this code, you will see that it does look like a class or structure, but notice the first line. There is no name. You have the keyword extension followed by the class you are extending. After that, nothing else is different. To use the new extension, you simply invoke the `reverse()` method as if it were part of the class. Copy this code into your `main.swift` and run the program again. You will see the following output:

```
The String is now reverse
```

Generics

Generics have been around for a long time in languages such as Java, but they have been missing on the Mac and iOS side. Swift solves this problem with its own implementation of generics.

Generics allow you to write code that is both flexible and reusable. Generics are one of the most interesting features of Swift. Let's dig in and see what generics are and how you can leverage them to make your coding life easier.

```
func orderTwoNumbersAscending(num1: Int,
                        num2: Int) -> (lesser: Int, greater: Int) {

    if num1 > num2 {

        return (num2, num1)
    }
    return (num1, num2)
}

var numbers = orderTwoNumbersAscending(10, 7)
println("\(numbers.lesser) < \(numbers.greater)")
```

This is a bit of a contrived example, but it will serve its purpose. In this snippet, you have a function that takes two `Int`s, compares them, and returns a tuple with the numbers in ascending order. If you run this, you will see the following output:

```
7 < 10
```

It's pretty straightforward, but what if you wanted to compare `String`s? You would have to write a whole new function. Generics solve this problem. Generics have the following syntax:

```
func functionName<T>(param : T)
```

The definition starts normally enough. The differences start after the function name. Here you have a T surrounded by less-than and greater-than signs, `<T>`. This T represents a generic type that will be determined by the type passed to this function at the parameter position where there is a T. If you passed an `Int` in this position, then wherever a T was found in the function definition, the compiler would expect another `Int`. The compiler would see something like this:

```
func functionName<Int>(param : Int)
```

If you wanted to pass in two params of different types, you would have the following definition:

```
func functionName<T, G>(param : T, param2 : G)
```

And if you wanted to return the same type, you add a generic return definition to your function.

```
func functionName<T>(param : T) -> T
```

Finally, if you wanted to restrict the types that could be represented by the generic, you would add a where clause.

```
func functionName<T where T: type>(param : T) -> T
```

The type in the where clause can force the type to implement a protocol, require two types to be the same, or even require a class to have a particular superclass. Let's look at some code that will make this a little clearer: Take a look at the following code:

```
func orderTwoValuesAscending<G where G: Comparable>(val1: G, val2: G)
    -> (lesser: G, greater : G) {

        if val1 > val2 {

            return (val2, val1)
        }
        return (val1, val2)
}

var numbers = orderTwoValuesAscending(10, 7)
println("\(numbers.lesser) < \(numbers.greater)")

var characters = orderTwoValuesAscending("f", "d")
println("\(characters.lesser) < \(characters.greater)")
```

Let's examine the new function. You will see that the new function is similar to the earlier function orderTwoNumbersAscending(). The first thing you will notice is this function uses a G to represent its generic type (I chose another letter just to show that the character used is arbitrary). This generic, G, is used for both parameters and values in the returned tuple, and it is restricted to the Comparable protocol. Now, because both Strings and Ints adopt the Comparable protocol, the new function can operate on Ints and Strings. Go ahead and give it try. You will see the following output:

```
7 < 10
d < f
```

Index

■ A

Acceleration property, 88
Ambient light, 172
Angle property, 88
Animation
    boxNode, 185–186
    cylinder node, 188
    globeNode, 183–184, 187
    pyramidNode, 182
    Scene Kit, 181
    tubeNode, 184–185
Assistant pop-up menu, 214

■ B

Behavior setting sound, 216
Birthrate and Maximum properties, 86
BlackHole node
    addBlackHolesToForeground(), 65, 68
    addOrbsToForeground(), 65
    CollisionCategoryBlackHoles, 67
    didBeginContact(), 67
BoxNode, 186
BoxNode materials, 175

■ C, D

Cartesian coordinate system, 145
Cocoa and Cocoa touch features, 219
Collada file, 176
CollisionCategoryBlackHoles, 67
Collision detection
    dynamic, 196
    kinematic, 196
    SCNPhsicsContact protocols, 200
    SCNPhysicsBody, 196
    SCNPhysicsBody categoryBitMask and
        collisionBitMask, 198–199
    SCNPhysicsBody class initialization, 197

SCNPhysicsWorld didBeginContact
    protocol, 200
SharedConstants.swift contents, 198
static, 196
createMainScene() method, 171, 180

■ E, F

Emission, 173

■ G

GameOverlay
    startTimer(), 203
    stopTimer, 203
GameOverView, 206
GameScene
    backgroundNode, 48
    code changes, 47
    foregroundNode, 47
    impulseCount property, 49
    modified scene with
        additional orbs, 51
    orbNode, 49, 50, 52
    player movement control with
        accelerometer, 54–57
    playerNode and orbNode, 48
    scrolling the scene, 52–54
    touchesBegan() method, 48
GameScene Class
    GameScene.swift file, 11
    init() methods, 12
GameScene, planet's surface
    backgroundNode declaration, 71–72
    colorizeAction, 77
    layer of stars, 74
    parallelaxation, 74
    position of playerNode, 74
    SKSpriteNode declaration, 74
    update() method, 72

GameViewController, 152, 190,
    195, 200, 204
GameViewController Class
    iOS Swift applications, 9
    scaleMode properties, 11
    scene variable, 10
    SKView, 10
    super.viewDidLoad(), 10
    UIViewController, 10
    viewDidLoad() method, 10
GlobeNode, 183–184, 187
GlobeNode lightening enhancements, 175

H

Hit testing
    CoreMotion framework, 194
    enemy node, 195
    GameView.swift, 189–190
    positionCameraWithSpaceman(), 193
    Render delegate method, 192
    Scene Kit render cycle, 191
    setupAccelerometer function, 194–195
    setupEnemy(), 196

I, J, K

init() method, 60

L, M

Lighting, camera and material effects
    ambient light, 172
    BoxNode materials, 175
    diffuse shading, 172
    globeNode lightening
        enhancements, 175
    multiply, 174
    normal lighting, 173
    pyramidNode material, 174
    reflective lighting, 173
    remaining obstacle materials, 175–176
    scene editor, 177–178
    scene kit camera usage, 179
    SCNLightTypeAmbient, 169
    SCNLightTypeDirectional, 170
    SCNLightTypeOmni, 170
    SCNLightTypeSpot, 170
    setupLighting() method, 170
    specular, 172
    transparent, 174

N

Node tree, SKScene
    enumerateChildNodesWithName()
        method, 27
    GameScene.init() method, 25
    memory property, 27
    nested nodes, 25
    overlapping player nodes, 26
    SKNode.name property, 26
Normal mapping, 211

O

Orb node layout, 59–61, 63

P, Q

Parallelaxation, 74
Particle emitters
    choosing file options dialog, 83
    choosing template dialog, 83
    creation, 82–84
    description, 80
    exhaust trail, 90–94
    generated spark particle emitter, 84
    properties, 84, 86–89
    SKEmitterNode object, 80
    templates, 82
    Xcode's Particle Emitter Editor, 81
Particle life-cycle properties, 86
Particle movement properties, 87
Position Range property, 87
PyramidNode, 182–183
PyramidNode material, 174

R

RandomPosition() method, 209
Reflective lighting, 173
Render delegate method, 161
Rendering loop, SKScene
    didEvaluateActions() method, 21
    didSimulatePhysics() method, 21
    iOS application, 20
    update() method, 21

S

Scene building
    Collada file, 158
    editor, 157
    graph properties editor, 158–159
    render cycle, 161
    scene graph, 155–156
    scene Kit geometries, 161
    scene nodes, 156
    SCNText, 167
    submenu, 160
Scene graph, 143–144
Scene Kit. See also Sprite Kit
    2D scene, 201
    animation, 144
    Apple's Scene Kit library, 209
    art assets, 150
    Cartesian coordinate system, 145
    classes, 144
    coordinate system, 145
    euclidean space, 145
    floorNode, 153
    GameViewController, 149, 203
    iPhone, 154
    options, 147
    point, 145
    resources, 149
    sample application, 147–148
    scene graph, 143
    SCNNode, 152–153
    spaceman in 3D, 151
    spaceman standing, floor, 153
    SuperSpaceMan3D device, 148–149
    Swift, 146
    template dialog, 146
    transformations, 145
    vectors, 145
    viewDidLoad() method, 150
    wiring Up and building, 148
Scene transitions. See SKTransition
sceneView.overlaySKScene, 207
SCNGeometry objects
    Obstacles Class, 165–166
    pyramidNode, 164–165
    SCNBox, 162
    SCNCapsule, 162

SCNCone, 162
SCNCylinder, 162
SCNFloor, 162
SCNPlane, 162
SCNPyramid, 162
SCNShape, 163
SCNSphere, 163
SCNText, 163
SCNTorus, 163
SCNTube, 163
setupCameras() method, 180
SetupLighting() method, 171
SKLabelNodes
    adding impulse counter, 108–110
    adding scoring, 105–107
    adding simple sounds, 110–112
    description, 97
    horizontalAlignmentMode, 99–100
    init() method, 98
    simple SKLabelNode, 99
    VerticalAlignmentMode, 101, 103–104
SKNode
    collision detection
        didBeginContact(), 39
        didEndContact(), 39
        playerNode and orbNode, 39
        removeFromParent(), 43
        SKPhysicsContactDelegate, 39
    GameScene.init(size\: CGSize), 42
    GameScene.swift, 43–44
    orbNode.physicsBody.static and
        dynamic, 38
    physicsBody.allowsRotation, 39
    POWER_UP_ORB, 42
    SKPhysicsBody, 40–41
    SKPhysicsContact properties, 42
    sprites.atlas, 38
SKPhysicsBody
    active nodes, 33
    applyForce(), 35
    applyImpulse(), 35
    bit mask properties, 40
    bit masks, 40
    CGFloat, 34
    CGVectorMake, 35
    CollisionCategoryPowerUpOrbs, 40
    contactTestBitMask, 41

SKPhysicsBody (*cont.*)
    dynamic and static volume, 33
    fluid or air friction simulation, 36
    GameScene.init(size\: CGSize), 41
    GameScene's, 34
    GameScene.swift, 37
    linearDamping, 36
    playerNode, 34
    player setup code, 34
    polygonFromPath, 34
    rectangleOfSize, 34
    render loop, 33
    super.init(size\: size), 35
    SuperSpaceMan application, 36
    UIResponder.touchesBegan(), 36
    Xcode, 34
SKSpriteNode coordinates
    GameScene.init() method, 27–28
    playerNode, 28–30
    size property, 28
SKTransition
    adding new scene, 116–117
    adding the transition, 121, 123–124
    ending the game, 118
    losing the game, 119–121
    pausing scenes, 115
    scene detection, 115
    transitioning between scenes, 113–115
    winning the game, 118–119
Specular light, 172
Speed property, 88
Sprite Kit
    addBlackHolesToForeground()
        method, 131
    addOrbsToForeground() method, 130
    Apple's Scene Kit library, 209
    bonus, 208–209
    creating own nodes, 127–129
    didBeginContact method, 207
    didSimulatePhysicsAtTime Protocol, 205
    enemy node enhancement, 207
    externalizing game data, 135–137
    GameOverlay class, 202
    GameOverView class, 206
    GameViewController, 204–205
    NSNumberFormatter, 202
    OpenGL context, 201

overlaySKScene parameter, 207
overlay timer, 204
overridden init(size\: CGSize)
    function, 202
removing unnecessary nodes, 137–139
restart the game, 207
reusing textures, 132, 134
scoreboard, 201
SKLabelNode object, 202
SKLabelNode.setup, 202
startTimer() function, 203
stopTimer(), 203, 205
timer running, 205
Sprite Kit actions
    BlackHole node, 64–65, 67–68
    definition, 63
    moveToX, sequence and
        repeatForever, 64
    SKTexture and SKTextureAtlas, 69–70
    steps, 63
    uses, 63
Sprite Kit game
    anchorPoints, 16
    backgroundNode, 14–15
    custom class, 9
    GameScene.init() method, 16
    GameScene.swift, 7
    GameViewController.swift, 7, 9
    image assets, 13–14
    Images.xcassets, 15
    Intel-based Macintosh, 3
    iOS app, 9
    Main.storyboard, 8
    playerNode, 14
    portrait mode running, 6
    SKSpriteNodes, 15
    SpaceShip asset, 13
    spites.atlas, 12
    SuperSpaceMan, 4
    target settings, 6
    UIViewController, 8
    visual elements, 14
    Xcode simulator, 3
SpriteKit particle emitter properties, 85
Sprite Kit scenes
    anchorPoint properties, 30, 32
    coordinate systems, 19, 31

gameScene's children property, 23
GameViewController.viewDidLoad(), 20
insertChild(), 22
nested nodes, 24
node2.removeFromParent(), 24
playerNode, 32
removeFromParent() method, 22–23
rendering loop. *See* Rendering loop,
        SKScene
scaleMode property, 20
SKEffectNode, 19
SKScene.addChild() method, 22
Start and Range properties, 87
SuperSpaceMan3D device, 149
Swift functions
    basic syntax, 226
    catTwoWords(), 226
    inout Parameters, 232
    nested functions, 228–229
    pass functions
        Int parameter, 231
        mathFunction, 231
    returned function, 229–231
    tuples, 227
    variadic parameters, 227
Swift programming language
    classes
        computed properties, 237–238
        dot (.) operator, 234
        extending classes, 236
        Xcode project, 234
    closures, 233
    Cocoa and Cocoa touch features, 219
    enumerations, 239–240
    extensions, 242
    for loops
        for-conditional-increment, 224
        for-in, 224–225
    functions, 226–227, 229–230, 232
    generics, 243–244
    if statement, 222
    LLVM compiler, 219
    protocols, 240, 242
    structures, 238
    Swift project, 220

switch statement, 222–223
variables and constants, 220–221
while loops
    do-while, 226
    while, 225
Swift Sprite Kit project
    rotating space, 6
    templates, 4
    Xcode, 4

▪ T, U

3D graphic programming
    assistant pop-up menu, 214
    Behavior new type, 217
    Behavior setting sound, 216
    hotkeys, 213
    normal mapping, 211
    Scene Kit, 212
    SCNMatrix4Invert, 212
    SCNMatrix4MakeRotation, 212
    SCNMatrix4MakeScale, 212
    SCNMatrix4MakeTranslation, 212
    SCNMatrix4Mult, 213
    SCNMatrix4Rotate, 212
    SCNMatrix4Scale, 212
    SCNMatrix4Translate, 212
    Swift best practices, 211
    vectors, 211
    Xcode Behaviors section, 215
    Xcode clean layout, 218
    Xcode edItor, 213
Tube node, 184–185

▪ V, W

viewDidLoad() function, 167
viewDidLoad() method, 150,
        152–153, 195

▪ X, Y, Z

Xcode Behaviors section, 215
Xcode clean layout, 218
Xcode editor, 213
Xcode IDE, 216–217

Get the eBook for only $10!

Now you can take the weightless companion with you anywhere, anytime. Your purchase of this book entitles you to 3 electronic versions for only $10.

This Apress title will prove so indispensible that you'll want to carry it with you everywhere, which is why we are offering the eBook in 3 formats for only $10 if you have already purchased the print book.

Convenient and fully searchable, the PDF version enables you to easily find and copy code—or perform examples by quickly toggling between instructions and applications. The MOBI format is ideal for your Kindle, while the ePUB can be utilized on a variety of mobile devices.

Go to www.apress.com/promo/tendollars to purchase your companion eBook.